Gilded Age
and Progressive Era

Biographies

Gilded Age
and Progressive Era

Biographies

Rebecca Valentine

Lawrence W. Baker, Project Editor

U·X·L
An imprint of Thomson Gale,
a part of The Thomson Corporation

THOMSON
GALE

Detroit • New York • San Francisco • New Haven, Conn. • Waterville, Maine • London

Gilded Age and Progressive Era: Biographies

Rebecca Valentine

Project Editor
Lawrence W. Baker

Rights and Acquisitions
Margaret Abendroth, Emma Hull,
Jackie Jones

Imaging and Multimedia
Dean Dauphinais, Lezlie Light,
Michael Logusz

Product Design
Pamela Galbreath, Jennifer Wahi

Composition
Evi Seoud

Manufacturing
Rita Wimberley

LIBRARY OF CONGRESS CATALOGING-IN-PUBLICATION DATA

Valentine, Rebecca.
  Gilded Age and Progressive Era reference library / Rebecca Valentine; Lawrence W. Baker,
project editor.
    v. cm.
  Includes bibliographical references zand index.
  Contents: [1] Almanac -- [2] Biographies -- [3] Primary sources.
  ISBN-13: 978-1-4144-0193-5 (set : alk. paper) --
  ISBN-10: 1-4144-0193-0 (set : alk. paper) --
  ISBN-13: 978-1-4144-0194-2 (Almanac : alk. paper) --
  ISBN-10: 1-4144-0194-9 (Almanac : alk. paper) --
  [etc.]
  1. United States -- History -- 1865-1921 -- Juvenile literature. 2. United States -- History --
1865-1921 -- Biography -- Juvenile literature. 3. United States -- History -- 1865-1921 --
Sources -- Juvenile literature. 4. Almanacs, American -- Juvenile literature. I. Baker,
Lawrence W. II. Title.
  E661.V35 2006
  973.8 -- dc22
                                                                      2006022839

ISBN-13:

978-1-4144-0193-5 (set)
978-1-4144-0194-2 (Almanac)
978-1-4144-0195-9
  (Biographies)

978-1-4144-0196-6
  (Primary Sources)
978-1-4144-0197-3
  (Cumulative Index)

ISBN-10:

1-4144-0193-0 (set)
1-4144-0194-9 (Almanac)
1-4144-0195-7
  (Biographies)

1-4144-0196-5
  (Primary Sources)
1-4144-0197-3
  (Cumulative Index)

This title is also available as an e-book.
ISBN-13: 978-1-4144-1046-3, ISBN-10: 1-4144-1046-8
Contact your Thomson Gale sales representative for ordering information.
Printed in the United States of America
10 9 8 7 6 5 4 3 2 1

Contents

Reader's Guide

The Gilded Age and Progressive Era in American history blended so seamlessly into one another that they can hardly be thought of separately. The Gilded Age was a major turning point in the nation, as it marked the rise of industrialism (an economy based on business and industry rather than agriculture) and the decline of an economy based on agriculture. Roughly 1877 to 1900, the Industrial Revolution made celebrities of robber barons such as oil magnate John D. Rockefeller and railroad tycoon Cornelius Vanderbilt. It encouraged the growth of a middle class as more and more Americans became members of the working class. It fostered competition in business even as it grew through the questionable practices of forming trusts and monopolies, and it made unimaginable wealth for a handful while sending millions of others into unrelenting poverty.

The Gilded Age was a time of great discontent as angry workers gave birth to the labor movement and muckraking journalists such as Ida M. Tarbell exposed big business for what it really was. The 1890s was a decade of economic depression for the entire nation; American farmers and laborers were so desperate that they took the radical measure of forming their own political party, the Populist Party. In no other era in history has America been led by so many presidents that time seems to have forgotten, and yet the Gilded Age led directly to the Progressive Era, which was ushered in by one of the most passionate, deliberate, incorrigible presidents: Theodore Roosevelt.

The Progressive Era, approximately 1900 to 1913, was a time of great reform in a nation that was just beginning to understand who it was, who it no longer could be, and who it just might become, given the right circumstances. The temperance movement eventually led to

Prohibition (when the Eighteenth Amendment banned the manufacture and sale of alcohol). Labor laws gave rights to workers, and concerned citizens such as child labor photographer Lewis Hine and photojournalist Jacob Riis used their talents to secure improved living and working conditions for the urban poor and their children.

America in the Progressive Era was a melting pot that included millions of immigrants from around the world. As cities became overpopulated with people living in poverty, those who could moved to the outskirts of town, and suburban America was born. Those who could not escape the city led lives of intense hardship and heartache, but their underpaid and underappreciated labor kept America's economy going, even through the Panic of 1907. Reformers such as Jane Addams and Hannah Solomon dedicated their lives to helping where help was most needed: in urban slums.

Coverage and features

Gilded Age and Progressive Era: Biographies tells the story of this everchanging period in history through the personal accounts of the lives of twenty-five influential people. Between the covers of this volume, students will find information on such well-known Americans as Mark Twain, Theodore Roosevelt, and Thomas Edison. But they will also be introduced to movers and shakers who have, perhaps, escaped their attention before: Edward Harriman, a railroad tycoon who made important contributions to science; Emma Goldman, an anarchist and social activist; and Thomas Nast, a famous political cartoonist upon whom America depended for insight and a laugh or two. Readers will learn about financier Jay Gould, activist Frances Willard, and suffragist Elizabeth Cady Stanton.

Through sidebars, the *Biographies* volume highlights other interesting people and details of the Gilded Age and Progressive Era, including: Native American warrior Geronimo, the history of baseball cards, and the San Francisco Earthquake of 1906. By reading about the lives of the famous and not-so-famous, students will understand that history is made not only through major events such as wars and political administrations, but through activities as seemingly insignificant as drawing a cartoon or taking a photograph.

Within each full-length biography, boldfaced cross-references direct readers to other individuals profiled in the volume, helping readers understand that people of various backgrounds and with different goals often found themselves related by events and circumstances. The *Biographies* volume contains nearly eighty photographs and illustrations. The volume includes a timeline of important events and dates, a "Words to Know" section, a general bibliography, and a subject index of people, places, and events discussed throughout *Gilded Age and Progressive Era: Biographies.*

U•X•L Gilded Age and Progressive Era Reference Library

Gilded Age and Progressive Era: Biographies is just one component of a three-volume U•X•L Gilded Age and Progressive Era Reference Library. The other titles in this set are:

Gilded Age and Progressive Era: Almanac gives comprehensive coverage of these decades by examining them from political, social, and cultural perspectives. Unlike other periods in history, these were not so directly informed by major wars or other political events (though war was certainly a contributor to the times), but by other more socially centered influences. The *Almanac* paints the Gilded Age and Progressive Era as they were: times of great sorrow and grand luxury. The eleven chapters begin with a brief review of Reconstruction, when the United States rebuilt itself following the Civil War (1861–65). In doing so, readers understand just how tumultuous a time in history the Gilded Age was. From there, students are given a tour of the business of doing business, including the struggles within the new labor movement. Immigration and its impact on the nation are detailed as it occurred, from sea to sea. The *Almanac* gives readers an understanding of the myth of the Wild West versus its reality as it concerned Native Americans. Students may also analyze the plight not only of the late nineteenth century farmer, but also of the African American in the South who was emancipated but not truly freed. Populism leads to Progressivism as readers see how a change in one aspect of life—whether business, social, cultural, or political—affects every other.

Gilded Age and Progressive Era: Primary Sources informs not through narrative, but by presenting actual documents, photographs, and other primary sources of the time. Eighteen entries show just how transitional this time period was to the United States. Included are texts of important legislation, such as the Dawes Severalty Act and the ruling from *Plessy vs. Ferguson.* Students will read a portion of the groundbreaking novel *The Jungle,* which led directly to the passage of several important laws concerning the food and drug industries. Readers will become acquainted with the famous Gibson Girl illustrations, and have the opportunity to peruse original images from the Sears Modern Homes catalog of the early twentieth century.

A cumulative index of all three titles in this set is also available.

Acknowledgments

My deep gratitude goes to copyeditor Theresa Murray; proofreader Amy Marcaccio Keyzer; the indexers from Factiva, a Dow Jones & Reuters Company; and typesetter ITC/International Typesetting & Composition. I would be remiss if I failed to thank Larry Baker, project editor extraordinaire, and my family, who made do with less of my attention for longer than they would have liked.

Special thanks are due for the invaluable comments and suggestions provided by U•X•L's Gilded Age and Progressive Era Reference Library advisors and consultants:

- Sally Collins, Library Media Specialist, Highland Park Middle School, Dallas, Texas
- Nina Levine, Library Media Specialist, Blue Mountain Middle School, Cortlandt Manor, New York
- Bernadette Monette, Library Media Specialist, Sacopee Valley High School, Hiram, Maine

Comments and suggestions

We welcome your comments on *Gilded Age and Progressive Era: Biographies* and suggestions for other topics in history to consider. Please write: Editors, *Gilded Age and Progressive Era: Biographies,* U•X•L, 27500 Drake Road, Farmington Hills, MI 48331-3535; call toll-free 800-877-4253; fax to 248-699-8097; or send e-mail via http://www.gale.com.

Timeline of Events

1873 **Mark Twain** publishes his novel titled *The Gilded Age;* this term is used as the name of the era characterized by robber barons and their ostentatious displays of wealth.

1877 The Industrial Revolution begins, shifting America's economic focus from one of agriculture to industry.

January 4, 1877 The original robber baron, **Cornelius Vanderbilt,** dies with an estate worth $100 million.

July–August 1877 The Great Railroad Strike takes place across the nation, after the Baltimore & Ohio Railroad had cut wages for a second time in one year. The strike soon spread throughout the nation, and federal troops were called in. It is the first major strike of a newly industrialized nation. Forty-five days later, the strikes were put down.

1878 **Thomas Edison** founds the Edison Electric Light Company. It puts rival companies out of business and becomes General Electric.

January 10, 1878 The "Anthony Amendment," named after women's rights pioneer Susan B. Anthony, is introduced to Congress. It requests giving women the right to vote.

April 12, 1878 Politician William "Boss" Tweed, the corrupt leader of New York's Tammany Hall, dies in prison. Political cartoonist **Thomas Nast** was largely credited with Tweed's arrest.

1879 California passes a law forbidding the employment of Chinese laborers.

1879 **Frances Willard** is elected president of the Woman's Christian Temperance Union, an organization that works to minimize the consumption of alcohol and for the health and safety of women and children.

September 1879 Terence V. Powderly becomes grand master workman and leader of the Knights of Labor, a powerful labor union.

December 31, 1879 Thomas Edison demonstrates the progress of his newly invented incandescent lightbulb on the grounds of his lab in Menlo Park, New Jersey. He installed sixty lamps outdoors, and lit them all at once to an astonished and impressed public.

1880 The National Farmers' Alliance is formed. Farmers find themselves in tragic circumstances due to drought and flood, high interest rates on loans, and unfair railroad rates.

1880 The U.S. population reaches 50.1 million. More than 6 million are foreign born.

1880 The Arts & Crafts movement begins, hailing a return to furniture and interior decoration based on simplicity.

1880 The Alaska gold rush begins.

1880 Financier and railroad tycoon **Jay Gould** owns 10,000 miles (16,000 kilometers) of railway, roughly one-ninth of the country's railway mileage.

1880 Andrew Carnegie monopolizes the steel industry.

1881 President Rutherford B. Hayes forbids the sale of alcoholic beverages at military posts. His wife had already acquired the nickname "Lemonade Lucy" for her refusal to serve alcohol in the White House.

1881 Native American rights activist Helen Hunt Jackson publishes *A Century of Dishonor.*

1881 **Booker T. Washington** founds the Tuskegee Normal and Industrial Institute.

March 4, 1881 U.S. representative James A. Garfield of Ohio becomes president; New York politician Chester A. Arthur is vice president.

May 1881 Kansas becomes the first state to outlaw the sale of liquor.

July 2, 1881 President James Garfield is shot in a Washington, D.C., train station. He dies in September; Vice President Chester A. Arthur becomes president.

July 14, 1881 Famous criminal Billy the Kid is shot and killed.

1882 John D. Rockefeller organizes the Standard Oil Trust. The trust gets him around the laws of each state and becomes the model for future corporations.

1882 The first parade is held in New York City in observance of Labor Day, as ten thousand workers take the day off to march.

1882 The first commercial electric light system is installed on Pearl Street in New York City.

1882 Congress sets restrictions on immigration standards. Exceedingly poor people, convicts, and those declared insane are no longer welcome at Ellis Island.

May 6, 1882 The Chinese Exclusion Act passes. Chinese immigrants are no longer welcome in the United States. The law would be repealed ten years later.

1883 The Brooklyn Bridge is completed. After taking fourteen years to build, New Yorkers consider it the eighth wonder of the world.

1883 Frances Willard founds the World Woman's Christian Temperance Union.

1883 Jewish poet Emma Lazarus writes the poem "The New Colossus," which is engraved on a plaque and hung at the base of the Statue of Liberty.

January 16, 1883 The Pendleton Act is passed, transforming the Civil Service to an agency of qualified employees who must pass tests in order to be hired.

1884 The Home Life Insurance building in Chicago, Illinois, is constructed. It is the world's first skyscraper. It is also the first building to have a steel frame upon which floors and walls are hung.

1884 Mark Twain publishes the popular novel, *The Adventures of Huckleberry Finn.*

November 1884 New York governor **Grover Cleveland** is elected president.

1886 Riots against the Chinese occur in Washington. At least four hundred Chinese are forced from their homes. Federal troops intervene to restore order.

1886 Samuel Gompers organizes the American Federation of Labor.

1886 Cartoonist and illustrator Thomas Nast severs professional ties with *Harper's Weekly,* the newspaper for which he had worked for more than twenty-five years.

1886 Jay Gould fires a Knights of Labor union employee on his Texas & Pacific Railway line. All KOL employees of the company go on strike, and soon other labor union workers on other railroads in the region strike as well. Gould refuses to negotiate and violence erupts.

May 4, 1886 The Haymarket Square Riot takes place in Chicago, Illinois. About fourteen hundred people gather to protest police brutality against workers on strike. Nearly two hundred police arrive to break up the crowd. A bomb is thrown into the midst of the police. The nation begins to equate workers on strike with violent anarchists.

June 2, 1886 Grover Cleveland becomes the first president to marry in the White House.

October 28, 1886 President Grover Cleveland accepts the Statue of Liberty from France and delivers his dedication address.

February 4, 1887 The Interstate Commerce Act becomes law. A commission is created to ensure fair and reasonable rates for freight carriers.

February 8, 1887 Congress passes the Dawes Severalty Act. Every Native American family is to be given 100 acres of land to farm.

1888 Congress establishes a Department of Labor.

1888 Susan B. Anthony founds the National Council of Woman of the United States.

January 12, 1888 The Schoolchildren's Blizzard claims the lives of between 250 and 500 immigrants on the Dakota-Nebraska prairie; most of them are children.

November 1888 Former U.S. senator **Benjamin Harrison** of Indiana is elected president.

1889 North Dakota, South Dakota, Montana, and Washington become states.

1889 **Jane Addams** opens Hull-House in Chicago, Illinois, the first social services system.

1889 Land in Oklahoma that was given to the Native Americans is opened to white settlers, furthering antagonizing the relationship between Native Americans and whites.

May 31, 1889 The Johnstown flood claims the lives of more than two thousand Pennsylvanians.

June 1889 Andrew Carnegie publishes his famous philosophy, the "Gospel of Wealth."

1890 The American Women's Suffrage Association merges with the National Women's Suffrage Association, bringing solidarity to the suffrage movement.

1890 The McKinley Tariff Act is passed, establishing record-high tariffs on many imported goods.

1890 Photojournalist Jacob Riis publishes *How the Other Half Lives*, a book that provides a glimpse into the lives and hardships of America's urban poor and reveals the squalor of New York City's tenement homes. At the time, **Theodore Roosevelt** was the police commissioner of New York. He was moved by Riis's exposé and joined in the efforts to clean up the city.

January 25, 1890 Journalist Nellie Bly completes her trip around the world, which took her seventy-two days, six hours, and eleven minutes.

July 2, 1890 The Sherman Anti-Trust Act is passed, making it unlawful for businesses to form trusts that prohibit competition.

July 10, 1890 Wyoming becomes a state; later, it becomes the first state to give women the right to vote.

July 14, 1890 The Sherman Silver Purchase Act is signed by President Benjamin Harrison. The law increased the amount of money in circulation in the economy, but it also put a serious strain on the federal gold reserve.

October 1, 1890 Yosemite Park is created. Congress set aside 1,500 square miles of reserved forest lands.

December 15, 1890 Chief **Sitting Bull** is fatally wounded by one of his own men.

December 29, 1890 The Massacre at Wounded Knee officially closes the American frontier.

1891 Thomas Edison receives a patent for the first motion picture camera.

1892 Conservationist **John Muir** helps establish the Sierra Club. He remains its president until his death in 1914.

1892 Nearly 2 million acres of Crow Indian reservation in Montana are given to white settlers.

1892 Lizzie Borden is accused of murdering her father and stepmother with an axe. Though later found not guilty, her alleged crime remains one of the country's great unsolved mysteries.

January 1, 1892 Ellis Island opens to become the port of entry for all immigrants entering America via the Atlantic Ocean.

June 29, 1892 Carnegie Steel workers are locked out, an event that began the Homestead Steel Strike, one of the bloodiest work strikes in industrial history.

July 1892 The Populist Party is formed.

1893 **Hannah Solomon** establishes the National Council of Jewish Women.

1893 Frederick Jackson Turner delivers his lecture called "The Significance of the Frontier in American History."

1893 **Ida B. Wells** publishes a pamphlet on racism for distribution at the Chicago World's Fair. "The Reason Why the Colored American Is Not in the World's Columbian Exposition" was written by Wells, reformer Frederick Douglass, and other activists, and includes information on lynching, unfair legislation, and the convict lease system as well.

March 1893 Grover Cleveland is inaugurated to serve his second term as president of the United States. He is the first president to serve non-consecutive terms.

May 1, 1893 The World's Columbian Exposition, also known as the Chicago World's Fair, opens.

May 4, 1893 The New York Stock Exchange crashes, beginning the worst economic depression in American history to that point. The economy would not begin to recover until 1896.

May 24, 1893 The Anti-Saloon League is founded in Oberlin, Ohio.

June 1893 President Grover Cleveland successfully calls upon Congress to repeal the Sherman Silver Purchase Act.

June 20, 1893 Eugene V. Debs establishes the American Railway Union, the first industrial union in the United States.

September 1893 Anarchist **Emma Goldman** is jailed on charges that she started a riot.

1894 Educational philosopher **John Dewey** opens an experimental school in Chicago, Illinois.

1894 Congress officially declares the first Monday of every September to be Labor Day. This declaration is a sign of the growing importance of and concern given to American labor.

1894 Charles Dana Gibson's first illustration of the All-American Girl appears in print. His "Gibson Girl" was the symbol of America's modern woman through World War I (1914–18).

March 25, 1894 Jacob Coxey leads one hundred men from Ohio to Washington, D.C., in protest of the economic depression and with a demand that the government aid its citizens by creating jobs. "Coxey's Army" grew to include more than five hundred men by the time they reached Washington on April 30. Some of the men were arrested for trespassing on the lawn of the Capitol.

May 11, 1894 Fifty thousand Pullman Palace Car Company employees strike in Chicago, Illinois. The strike eventually included railroad workers across the nation, and President Grover Cleveland called upon federal troops to break up the event. Violence erupted and many strikers were killed and wounded.

1895 Lillian Wald opens Henry Street Settlement House on New York's East Side.

1895 George Eastman introduces the first pocket Kodak camera.

1895 Suffragist **Elizabeth Cady Stanton** publishes the controversial book *Woman's Bible.*

May 18, 1896 In *Plessy v. Ferguson,* the U.S. Supreme Court approves racial segregation by upholding the "separate but equal" doctrine.

July 9, 1896 William Jennings Bryan delivers his rousing "Cross of Gold" speech.

November 1896 Ohio governor **William McKinley** defeats former U.S. representative William Jennings Bryan of Nebraska in the presidential election.

1897 The Dingley Tariff is passed, raising tariffs to a new high of an average of 50 percent.

November 1, 1897 The Library of Congress is housed in its own building for the first time.

February 15, 1898 The *U.S.S. Maine* explodes and sinks, killing 266 crew members. This event triggers the Spanish-American War, which lasts for one hundred days.

June 15, 1898 The Anti-Imperialist League forms to fight America's territorial expansion policy. Famous members include Mark Twain, Andrew Carnegie, Jane Addams, and Samuel Gompers.

July 1, 1898 Theodore Roosevelt leads his Rough Riders in the Battle of San Juan Heights during the Spanish-American War in Cuba. No military unit suffered as many casualties in that war as did the Rough Riders, who sacrificed 37 percent of their men before coming home.

July 7, 1898 America annexes Hawaii.

1899 President William McKinley advocates an "Open Door" policy with China.

1899 Southern regionalist writer Kate Chopin publishes her scandalous novel, *The Awakening.*

1899 Pianist **Scott Joplin** writes and publishes the *Maple Leaf Rag,* his best-known composition.

February 4, 1899 The Philippine-American War breaks out. America had purchased the Philippine Islands after defeating the Spanish in Cuba. But the Philippines did not want to go from being ruled by one country to being ruled by another, so they rebelled. The bloody war lasted until July 4, 1902, when America won and did its best to modernize the Philippines. The islands gained their independence in 1946.

May 31, 1899 Railroad tycoon **Edward Harriman** embarks on a two-month cruise to Alaska.

1900 The average American family has three or four children, compared to 1800, when it included seven or eight.

1900 Ragtime becomes the most popular genre of music in America. It has its roots in African American music and features fast tempos with syncopated rhythms.

May 25, 1900 Congress passes the Lacey Act, which protects particular animals and their habitats and outlaws the interstate shipment of wildlife that has been hunted illegally.

June 1900 The Boxer Rebellion takes place in China and lasts until August.

1901 Steel magnate Andrew Carnegie sells his steel mill to U.S. Steel and becomes the world's wealthiest man.

1901 J. P. Morgan incorporates the United States Steel Company, giving America its first billion-dollar company.

1901 The Tenement House Act is passed, improving the construction and safety of New York City's housing for the poor.

September 2, 1901 Vice President Theodore Roosevelt delivers a speech at the Minnesota State Fair in which he explains his stance on foreign policy by quoting an African proverb that says, "Speak softly and carry a big stick."

September 5, 1901 President William McKinley is shot by immigrant Leon Czolgosz. Nine days later, McKinley dies from his wounds and Vice President Theodore Roosevelt is sworn in as president.

October 16, 1901 Reformer Booker T. Washington dines with President Theodore Roosevelt at the White House. It is the first time a president has invited an African American to the White House.

1902 President Theodore Roosevelt dissolves the Beef trust and the Northern Securities Company (a railroad monopoly).

1902 Suffragist Carrie Chapman Catt organizes the National American Woman Suffrage Association.

1902 Muckraker Ida Tarbell publishes the first chapter of her exposé on the Standard Oil Company.

May 12, 1902 Anthracite coal miners walk off their jobs in Pennsylvania. The strike lasted 164 days and ended when President Theodore Roosevelt intervened and appointed J. P. Morgan to arbitrate the dispute.

June 17, 1902 President Theodore Roosevelt passes the Newlands Act, which allows for the use of money from the sale of public lands in sixteen western states to be used to restore those states to a balanced ecosystem.

1903 The Women's Trade Union League is formed.

1903 Reformer and activist W. E. B. Du Bois publishes his famous treatise, *The Souls of Black Folk,* in which he challenges the philosophy of Booker T. Washington and proposes his own "Talented Tenth" philosophy.

1903 The first Teddy Bear, named after president Theodore Roosevelt, is introduced on the market and becomes an immediate best-seller.

1903 Writer **Jack London** publishes a best-selling novel, *Call of the Wild.*

1903 John Muir acts as guide to President Theodore Roosevelt on a hike through the Sierra Nevada. The two men develop a life-long friendship.

December 17, 1903 Wilbur and Orville Wright make history by becoming the first humans to ever fly. Their first flight lasted 12 seconds and went a distance of 120 feet (3.7 meters).

1904 The National Child Labor Committee forms and works tirelessly to campaign for child labor laws.

1904 President Theodore Roosevelt initiates the building of the Panama Canal. The project would take ten years and thirty thousand workers to be completed; the canal opened for business on August 15, 1914.

1904 Breaker boys (boys aged 7 to 13 who worked in the coal mining industry) earn 45 to 50 cents for a day's work. Each work day lasted ten to twelve hours.

February 8, 1904 Japan attacks Port Arthur and conducts a quick series of victorious attacks on Russian naval fleets, marking the start of the Russo-Japanese War. The war ended in defeat for Russia in 1905.

October 27, 1904 The New York subway opens.

1905 The Victrola disc player is first sold on the market; by 1911, this early version of the record player could be found in millions of homes across America.

March 3, 1905 President Theodore Roosevelt gives the Bureau of Forestry a new name: the Forest Service; he appoints conservationist Gifford Pinchot as its director. Under Pinchot's leadership, the country's forests grew from 56 million acres to 172 million acres.

August 1905 The Detroit Tigers baseball team purchases center fielder **Ty Cobb;** he would play there for twenty-one years.

1906 **Upton Sinclair** publishes his muckraking novel *The Jungle*. It is an immediate best-seller and leads to federal reform in the food industry.

1906 The Meat Inspection Act is passed, providing hygiene standards in the meatpacking industry.

1906 The Pure Food and Drug Act is passed, requiring manufacturers to label their products with a list of ingredients.

April 18, 1906 San Francisco experiences one of the most significant earthquakes of all time. Resulting fires burned for more than three days. Hundreds of thousands of the city's residents were left homeless, and the death toll ranged between five hundred and three thousand.

June 29, 1906 Theodore Roosevelt signs the Hepburn Act, which added two more members to the Interstate Commerce Commission.

December 10, 1906 President Theodore Roosevelt accepts the Nobel Peace Prize for his peacekeeping efforts in negotiating an agreement between Russia and Japan.

1907 Several large businesses and banking institutions file bankruptcy, causing an economic crisis known as the Panic of 1907. The crisis lasted just a few weeks because President Theodore Roosevelt worked with financier J. P. Morgan to provide assistance to needy firms so they could avoid bankruptcy.

1908 Henry Ford introduces the Model T automobile.

1908 Sears, Roebuck & Co. begins selling home-building kits through the mail.

1908 **Lewis Hine** joins the National Child Labor Committee as its official photographer.

June 8, 1908 The American Antiquities Act is passed, giving the president of the United States the authority to designate specific lands as historic monuments, thereby giving them federal protection for the purposes of preservation.

July 26, 1908 The Federal Bureau of Investigation (FBI) is established.

November 1908 Former U.S. secretary of war William Howard Taft is elected president of the United States.

December 26, 1908 Jack Johnson becomes the first African American boxer to win the heavyweight championship.

1909 The National Association for the Advancement of Colored People (NAACP) is established.

April 6, 1909 Explorer Robert Peary becomes the first human to reach the North Pole.

1910 Hannah Solomon founds the Chicago Women's City Club.

1911 Baseball is known as "America's favorite pastime."

March 25, 1911 The Triangle Shirtwaist Factory fire claims the lives of 146 immigrant workers, most of them young girls. It is the largest industrial accident to date in the country.

1912 The Progressive, or "Bull Moose," Party is established. Former president Theodore Roosevelt becomes that party's presidential candidate in the 1912 election after losing the Republican Party nomination to incumbent president William Howard Taft.

April 9, 1912 President William Howard Taft creates the Federal Children's Bureau, which provided much-needed money to help maintain the health and well-being of children throughout the nation.

April 15, 1912 The ocean liner *Titanic* sinks into the Atlantic Ocean, killing 705 passengers.

November 1912 New Jersey governor Woodrow Wilson is elected the twenty-eighth president of the United States by defeating incumbent president William Howard Taft and former president Theodore Roosevelt.

1913 The Armory Show is presented in New York and attended by five thousand people. The exhibit featured art by the Ashcan School artists as well as Pablo Picasso and Marcel Duchamp. America was appalled by the new style of painting, but within a few years, the Modernist style would be all the rage.

1913 Miners in Ludlow, Colorado, go on strike. Events lead to the murder of the miners and their families at the hands of federal troops on April 20, 1914.

December 23, 1913 President Woodrow Wilson passes the Federal Reserve Act, which calls for banking and currency reform.

July 28, 1914 World War I, also known as the Great War, begins. America remains neutral until April 2, 1917, when President Woodrow Wilson declares war on Germany. The war ends on November 11, 1918.

Words to Know

A

abolitionists: People who worked to end slavery.

aeronautics: The study of flight and aircraft.

Ancient Order of Hibernians (AOH): A Catholic organization formed in America in 1836. Some of its members came from various organizations created centuries earlier in Ireland. The purpose of the AOH was to help Irish Catholic immigrants settle in America and to defend them from persecution. One way the AOH defended its members was to keep its meetings and actions secret.

anti-Semitism: Prejudice against Jewish people.

antitrust: Against the formation of monopolies or trusts.

B

bimetallism: A movement of the late nineteenth century aimed at expanding the amount of money in circulation by backing it with silver as well as gold. Also sometimes referred to as free silver.

boomtowns: Towns that were built quickly by gold-seekers.

C

capitalism: An economic system in which property and goods are privately owned, produced, and distributed.

civil service: The system in which civilians work for various government agencies and departments. Before civil service reform, people were appointed to positions depending on whom they knew in politics and business. After reform, people had to apply for a job and pass examinations in order to qualify.

conspicuous consumption: The buying of expensive and unnecessary items as a way of displaying one's wealth.

coolies: Unskilled Asian workers.

deflation: A decline in the prices of goods and services.

Democratic Party: One of the oldest political parties in the United States. Originally linked with the South and slavery, it transformed into one associated with urban voters and liberal policies.

depression: A long-term economic state characterized by high unemployment, minimal investment and spending, and low prices.

electoral votes: The votes a presidential candidate receives for having won a majority of a state's popular vote (citizens' votes). The candidate who receives the most popular votes in a particular state wins all of that state's electoral votes. Each state receives two electoral votes for its two U.S. senators and a figure for the number of U.S. representatives it has (which is determined by a state's population). A candidate must win a majority of electoral votes (over 50 percent) in order to win the presidency.

farm tenancy: An arrangement whereby farmers who no longer owned their own farm farmed someone else's land and were paid a share of the harvest.

Gilded Age: The period in history following the Civil War and Reconstruction (roughly the final twenty-three years of the nineteenth century), characterized by a ruthless pursuit of profit, an exterior of showiness and grandeur, and immeasurable political corruption.

grubstake: To advance money or supplies to miners in exchange for a percentage of profits from any discoveries.

horizontal integration: A business strategy in which one company buys out the competition; commonly known as a merger.

immigration: Leaving one's country to live in another.

imperialism: The practice of one country extending its control over the territory, political system, or economic system of another country.

Indian agents: Representatives of the U.S. government who worked with Native Americans. Their responsibility was to resolve conflicts and take the Native Americans' concerns to the government.

industrialism: An economy based on business and industry rather than agriculture.

inflation: A rise in the prices of goods and services.

Interstate Commerce Act: Passed in 1887, this law created the Interstate Commerce Commission (ICC), the first federal regulatory agency. It was designed to address railroad abuse and discrimination issues.

Ku Klux Klan: An organization of whites who believed in white superiority and who terrorized African Americans and their supporters in the South after the Civil War.

labor strike: A refusal of workers to work until management agrees to improvements in working conditions, wages, and/or benefits.

labor union: A formally organized association of workers that advances its members' views on wages, work hours, and labor conditions.

Molly Maguires: A secret society of workers established in Ireland in the 1840s whose mission was to fight discrimination. Some of its members immigrated to America later in the century. The Mollies were blamed for violence in the coal regions, though evidence against them was nonexistent.

monopoly: A condition created when one company dominates a sector of business, leaving the consumer no choices and other businesses no possibility of success.

mortgage: A loan of money to purchase property, such as a farm. The property is used as security for repayment of the loan; that is, if the borrower fails to pay, the property is seized.

muckrakers: Journalists who exposed scandal in Gilded Age society. These scandals usually involved public figures and established institutions and businesses, and focused on social issues such as child labor, political corruption, and corporate crime. The term "muckraking" was coined by President Theodore Roosevelt in 1906.

Mugwumps: A breakaway group of the Republican Party whose goal was to return Ulysses S. Grant to the White House.

naturalization: The process by which a person becomes a citizen of a country other than the one in which he or she was born.

patent: A grant by the government of the ownership of all rights of an invention to its creator.

patronage system: Also known as the spoils system. In patronage, someone donates large sums of money to help ensure the election of a candidate. That candidate repays the favor by making job appointments or by passing and proposing legislation that safeguards the interests of the business or person who donated the money.

philanthropy: Community service, financial donations, and volunteerism to promote human well-being.

political boss: A politically powerful—and often corrupt—person who can direct a group of voters to support a particular candidate.

popular vote: The result of the total number of individual votes in an election.

port: For an immigrant, the point of entry into a country.

poverty line: The least amount of income needed to secure the necessities of life. If someone lives below the poverty line, he or she cannot afford to purchase the basics needed to live, such as food, shelter, or medical care.

Progressive Era: A period in American history (approximately the first twenty years of the twentieth century) marked by reform and the development of a national cultural identity.

prospector: An explorer looking for minerals, such as gold.

reform: Change intended to improve a situation.

Republican Party: One of the oldest political parties in the United States. Founded as an antislavery party in the mid-1800s, it transformed into one associated with conservative fiscal and social policies.

reservations: Specific land allotted to the Native Americans by the U.S. government, as part of the solution to the "Indian Problem." The tribes did not own the land, but they managed it. These areas were the only places the Native Americans were allowed to live in the nineteenth century.

robber barons: The negative label given to powerful industrialists who amassed personal fortunes during the late nineteenth century, generally through corrupt and unethical business practices.

rustlers: Cattle thieves.

"Separate but Equal" doctrine: A policy enacted throughout the South that theoretically promoted the same treatment and services for African Americans as for whites, but which required the two races to use separate facilities.

settlement house: A center that provides community services to the poor and underprivileged in urban areas.

severalty: Individual ownership of land, as opposed to tribal ownership.

sluice: A wooden trough for washing gold. Soil is shoveled into a steady stream of water. Gold and other larger particles get caught in the bottom. Smaller sluices called rockers were often used during the gold rush. These sluices could be rocked back and forth to hasten the process of separating the gold from the soil.

Smithsonian Institution: A government institution with most of its grounds located in Washington, D.C. It includes 16 museums, 7 research centers, and 142 million items in its collections.

socialism: An economic system in which the government owns and operates business and production as well as controls the distribution of wealth.

sojourners: Immigrants who planned to stay in the United States temporarily; they usually stayed for a particular season or for a pre-determined number of years before returning to their homeland.

Spanish-American War: A war fought in 1898 in Cuba. Cuba wanted independence from Spanish rule. The United States fought on the side of Cuba and beat Spain within three months.

stampeders: Gold-seekers.

stock: A share of ownership in a business.

strike: A work stoppage by employees in protest of unfair treatment.

strikebreakers: Companies or individual employees who provide work during a strike; sometimes called scabs.

suffrage: The right to vote.

tariffs: Taxes imposed on goods imported from other countries.

temperance: A movement that campaigned for the public to refrain from drinking alcohol.

transcontinental railroad: The railroad system that traveled across the entire United States; this included five routes through the West. The last stake was driven into the railroad on May 10, 1869.

trust: The concept of several companies banding together to form an organization that limits competition by controlling the production and distribution of a product or service.

Gilded Age
and Progressive Era

Biographies

Jane Addams

BORN: September 6, 1860 • Cedarville, Illinois

DIED: May 21, 1935 • Chicago, Illinois

Social reformer; peace activist

"Old-fashioned ways which no longer apply to changed conditions are a snare in which the feet of women have always become readily entangled."

J ane Addams dedicated her life to helping others. She was the founder of Hull-House, one of the first settlement houses (community centers) in America. Hull-House was built in the center of the poorest section of Chicago, Illinois. Opened on September 8, 1889, the center quickly became the heart and soul of its immigrant (foreign-born) neighborhood. By its second year of operation, Hull-House served two thousand people each week. Young children could attend kindergarten there, while older children participated in academic and social clubs. Adults could learn basic skills such as reading and writing, but they also were taught important skills such as how to balance budgets and how to keep their homes and children healthy and safe. Eventually, thirteen buildings were added to the original structure, and Hull-House occupied an entire block in its Chicago neighborhood.

Jane Addams.

Freed by ideas, imprisoned by expectations

Born on September 6, 1860, Laura Jane Addams was the eighth child of Sarah and John Addams. The Cedarville, Illinois, family prospered, thanks to the good business sense of Addams's father, who owned a mill and, eventually, a bank. He was also a politician who served in the state senate for sixteen years; his influence helped build Cedarville into a thriving town. Jenny, as Addams was called in her childhood, lost her mother to illness before her third birthday. Her eldest sister, Mary, took over the responsibility of raising the seven other Addams children.

Addams was born with curvature of the spine. She spent much of her childhood suffering from strong feelings of insecurity and ugliness. She did not engage in physical activity as young children usually do, but spent a great deal of time instead alongside her father. The two formed a close relationship. From her father, Addams learned the importance of hard work and equality for all people. John Addams also gave his daughter a strong sense of morality and of the responsibility to help other people.

Young Jane Addams dealt with inner conflict because of the teachings of her father. She believed that her life had a higher purpose, that she had a duty—because of her good fortune and life of comfort—to help others less fortunate than herself. Yet she lived in an era when women were expected to do nothing more than marry and raise children. Even as her father encouraged her to read and learn, he did so only because he believed this knowledge would make her a better wife and mother. Addams longed to attend college in the eastern United States where she might make a life of her own; instead, her father sent her to nearby Rockford Female Seminary. She graduated as valedictorian (highest ranking student) of her class in 1881 with plans to attend medical school in Philadelphia, Pennsylvania. These plans directly conflicted with her father's wishes, but their relationship was such that he respected her enough to let her make this major decision.

Addams did not last long in medical school. Her father died suddenly of a burst appendix. Around that same time, Addams's own health took a turn for the worse. She spent years in and out of the hospital and after spinal surgery needed six months of bed rest. After her recovery, Addams traveled around Europe for nearly two years. She took another two years to write and figure out what she wanted to do with her life.

Finds inspiration in England

During a second trip to Europe, this time in 1888, twenty-seven-year-old Addams and her close friend Ellen Gates Starr (1859–1940) visited a settlement house in London. Toynbee Hall was Britain's first university settlement. There, college students worked together to help improve the lives of the city's poverty-stricken population. Addams and Starr were so impressed with the settlement project that they returned to America determined to develop their own settlement house.

The following year, the two women leased a large, rundown building on the corner of Polk and Halsted Streets, in the heart of Chicago's immigrant slum (a district marked by intense poverty and filth). Starr and Addams moved into the building with the goal of restoring it and providing the families of the neighborhood with a place to go where they could improve themselves while at the same time form a

Hull-House cofounder Ellen Gates Starr. THE LIBRARY OF CONGRESS.

sense of community with one another. Although Hull-House was not the first settlement house in America, it would be the most famous (see box).

The birth of Hull-House

Addams and Starr gave public speeches about their intentions for Hull-House and raised money to help fund the renovations. They addressed political leaders, civic clubs, clergy, and women's clubs about the importance of the settlement experience. They convinced the young women of well-to-do families to donate their time to help out at the center. Starr and Addams themselves took on many roles: teacher, caretaker, counselor, advisor, nurse. There was nothing those two women would not do for the visitors of Hull-House.

The settlement became a key component of the immigration experience in Chicago. In 1890, historians estimate that 68 to 80 percent of Chicago's population was foreign born. Immigrants who sailed to America's shores and headed for Chicago went directly to Hull-House,

Lillian Wald: New York's Version of Jane Addams

Social worker Lillian Wald. THE LIBRARY OF CONGRESS.

Although she never achieved the same recognition as her peer Jane Addams did, Lillian Wald had as much an impact on New York's East Side as Addams did on Chicago.

Wald was born in Cincinnati, Ohio, on March 19, 1867, to a wealthy German Jewish family. Wald attended and graduated from New York Hospital's School of Nursing. Early in her career, she began teaching a class in home nursing. Soon, she experienced for the first time the poverty and overcrowded conditions of New York's East Side immigrants when she made a home visit to treat a person.

That experience inspired Wald to decide to dedicate her life to helping the immigrant poor. With the help of another nurse friend, Wald began working out of a fifth-floor apartment. The two women worked all hours of the day and night, making themselves available to anyone and everyone. Those who could afford the nurses' small fee paid it. Those who could not pay the fee received treatment at no charge. Wald soon became known around the East Side as someone who could be counted on and trusted.

Wald needed money to continue to offer her much-needed services. She approached the wealthy members of the German Jewish community with her request for funding. They did

where they knew they could find trustworthy people to help them locate jobs, homes, and food. That year, Hull-House serviced two thousand people each week. The settlement house worked on a number of levels because it did what few other charitable organizations of the time did: It recognized the poverty and squalor (dirty, run-down conditions) that its clients lived in, and it gave them a place to nurture their desire to rise above their economic conditions. With that hope came the means to better themselves, through education and encouragement.

Once Hull-House proved itself a worthy cause, Addams and Starr had little problem securing monetary donations to help keep it running.

not disappoint her and gave generously. With that money, Wald was able to expand her services. She hired more nurses and even managed to pay them each $15 a month for their work. Some of them refused payment.

Wald realized she would need larger offices. In 1893, she found a house at 265 Henry Street. The house was named Henry Street Settlement. By 1898, Wald employed eleven full-time workers, nine of whom were nurses. By 1916, she had a staff of more than one hundred nurses, yet still managed to keep the services personalized.

Wald convinced insurance companies to provide visiting nurses to their policyholders. In 1903, Metropolitan Life Insurance Company was the first to use her suggestion. The program soon became standard with most major insurance companies. With Wald's encouragement, New York developed a public nursing program. In 1913, Wald placed a nurse from her staff in each public school in the city. The idea was well received, and the New York Board of Health organized and staffed the first public school nursing system in the world.

The Henry Street Settlement acted much like Addams's Hull-House in that it provided free education and clubs for children as well as academic classes and life-skills instruction for adults. In 1915, Wald founded the Neighborhood Playhouse, also on New York's East Side, in an effort to meet the cultural needs of the district's citizens.

The reformer's achievements were many. She persuaded U.S. president Theodore Roosevelt to develop a Federal Children's Bureau to protect children from abuse. She was a key figure in getting labor protection in the form of federal laws for women and children. Wald was a supporter of birth control and women's suffrage. She convinced Columbia University to appoint the first professor of nursing at an American college or university; before that, nursing was taught only in hospitals.

In the 1920s and 1930s, Wald received well-deserved public recognition for her efforts. Among her many awards was her recognition in 1922 by the *New York Times* as one of the Twelve Greatest Living American Women.

Wald died on September 1, 1940. Her settlement house remains in operation in the twenty-first century and continues to offer social services and arts programming to more than one hundred thousand New Yorkers every year.

Free medical care was provided, as was relief for the unemployed. Addams made sure Hull-House clients received education not only in academic subjects but also in skills necessary for daily life. She and others taught immigrants the English language and how to count money and perform simple math calculations. She taught them how to read so that they would know if someone—a landlord, a merchant—was trying to take advantage of them. She made sure they learned how to use the political system to their advantage so that city taxes would be used to help those who truly needed it rather than those who were close friends with local politicians.

Children enjoy their pottery class at Jane Addams's Hull-House in 1937. © BETTMANN/CORBIS.

One building at a time, the Hull-House settlement grew. The first building added to it was an art gallery, followed by a public kitchen, a coffee house, and a gymnasium. Next came a swimming pool, a cooperative boarding club for girls, a book bindery, an art studio, a music school, and a drama group. Lastly came a public library, an employment bureau, and a labor museum. While parents were inside learning life skills such as cooking and sewing, their babies were in the nursery, and their older children were on the playground or in classes and clubs of their own.

Through the decades, Hull-House continued to provide a safe gathering place for its neighborhood citizens. Under various leaderships and directorships, the settlement project experienced funding and policy conflicts, but these issues always managed to be resolved. In 1961, the

University of Illinois at Chicago decided it would build its campus on the site where Hull-House stood. Although the neighborhood fought the decision, Hull-House officially closed its doors in 1963. At that same time, ten thousand urban Americans were evicted from their homes, forced to find somewhere else to live.

Addams goes national

When it became clear that the "experiment" of Hull-House was a success, settlement houses began appearing in every major city across the country. Social reformers used Hull-House as a meeting place. National campaigns on issues such as women's suffrage (right to vote) were planned and developed there. Hull-House far exceeded the expectations of Starr and Addams.

Addams also exceeded her expectations for herself as her reputation grew. In 1905, she was appointed to the Chicago Board of Education and elected as Chairperson of the School Management Committee. Three years later, she helped found the Chicago School of Civics and Philanthropy (charitable giving). She became the first woman president of the National Conference of Charities and Corrections in 1909. That same year, Addams helped establish the National Association for the Advancement of Colored People (NAACP) to promote equality between the races; the organization is still active in the twenty-first century. From 1911 to 1914, Addams was vice president of the National American Women's Suffrage Association, one of the key women's organizations of the era. All the while, she remained at the center of social reform in her beloved Chicago. Addams headed investigations involving city sanitation issues and even accepted a position as garbage inspector for the Nineteenth Ward. (Cities were divided into areas called wards for political and civic reasons.) For her efforts in that position, she received an annual sum of $1,000.

Through it all, a feminist

With roots reaching back to the days when her father taught her that all people were equal, Addams's feminist philosophy motivated her throughout her life, including her endeavors at Hull-House. She believed women should have voting rights. Taking the idea of feminism one step further than most of her peers did during the early twentieth century, she encouraged women to create their own opportunities for growth and development.

Addams was also a pacifist (someone who does not believe in violence of any kind). She traveled the country speaking out on the importance of peace. She gave lectures against America's involvement in World War I (1914–18) and was made chairperson of the Women's Peace Party in 1915. Shortly after that, she was elected president of the Women's International League for Peace and Freedom; she held that position until 1929 and was honorary president until her death in 1935.

Addams's public disapproval of America's involvement in the war brought attacks upon her in newspapers and political magazines. As recorded on *Spartacus Schoolnet,* former U.S. president **Theodore Roosevelt** (1858–1919; served 1901–9; see entry) called Addams and her colleagues "hysterical pacifists," and even some of her former supporters rejected her. Addams did not let the controversy weaken her position; she chose instead to work with soon-to-be-elected U.S. president Herbert Hoover (1874–1964; served 1929–33) in a program that provided food supplies to the women and children of America's enemies in the war. For her many tireless humanitarian efforts, Addams was awarded the Nobel Peace Prize in 1931.

Despite her many social and political activities, Addams found time to write. The activist and reformer authored numerous magazine articles on social reform issues and published seven books on social reform and pacifism. Never having married or had children of her own, Addams died, surrounded by friends, on May 21, 1935, three days after an operation revealed that she had cancer.

For More Information

BOOKS

Addams, Jane. *The Second Twenty Years at Hull-House.* New York: Macmillan, 1930.

Addams, Jane. *Twenty Years at Hull-House.* New York: Macmillan, 1910. Reprint, New York: Signet Classics, 1999.

Davis, Allen F. *American Heroine: The Life and Legend of Jane Addams.* New York: Oxford University Press, 1973. Reprint, Chicago: Ivan Dee, 2000.

Elshtain, Jean Bethke, ed. *The Jane Addams Reader.* New York: Basic Books, 2002.

WEB SITES

Harvard University Library: Open Collections Program. "Jane Addams (1860–1935)." *Women Working, 1800–1930.* http://ocp.hul.harvard.edu/ww/people_addams.html (accessed on August 17, 2006).

Henry Street Settlement. http://www.henrystreet.org/site/PageServer (accessed on August 17, 2006).

"Jane Addams." *Spartacus Schoolnet*. http://www.spartacus.schoolnet.co.uk/USAaddams.htm (accessed on August 17, 2006).

"Jane Addams—Biography." *Nobelprize.org*. http://nobelprize.org/peace/laureates/1931/addams-bio.html (accessed on August 17, 2006).

Krain, Jacob B. "Lillian Wald." *The Jewish Magazine*. http://www.jewishmag.com/51mag/wald/lillianwald.htm (accessed on August 17, 2006).

"Lillian D. Wald." *National Association for Home Care & Hospice*. http://www.nahc.org/NAHC/Val/Columns/SC10-4.html (accessed on August 17, 2006).

PBS. "People & Events: Jane Addams (1860–1935)." *American Experience: Chicago, City of the Century*. http://www.pbs.org/wgbh/amex/chicago/peopleevents/p_addams.html (accessed on August 17, 2006).

Ryan, Alan. "Founding Mother." *The New York Review of Books*. http://www.nybooks.com/articles/18951 (accessed on August 17, 2006).

University of Illinois at Chicago. *Urban Experience in Chicago: Hull-House and Its Neighborhoods, 1889–1963*. http://www.uic.edu/jaddams/hull/urbanexp/ (accessed on August 17, 2006).

Grover Cleveland

BORN: March 18, 1837 • Caldwell, New Jersey
DIED: June 24, 1908 • Princeton, New Jersey

U.S. president

Grover Cleveland.
© CORBIS.

"I have tried so hard to do right."

Grover Cleveland was the twenty-second and the twenty-fourth president of the United States. Although elected to serve two terms, historians generally do not consider him to be among the great presidents. He is, however, respected for his success in restoring power to the executive branch (the departments of the federal government responsible for executing and enforcing laws).

Humble beginnings

Stephen Grover Cleveland was born on March 18, 1837, in Caldwell, New Jersey. He was the fifth of nine children born to Richard and Anne Cleveland. Cleveland's father was a Presbyterian minister who never made much money; the family remained poor throughout Cleveland's childhood. The Cleveland family moved to upstate New York when Grover was a young boy. Cleveland was just sixteen years old when his father died. The teen had to put his dreams of college on hold so that he could find a job to help support the large family. He found work in Buffalo as a clerk in a law office. Although he never

11

received a day of formal law education, he was admitted to the state bar in 1858, at the age of twenty-two.

During the Civil War (1861–65), Cleveland served as the assistant district attorney for Erie County in New York. The sole supporter of his family at the time, he paid someone $300 to take his place in the war, a legal and common arrangement at the time. However, this was a decision that would affect him negatively during his political years. His enemies would use it to paint him as unpatriotic for not serving in the military during wartime.

In 1870, Cleveland became sheriff of Erie County. During his three years in that position, he was also the county's executioner, and he personally hanged two criminals. In 1873, Cleveland returned to practicing law. By 1881 he had managed to save $75,000. His bank account was not the only thing that grew throughout the 1870s. The 5-foot, 11-inch attorney weighed 250 pounds (113.5 kilograms) and had earned the nickname Big Steve. Cleveland was not a man who enjoyed traveling, reading, or listening to music. He preferred poker games and evenings spent with friends at the local saloon. Cleveland also enjoyed hunting.

Becomes mayor and enters politics

As sheriff, Cleveland had avoided getting involved in politics, so it was a surprise to friends when he ran in Buffalo's mayoral race and won in 1881. So quick was he to clean up corruption among the city's various politicians that the Democratic Party nominated him to be governor of the state of New York.

By this time, Uncle Jumbo (as he was affectionately referred to by friends and family) weighed 280 pounds (127 kilograms). His weight did not deter him from success, however, and he was elected governor of New York in 1882. He served one two-year term and worked hard to fight corruption at the state level. Within his first year in the governor's mansion, Cleveland was already being talked about as a possible presidential candidate.

Cleveland's success as mayor and then governor gave him the confidence to seek the Democratic nomination in the 1884 presidential race. His Republican opponent was James G. Blaine (1830–1893) of Maine. Whereas Cleveland was popular throughout the entire Democratic party, Blaine had his share of Republican supporters, but nearly the same number of Republican enemies. Those who disliked Blaine were more reform-minded than their traditional Republican peers, and they favored Cleveland because of his obvious desire to challenge and defeat political corruption. Even with his foes, Blaine posed a considerable threat to Cleveland. He had served in the U.S. Senate from 1876 to 1881 and had been a member of the House of Representatives from 1863 to 1876. From 1869 to 1874, he served as Speaker of the House, one of the most influential positions after the president. He also had held the position of secretary of state in the administrations of James A. Garfield (1831–1881; served 1881) and Chester A. Arthur (1830–1886; served 1881–85).

Uncle Jumbo takes office

Although he gave only two campaign speeches and had to deal with a major scandal, Cleveland won the 1884 election. How he handled the scandal—with openness and honesty—helped cement his presidential victory.

During the 1884 campaign, word was leaked that Cleveland had fathered a son out of wedlock (while not married) in 1874. Although there was no way to prove with complete certainty that Cleveland was the father, he accepted responsibility and was helping financially to raise the boy, Oscar Folsom Cleveland. There was an equal chance that Cleveland's former law partner, Oscar Folsom (1837–1873), was the father. When Blaine's campaigners confronted Cleveland with the rumor, the presidential candidate publicly acknowledged that he had indeed engaged in sexual relations outside of marriage. Having responded to the scandal with honesty, Cleveland won the election, though just barely. He received 48.5 percent of the votes compared with Blaine's 48.2 percent.

Cleveland was the first Democrat elected to the White House since before the Civil War. At the time he took office, the patronage system was still quite powerful, despite the best efforts of former president Arthur's attempts to limit its influence. Cleveland spent the majority of his first term trying to keep Congress from granting undeserved privileges to big businesses. To do so, he replaced unqualified people with qualified officials as heads of departments of the federal government. Cleveland believed the job of the government was not to meddle or interfere in the everyday lives of citizens. By hiring capable, knowledgeable men, he built a government focused more on enforcing existing legislation than on introducing new laws.

Garfield and Arthur: Lost Presidents

There are four presidents that historians generally call the Lost Presidents, those who served rather uneventfully after the Civil War. They include Rutherford B. Hayes (1822–1893; served 1877–81), James A. Garfield, Chester A. Arthur, and Benjamin Harrison.

During his brief time as America's twentieth president, the Republican Garfield challenged corrupt politician Roscoe Conkling (1829–1888). Conkling was a U.S. senator from New York who believed men in his position should have personal control over assigning federal positions within state boundaries. Conkling had complete authority over the New York Customs House, which is the location where all imports and exports traveled through and were taxed. In an effort to reduce Conkling's corrupt power, Garfield nominated another man to run the Customs House, Conkling's rival, New York state senator William H. Robertson (1823–1898). With endless patience, Garfield maintained his stance, and eventually Robertson was elected to the position.

On July 2, 1881, just four months into the Garfield presidency, Charles J. Guiteau (1841–1882), an enraged attorney who had unsuccessfully sought a government position, shot Garfield. He clung to life for two-and-a-half months. During that time, inventor Alexander Graham Bell (1847–1922) tried to find the bullet lodged in Garfield's body using an electrical

device he had designed. His attempts failed, however, and Garfield's body finally gave in to infection and internal bleeding, and he died on September 19, 1881.

Chester A. Arthur, Garfield's vice president, took over the presidency upon Garfield's death. While vice president, Arthur had not joined Garfield in his battle against Conkling but had instead supported Conkling in his underhanded dealings. Once he reached the presidency, though, he wanted to prove himself trustworthy. He stopped spending time with old friends who knew him before his change of heart and began to support civil service reform.

Arthur was responsible for passing the first federal immigration law in 1882. The law barred criminals, lunatics, and paupers (extremely poor people) from entering America. That same year, Congress passed the Chinese Exclusion Act, which put severe restrictions on Chinese immigrants.

In 1883, Congress passed the Pendleton Act, which established a Civil Service Commission that required applicants to positions within government agencies and departments to pass a test. No longer would a friendship with a politician influence who was hired, a concept known as patronage. The act also protected government employees from being fired for reasons

Angers supporters

Democrats as well as Republicans depended on the patronage system. When it became clear that Cleveland would not tolerate this unjust practice, he angered thousands of Democrats who expected to be handed jobs simply because they shared the same political party as the president.

other than job performance. The Pendleton Act angered Republicans because it allowed Democrats to secure powerful positions in the civil service.

Angering his own party did not seem to be a major concern of Arthur's. He also sought to lower taxes so that the federal government did not have an embarrassingly high surplus of revenue each year. Republicans were traditionally in favor of high taxes, and they were furious over the signing of the Tariff Act of 1883. The law brought a gradual reduction in import taxes over the next decade.

A year after he became president, Arthur learned that he had a fatal kidney disease. He kept this information from becoming public knowledge, and in 1884, he sought reelection so as not to appear to be afraid of being beat. He failed to receive his party's nomination, however, and died in 1886.

An 1880 campaign poster showing Republican presidential candidate James A. Garfield and his running mate, Chester A. Arthur. © CORBIS.

Democrats had been at the mercy of Republican rule for twenty-four years; they were ready to make some money and wield some power. In spite of his fellow Democrats' obvious displeasure, Cleveland continued in the steps of President Arthur to reform the civil service (the system by which civilians are appointed to positions in various government agencies and departments). In 1887, Congress repealed the Tenure of

Office Act, which prohibited the president from removing any officials from office without the approval of the Senate. Even before their terms had expired, Cleveland was ridding the government of corrupt officials.

As president, Cleveland had the power to veto (vote down) a bill or piece of legislation. All the presidents before him used their veto power 204 times combined. In his first term alone, Cleveland exercised his power to veto 414 bills. By the end of his second term, that number increased to 584.

The bachelor marries

When Cleveland became president, he was a bachelor (unmarried). His unmarried sister, Rose Cleveland (1846–1918), took on the role of First Lady. Rose hated her duties; she was more interested in pursuing scholarly activities than she was hosting parties and entertaining dignitaries. She was relieved from her obligations in 1886, when Cleveland married Frances Folsom (1864–1947), the twenty-one-year-old daughter of his former law partner.

It was a surprise to no one when it was announced that the president had married a Folsom. Cleveland's partner's widow, Emma Folsom, and her daughter Frances were frequent visitors at the White House. But the public was quite certain it would be Emma that Cleveland would marry. Society was shocked when the forty-eight-year-old president chose a bride less than half his age.

Cleveland became the first president to marry in the White House when, on June 2, 1886, he exchanged wedding vows with Frances in front of forty close friends. The idea of a wedding at the White House enthralled Americans, and Frances Cleveland almost immediately became a celebrity. She received so many fan letters from the moment she became First Lady that she had to hire a social secretary to help her answer them.

Although she avoided getting involved in politics, Frances was an ideal president's wife. She showered her husband with attention and was a most gracious hostess who willingly shook hands with thousands of people at White House presentations and at public appearances. Well schooled, she impressed visitors and politicians with her breadth of knowledge and her ability to speak French. The First Lady became known throughout the country as Frankie, and her likeness was used

Harper's Weekly *illustration shows the White House wedding of President Grover Cleveland and Frances Folsom, June 2, 1886.* THE LIBRARY OF CONGRESS.

in advertisements and labels to sell goods of all sorts. The Clevelands eventually had five children.

A busy first term

The year 1886 was important in another way for Cleveland, as it was the year of the dedication ceremony of the Statue of Liberty in New York. The following year was more controversial, however. In addition to repealing the Tenure of Office Act, the president used his veto power to refuse to pass a bill that would give disabled Civil War Union (Northern) veterans a regular pension (an income or regular payment received based on prior service). Most veterans who became disabled because of military service applied for their pensions through the federal Pension Bureau. The bureau investigated each case to confirm that the disability was war related and to determine how much money the veteran should receive. Some veterans' pension applications, however, were made in a private bill, meaning they applied for their pensions privately, rather than through the Pension Bureau. These cases were not usually investigated, so there were many chances for corruption. From 1885 to 1887, 40 percent of all bills passed by the House of Representatives and more than half of all those approved by the Senate were private pension bills. In the first four years of his presidency, Cleveland received 2,099 private pension bills and vetoed 288 of them. The president's refusal to pass such bills angered the veterans, who made up a large portion of the voting public. But Cleveland believed that passing the 1887 proposal would serve only to create an expensive, endless, and corrupt form of charity.

February of that same year saw the passage of the Interstate Commerce Act (February 4) and the Dawes Severalty Act (February 8). Cleveland did not initiate either piece of legislation.

Interstate Commerce Act Up until 1887, the railroads conducted their business with very few regulations. As a result, they were arguably the most corrupt industry in the country. Rather than compete with one another, owners of various railroads met and developed a pricing structure that allowed them all to profit and none to underprice one another. This practice was known as pooling. Railroads also charged higher freight rates to shippers sending goods a short distance than they did to those sending goods long distances, even though it cost railroads the same amount, regardless of miles shipped. Railroads gave out refunds to shippers who did a great deal of business with a particular railroad company, or to large companies that agreed to give that railroad all their shipping business. This refund was known as a rebate and was another form of rate discrimination.

These unethical practices made competing impossible for smaller companies and farmers. All the discounts and special benefits were reserved only for big business. Rate discrimination laws had been passed in 1842, but they were largely meaningless because there was no federal enforcement of them. By the 1870s, merchants were asking the government for regulations; even some railroad companies joined in the plea in the 1880s. Competition among them was fierce.

Congress responded by passing the Interstate Commerce Act. Along with the law came the establishment of the Interstate Commerce Commission (ICC). The commission comprised five members who would each serve a six-year term. There could be no more than three members belonging to the same political party. The new law banned pooling and rebates, and some of the rate differences for short and long hauls were eliminated. Unfortunately, the ICC was powerless to set rates or to punish companies that violated the law. Neither the railroads nor all the farm groups were happy. Railroad owners believed the government was too involved; farmers believed it was not involved enough.

Dawes Severalty Act The Dawes Severalty Act was passed on February 8. Also known as the Indian Emancipation Act, the law took away all tribal lands and divided them up for individual ownership. In doing so, the government took away the legal standing and rights of tribes. Native American individuals gave up their tribal status in exchange for American citizenship as well as a specific amount of land. But ownership was still restricted: Native Americans could not completely own the land they were "given" until twenty-five years had passed.

The purpose of the Dawes Act was to force Native Americans to assimilate into (fit into and adapt their ways of life into) American society. Reformers saw the tribes' nomadic lifestyle (frequent moving around) as an obstacle to be overcome in order to become Americanized. The Act seriously undermined the Native American way of life, but it did little to help anyone assimilate. After all land had been divided and given out, there were millions of acres of "leftover" land that was then sold to non–Native Americans. Before the Act, Native Americans owned about 138 million acres of land. After the law's passage, their holdings dwindled to about 78 million acres. It was not until 1934 that the policy was reversed. The surplus lands were returned to the Native Americans.

Foreign affairs

Cleveland was not in support of territorial expansion (gaining more land for the United States). He felt America had enough trouble with big business regulations and the Native American issue. As a result of his thoughts on expansion, Cleveland withdrew a treaty proposed during the presidency of Chester A. Arthur that would have given the United States the right to build a canal in Nicaragua to be owned by both countries.

President Cleveland did get involved in an issue involving fishing rights in the North Atlantic Ocean off the coasts of Canada and Newfoundland. These fishing rights had been a conflict between America and Great Britain (which owned Newfoundland at the time) for more than a century. By the time Cleveland took office, American fishermen were fishing the waters with the condition that Canadian fishermen could export their fish to the United States without paying taxes. Congress repealed the rights of Canadians to do so, and Canadian fishermen began seizing U.S. fishing boats. In March 1887, Cleveland signed a bill known as the Retaliation Act, which allowed him to forbid Canadian imports of any kind if the Canadians continued to harass American fishermen. In February 1888, the Bayard-Chamberlain Treaty was signed between America and Britain. This treaty allowed American fishermen to fish off the coasts of Canada and buy their fishing licenses there. If Congress ever lifted the taxation on Canadian exports, American fishermen would receive certain privileges. The treaty satisfied everyone involved.

Presidential positions on other issues

Cleveland believed African Americans were inferior to whites and refused to treat them as social or political equals. To him, civil rights was a social issue that should not be interfered with by the federal government. He considered himself an Indian reformer but looked upon Native Americans as children who needed a caretaker. As for women, he had little to say. Women during his presidency did not have the right to vote, and he never encouraged them to seek such a right.

Loses election, then wins again

Cleveland lost the 1888 presidential election to former U.S. senator **Benjamin Harrison** (1833–1901; served 1889–93; see entry) of Indiana. Harrison led a troubled administration, though, and Cleveland decided to run again in the campaign of 1892. His victory over Harrison gave Democrats the majority of power in both the Senate and the House of Representatives.

By 1894, the country was entering a major economic depression (a long-term state in which unemployment rates are high, prices and business activity are low, and people are fearful of the future). Nearly 18 percent of all workers were unemployed. Without money to pay bills, many Americans were hungry and homeless. Railroad construction dropped by 50 percent, and nearly two hundred railroad companies declared bankruptcy. (Bankruptcy refers to the legal declaration of the inability of an individual or a company to repay debt.) One in every ten banks did the same, as did dozens of steel companies.

Cleveland, still of the belief that the government should not support charity with its dollars, did nothing to help the crisis. Rather than provide relief dollars, he repealed the Sherman Silver Purchase Act. This bill, sponsored by U.S. senator John Sherman (1823–1900) of Ohio, had the U.S. Treasury purchase 4.5 million ounces of silver at market price each month. The silver was bought with Treasury notes that could be redeemed in either gold or silver. Holders of these notes were eager to turn them in for gold because they got more money per note that way. The act increased the production of silver, which sent silver prices down rather than up, which was the intent.

Repealing the act angered some members of the Democratic Party and caused them to consider Cleveland more Republican than many Republicans. This split within the party weakened its strength. On top of that, thousands of holders of government bonds and old silver certificates began cashing them in for gold, which depleted the nation's gold reserve. In response, Cleveland authorized four new government bonds between 1894 and 1896. These bonds allowed the government to pay its international debts. By turning to investment banker J. P. Morgan (1837–1913) to back the bonds with $62 million in gold, Cleveland was accused of siding with big business and betraying the working class. Morgan was known for his unethical business tactics and ruthless ambition. This common perception of Cleveland had a direct impact on the congressional election of 1894, in which Democrats lost in every region but the South. Now it was Cleveland's turn to feel betrayed.

The Pullman Strike

In addition to the Depression that began in 1893, Cleveland had to deal with serious labor unrest throughout his second term. In June 1894, a railroad strike at the Pullman Palace Car Company in Chicago, Illinois, created problems throughout the entire state of Illinois. Railroads stopped running, which put a halt to any business that relied on the railways for shipping. This work stoppage brought mail delivery service and passenger transportation to a standstill. State authorities realized the strike was beyond their control and called on the federal government for assistance. Cleveland's response made history when, for the first time, federal military troops became involved in a labor strike.

On July 4, President Cleveland sent in twenty-five hundred federal troops in an attempt to end the strike. Rioting occurred from July 7 through 9, when strikers attacked the military troops. These forces

The Fifteenth U.S. Infantry Company C, called in by President Grover Cleveland to help break up the Pullman Palace Car Company strike of 1894, poses beside a Rock Island Railroad patrol car in Blue Island, Illinois. © CORBIS.

responded with gunfire at point-blank range. About thirty strikers were killed and many more wounded. The number of troops on hand soon increased to fourteen thousand, as state and additional federal troops joined in the confrontation. The strikers were defeated within the week, and after several weeks of negotiating, Pullman reopened its doors on August 2.

Remains firm on territorial expansion

Cleveland retained his position that territorial expansion was not good for the United States. Protecting what America already owned, however, was not in question. His most controversial foreign policy decision involved a boundary dispute between Venezuela and Britain. Britain owned a profitable trade route through Venezuela, but Venezuela wanted to control its own region. When Britain refused negotiations, Venezuela called on the United States for help. This request made Britain unhappy. Cleveland was willing to help and proved his commitment by sending U.S. Navy ships to confront British warships near Venezuela. Americans feared an impending war, but Britain changed its mind and negotiated the dispute to Venezuela's satisfaction.

Cuba posed another challenge for the president. It had been under Spanish rule in 1895. America had received reports that Spanish troops were abusing Cubans. Although Cleveland wanted Cuba to gain its independence, he was not willing to aid them in their fight, so he refused to send in troops to support the Cubans. Instead, he tried to convince Spain to adopt reforms that would allow Cuba to gain its independence gradually. The Senate completely opposed Cleveland on this issue, and they passed pro-Cuba legislation whenever possible. When Congress threatened to recognize Cuba as an independent nation, Cleveland warned that he would view the decision as an act of defiance against his presidential authority. The issue never was resolved during Cleveland's second term.

Ultimate betrayal

Although Cleveland's response to the Pullman Strike in 1894 helped rebuild America's trust in its president, it was not enough to overcome the bitter resentment the public still held regarding his refusal to help during the Depression. Cleveland was not nominated by the Democrats in the 1896 presidential election, but was replaced by former U.S. representative William Jennings Bryan (1860–1925) of Nebraska. Bryan lost the election to **William McKinley** (1843–1901; served 1897–1901; see entry).

Following the end of his second term, Cleveland and his wife moved to a mansion in Princeton, New Jersey, where local residents treated them like a king and queen. He spent the early 1900s writing political commentary. In 1904, he published a book called *Presidential Problems*. That same year, his eldest daughter, Ruth, died. Those who knew him best said he never recovered from the loss.

In March 1908, Cleveland suffered a severe attack of a gastrointestinal disease he had lived with for years. He was secretly rushed to the hospital, where he died on June 24. His wife Frances was by his side.

For More Information

BOOKS

Cherny, Robert W. *American Politics in the Gilded Age: 1868–1900*. Wheeling, IL: Harlan Davidson, 1997.

Gaines, Ann. *Grover Cleveland: Our Twenty-Second and Twenty-Fourth President.* Chanhassen, MN: Child's World, 2002.

Kent, Zachary. *Grover Cleveland.* Chicago: Children's Press, 1988.

Laughlin, Rosemary. *The Pullman Strike of 1894.* Greensboro, NC: Morgan Reynolds Publishing, 2000. Reprint, 2006.

Rolde, Neil. *Continental Liar from the State of Maine: James G. Blaine.* Gardiner, ME: Tilbury House, 2006.

WEB SITES

"Chester Alan Arthur." *American President.* http://ap.beta.polardesign.com/history/chesterccrthur/biography/LifeBeforePresidency.common.shtml (accessed on August 17, 2006).

"Grover Cleveland." *The White House.* http://www.whitehouse.gov/history/presidents/gc2224.html (accessed on August 17, 2006).

"Grover Cleveland's Obituary." *New York Times* (June 25, 1908). Available online at http://starship.python.net/crew/manus/Presidents/sgc/sgcobit.html (accessed on August 17, 2006).

"James Abram Garfield." *American President.* http://www.americanpresident.org/history/jamesgarfield/ (accessed on August 17, 2006).

"Stephen Grover Cleveland." *American President.* http://americanpresident.org/history/grovercleveland/biography (accessed on August 17, 2006).

Ty Cobb

BORN: December 18, 1886 • Narrows, Georgia

DIED: July 17, 1961 • Atlanta, Georgia

Baseball player

Ty Cobb.
© BETTMANN/CORBIS.

"The great American game should be an unrelenting war of nerves."

Ty Cobb is considered by many baseball historians to be the greatest player ever to play the game. He is also viewed as one of the most controversial players in the history of the sport. Nicknamed the "Georgia Peach," Cobb was the first player elected to the Baseball Hall of Fame (1936). As of 2006, his career batting average of .367 has never been equaled.

A simple childhood

Tyrus Raymond Cobb was the first of three children born to Amanda and William Cobb. William was a schoolteacher and Baptist minister who had married his wife when she was just twelve years old. The family spent most of Cobb's childhood in Royston, Georgia. Here they lived on a farm, where Cobb learned the value of hard work. He worked side by side with his father, and developed a respect and reverence for him that would last his lifetime.

Cobb was never close to his mother, and when he was just eighteen years old, their relationship suffered a major blow. Rumors were circulating throughout their small hometown that Amanda was unfaithful to her husband. On the night of August 8, 1905, Cobb was out of town playing baseball, and his two younger siblings were staying overnight elsewhere. Cobb's father told his wife he had out-of-town business that would keep him away for the night, but what he really planned to do was check to see if the rumors about his wife were true.

Armed with a pistol, Cobb's father climbed the family home to the outside of his wife's bedroom window. When she heard someone trying to open the locked bedroom window, she took the loaded shotgun kept by her bedside and opened fire through the window, killing her husband. Although charged with voluntary manslaughter, an all-male jury found her not guilty. Her alleged faithlessness was never proved, and she never remarried.

His father's death at the hand of his mother devastated young Cobb. Ultimately, he used his unending respect for his father—and his own desire to make him proud, even in death—to fuel his motivation to be the best baseball player he could be.

Dreams of greatness

Cobb's father was never in favor of his eldest child pursuing a career in baseball. The sport was different during that time than it is in the twenty-first century. Many of its players built reputations of being hard-drinking, gambling, foul-mouthed womanizers. But Cobb spent much of his free time playing the game with neighborhood boys, and his natural abilities were immediately recognized. Young Cobb proved to be a fierce competitor for whom losing was not an option.

In 1903, Cobb grew weary of playing ball as a hobby. He wanted more and had the confidence in his own talent to believe he could do better. He wrote letters to managers of baseball clubs in the South Atlantic League. The one response he received came from the manager of the Augusta Tourists. If Cobb paid his own expenses, he could try out for a spot on the team the following spring.

Despite his father's reservations about a baseball career, Cobb received his blessings as well as six checks, each made out for $15. Cobb took his first step in the journey toward a career in professional baseball. In his autobiography, Cobb remembered his father's parting words. "You've chosen. So be it, son. Go get it out of your system, and let us hear from you."

Unimpressive beginnings

Cobb earned a spot on the Augusta Tourists team. As a center fielder, he did not impress his manager, who released Cobb early in the season. Not one to give up, Cobb followed a teammate to Anniston, Alabama, to try out for a semiprofessional team there. Worried what his father would say, Cobb phoned him and told him of his plans. According to his autobiography, Cobb's father told him to go after the job. "And I want to tell you one other thing," his father said. "Don't come home a failure." Those words would inspire Cobb to greatness.

Cobb made the team, and this time, his playing reflected his true abilities. He proved himself a more-than-capable batter. Within three months, he was asked to return to his old team, the Augusta Tourists. The team was under new management, so Cobb took a chance. He demanded a pay raise, which he got, and rejoined the team for the 1905 season.

Cobb did not enjoy playing under the team's new management, but he did not have to wait long for a leader he could respect. George Leidy took over the Tourists. Leidy immediately recognized great potential with Cobb. He helped Cobb focus and gave him the encouragement he needed. Together they worked on Cobb's batting skills. By August 1905, Cobb had shown much improvement. That month, however, would not be one of celebration for Cobb, who had to return home for his father's funeral. He did not finish the season with the Tourists, but instead learned he had been sold to the Detroit Tigers of the American League. He would stay with the team for the next twenty-one years, as both player and, later, as player-manager.

Rises to fame

Almost immediately, Cobb encountered difficulties with his new teammates. He was one of only a few southerners in the major leagues, and one of even fewer in Detroit. By nature a shy person, his quiet ways were mistaken for conceit, and his teammates did not appreciate his desire to spend his time alone. Fist fights and brawls with other team members were not uncommon. By the middle of the first full season in 1906, Cobb had to be hospitalized for a stomach ailment, the details of which have never been made clear. It was not an easy year for Cobb, who maintained the lowest batting average he would see in his career: .320 in ninety-eight games.

The following season was his first great year, and he helped his teammates reach the World Series. Although they were defeated by the Chicago Cubs, Cobb enjoyed a .350 batting average, which gave him the first of nine consecutive batting titles. He would eventually hold twelve batting titles. He also led the league that year with 212 hits, 49 steals, and 116 runs batted in (RBIs). The 1908 and 1909 seasons brought more of the same: each year, Cobb won the batting title and the Tigers won the pennant (league championship). But each time, they were again defeated in the World Series (in 1908, by the Cubs again; and in 1909, by the Pittsburgh Pirates). Despite an amazing career, Cobb would never again play in another World Series.

Around this time, Cobb developed a reputation as a violent, almost crazy, player. For his own part, Cobb did everything he could to encourage that reputation. In his mind, psychological warfare was as important as skill in the game of baseball, and he mastered the art of intimidation (making another timid or fearful). His tendency to be a loner further supported others' perception of him as a dangerous personality. He was known for his racism as well, the kind many white southerners embraced during that era. Anyone who disagreed with or was different from Cobb, he disliked. According to *ESPN.com,* he kept a list of people he did not like, and no one was off limits.

As a batter, Cobb often used his natural ability to hate. He would work himself into a state where he approached the plate with the intention to humiliate the pitcher in any way possible. Sometimes this meant bending over and picking at clumps of dirt, just as the pitcher was about to deliver the ball. Other times, he completely ignored the pitcher and took his time preparing for the pitch. Opposing team players came to despise Cobb not only because his talent was usually far greater than their own, but because he played mind games with them.

Cobb became as well known for his antics as he did for his abilities. Yet he was in demand as a player, because everyone would rather have him on their team than against them. Cobb cemented his popularity with fans in 1909 when he won the Triple Crown (the best batting average, most homeruns, and most RBIs) with a .377 batting average, 9 home runs, and 107 RBIs.

Baseball is war For Cobb, baseball was war. He used every tactic available to him not only to win but also to make his opponents feel as bad

Detroit Tigers Hall of Famer Ty Cobb slides into third base. NATIONAL BASEBALL HALL OF FAME LIBRARY/MLB PHOTOS VIA GETTY IMAGES.

as possible. He studied each individual pitcher and took advantage of his weaknesses. He practiced sliding until his legs were a bloody, raw mess. Pain was something to overcome, not give in to. On the official Ty Cobb Web site, he is quoted as having said, "I have observed that baseball is not unlike a war, and when you come right down to it, we batters are the heavy artillery." Although he agitated players in the major leagues with his racism and violent outbursts, he was respected for his ambition and dedication to the game.

Cobb's violence infiltrated his personal life as well. One of the longest-standing rumors is that he once killed a man when he and his wife stopped along the roadside to help three men whose car appeared broken down. The men reached into the car and began beating Cobb, who turned the tables on them and started to beat them back. According to legend, every time Cobb told the story of that event, it was slightly different. Sometimes the men recognized him and apologized, and there was no harm done. Telling the story at other times, he said that he got out of the car and chased them into an alley, where he beat them senseless, possibly to death. No official reports of beatings or any deaths for that day exist, so the story remains just another Ty Cobb legend.

The best years ever

As a hitter, Cobb enjoyed his best year ever in 1911, when he finished with a batting average of .420. This was also the year Cobb would be first featured on a baseball card.

The years immediate following were equally impressive, as Cobb continued to hold the batting average title. In 1915, he set a major league record when he stole 96 bases and scored 144 runs. The following year ended his nine-year streak as the batting-average king. His .361 average was just behind that of Tris Speaker (1888–1958), who batted .386. Cobb bounced back, however, and recovered his title for three more consecutive years, with averages of .383, .382, and .384.

Becomes manager

In 1921, thirty-four-year-old Cobb became Detroit's manager. He immediately initiated some changes regarding spring training (for example, he made arrangements for the team to stay at higher-quality hotels with better food) that were popular with the team and thus boosted his reputation in the eyes of his men. In his six seasons as the team's player-manager, the Tigers played above .500 in five, and Cobb remained in the top ranks of the league's hitters with batting averages that never dipped below .338.

Cobb's popularity as manager waned eventually, as players tired of his odd habits. He switched pitchers constantly, going back and forth between right- and left-handed men. He also slowed down the game considerably with his numerous visits to the pitcher's mound throughout the games. In November 1926, Cobb left the Detroit Tigers under questionable circumstances. He was accused by former teammate Dutch Leonard (1892–1952) of fixing (planning the victory or loss ahead of time) a 1919 game against the Cleveland Indians. Leonard claimed Cobb and

Cleveland Indians players Tris Speaker and Joe Wood (1889–1995) were in on the scheme. The matter was referred to baseball commissioner Kenesaw Landis (1866–1944), who judged the men not guilty. Cobb, however, resigned as manager shortly thereafter. The Tigers released him as a player in January 1927.

Final days

On February 8, 1927, Cobb signed with the Philadelphia Athletics. On July 18, 1927, he had his four thousandth hit. By the end of his career in 1928, Cobb would hold the league record with 4,191 hits. It remained the record until September 11, 1985, when Cincinnati Reds player Pete Rose (1941–) broke it.

After retiring in 1928, Cobb continued to behave in ways that contributed to his aggressive reputation. He frequently argued and spent his later years drinking heavily, habits that led his first wife of thirty-nine years to divorce him. He remarried at the age of sixty-two, but that marriage ended in divorce as well.

One of the highlights of Cobb's career came in 1936, when he earned 222 of 226 votes to be inducted into the Baseball Hall of Fame. He beat out the legendary Babe Ruth (1895–1948), a rival he disliked the most, which brought him great personal satisfaction. Ruth, since his entrance on the baseball scene in 1919, was the only player on the field who posed a real threat to Cobb's abilities. As Ruth's popularity grew, so did Cobb's disdain for him. Ruth became known as the home-run king, a fact that never ceased to annoy Cobb. Having earned 98.2 percent of the ballot into the Hall of Fame, Cobb felt that he had proved his superiority. That ballot record was not broken until 1992, when pitcher Tom Seaver (1944–) received 98.8 percent of the vote.

Cobb spent his later years alone; he had very few friends and two of his five children had already died. Having made wise investments with his money throughout his career, Cobb had an estate he wished to use to better the lives of those less fortunate. He donated $100,000 to his childhood town of Royston for a hospital to be built. He also established the Cobb Educational Fund, which awards college scholarships to needy students in Georgia. Another $100,000 went to that organization in 1953.

In the late 1950s, Cobb was diagnosed with cancer as well as Bright's disease, a fatal kidney disorder. By spring of 1961, the former baseball great was spending most of his time in the hospital getting treatments

A Brief History of Baseball Cards

As baseball gained in popularity in the 1860s, companies began producing trading cards that featured drawings of baseball teams or individual players on one side and advertising for a particular product on the other. Early trading cards reached the height of their popularity in the 1880s, when children began collecting and saving trading cards as a hobby.

Historians and collectors generally consider the sporting goods company Peck and Snyder to be the first publisher of baseball cards. It made sense: They sold baseball equipment, and the cards gave them an easy way to advertise. In the twenty-first century, a Peck and Snyder card is worth up to $20,000.

Trading cards were a smart way for businesses to get advertising into the hands of potential customers. Adults knew their children enjoyed collecting trading cards, so they made it a point to get them. Naturally, once in hand, parents would read the cards. It was an inexpensive way to communicate to consumers in an age before mass communication. By the turn of the century, trading cards lost their wide appeal as many businesses turned into mail-order companies and began printing catalogs.

By the 1880s, tobacco companies cornered the market on baseball cards. Between 1886 and 1890, they produced most of the century's cards that people immediately recognize as baseball cards. The companies competed with one another, but Goodwin & Co. is generally

considered the first major producer of "modern" baseball cards. Cards were inserted into cigarette packs, and the companies tempted smokers to buy their products by including coupons, which could be saved to be redeemed for a larger, higher-grade card. These were the first cards to feature photography rather than illustration or woodcut prints.

By 1895, the major companies within the tobacco industry had formed a monopoly (total control of an industry which does not allow for competition). Now that competition was no longer an issue, there was no need to produce baseball cards as a way to get people to buy their brand of tobacco. As a result, very few baseball cards were issued during those final years of the nineteenth century and the first few of the twentieth. At that time, federal regulations broke up the monopoly. Baseball cards once again became a means of beating out the competition.

Tobacco companies began issuing albums in which to store their cards. Each pack of cigarettes came with a coupon. Once a consumer had saved enough coupons, they could be redeemed for an album. But whereas the tobacco industry once was the only provider of baseball cards, now other industries were using the idea to attract customers. Candy manufacturers began including baseball cards in their packages of candy, and sports magazines included cards in each issue. The popular candy Cracker Jack, famous for the small toys and

for his cancer, which had moved into his spine and skull. It was not until the last few days of his life that he expressed regrets about some of the choices he had made and the way he had lived his life. He entered the hospital for the last time in June, and he took his final breath on June other items to be found in each box, used baseball cards as one of their first hidden prizes.

World War I (1914–18) changed America's economy, and card production was temporarily halted. They would not reappear on the market until the 1930s. In 1933, Goudey, a chewing gum company, began offering free cards with every gum purchase, and soon gum became associated with baseball cards. The major gum companies began competing for the rights to include specific players on their cards. Topps

became the number-one baseball-card producer for more than twenty years, well into the 1960s.

At that time, other food companies began offering cards with their products, including hot dogs, cereal, and gelatin desserts. In the 1980s, other bubblegum companies began issuing baseball cards. In the early twenty-first century, a company called Wizards of the Coast produced a line of collectible cards that could also be used in a playing-card game. As of 2006, only two companies marketed and sold traditional baseball cards: Topps and Upper Deck.

The front and back of a 1912 baseball card featuring Detroit Tigers outfielder Ty Cobb, issued by Miners Extra brand of chewing tobacco. THE LIBRARY OF CONGRESS.

17, 1961. Despite an admirable career that spanned more than twenty years, only three baseball players attended his small funeral. Cobb left one-quarter of his estate to the Cobb Educational Fund and the remaining $11 million to his children and grandchildren.

For More Information

BOOKS

Bak, Richard. *Peach: Ty Cobb in His Time and Ours.* Ann Arbor, MI: Sports Media Group, 2005.

Cobb, Ty, and Al Stump. *My Life in Baseball: The True Record.* Garden City, NY: Doubleday, 1961. Reprint, Lincoln: University of Nebraska Press, 1993.

Holmes, Dan. *Ty Cobb: A Biography.* Westport, CT: Greenwood Press, 2004.

Kramer, Sydelle. *Ty Cobb: Bad Boy of Baseball.* New York: Random House, 1995.

Okkonen, Mark. *The Ty Cobb Scrapbook: An Illustrated Chronology of Significant Dates in the 24-Year Career of the Fabled Georgia Peach.* New York: Sterling, 2001.

PERIODICALS AND OTHER MEDIA

Bak, Richard. "Forget the Babe, Baseball's Best Is Named Tyrus Raymond Cobb." *USA Today (Society for the Advancement of Education).* (September 2005). This article can also be found online at http://findarticles.com/p/articles/mi_m1272/is_2724_134/ai_n15727520.

Cobb. DVD. Ron Shelton. Hollywood, CA: Warner Home Video, 2003.

WEB SITES

"The Illustrated History of Baseball Cards: The 1800s." *Cycleback.com.* http://www.cycleback.com/1800s/ (accessed on August 21, 2006).

Library of Congress. "Baseball Cards: 1887–1914." *American Memory.* http://memory.loc.gov/ammem/bbhtml/bbhome.html (accessed on August 21, 2006).

The Official Web Site of Ty Cobb. http://www.cmgworldwide.com/baseball/cobb/bio.html (accessed on July 6, 2006).

Schwartz, Larry. "He Was a Pain…But a Great Pain." *ESPN.com.* http://espn.go.com/sportscentury/features/00014142.html (accessed on August 21, 2006).

"Ty Cobb." *Baseball Library.com.* http://www.baseballlibrary.com/baseballlibrary/ballplayers/C/Cobb_Ty.stm (accessed on August 21, 2006).

"Ty Cobb." *National Baseball Hall of Fame.* http://www.baseballhalloffame.org/hofers_and_honorees/hofer_bios/cobb_ty.htm (accessed on August 21, 2006).

Ty Cobb Educational Foundation. http://www.tycobbfoundation.com/ (accessed on August 21, 2006).

John Dewey

BORN: October 20, 1859 • Burlington, Vermont
DIED: June 1, 1952 • New York, New York

Philosopher; educational reformer

"We can have facts without thinking, but we cannot have thinking without facts."

John Dewey.
© BETTMANN/CORBIS.

John Dewey is considered by many historians to be the greatest educational philosopher of the twentieth century. His view of education is a theory called pragmatism. Pragmatism revolves around the concept that knowledge is valuable only if it is practical. Dewey acknowledged that each individual's experiences affected that practical application, and therefore, what one person knew as the truth might vary from another person's understanding of the truth. Pragmatism was in direct conflict with the traditional approach to education during the early Progressive Era (approximately 1900–13), which was authoritarian (unquestioning adherence to facts, with no consideration of individual experience). (The Progressive Era was a period in American history [approximately the first twenty years of the twentieth century] marked by reform and the development of a national cultural identity.) Dewey's revolutionary approach to learning changed the face of education forever. The value of his contribution continues to be debated in the twenty-first century.

Small-town childhood

John Dewey was the third of four sons born to Archibald Sprague Dewey and Lucina Artemesia Rich. He was born on October 20, 1859, in Burlington, Vermont, and spent his entire childhood in this small, rural (country) town, albeit one that included the University of Vermont. Dewey's father owned the one general store in town. The store was the gathering place for locals to discuss politics, current events, and any other topics that interested members of the community. Dewey grew up in this atmosphere of debate and discussion. His experience would continue to influence the philosopher throughout his lifetime.

Life in rural Vermont had a profound impact on Dewey's views toward education. Never a good student, he formed the opinion at an early age that the traditional approach to school—sitting at desks, being lectured, memorizing dates and names—was ineffective. Dewey believed the student should be an active learner, not the passive learner he or she was forced to be in an ordinary classroom. His perception of school was not completely negative, however. His social experiences at school, coupled with the stimulating discussions at his father's store, instilled in him a belief that the day-to-day contact one has with one's peers provides a real chance for significant learning, whether it be in the area of politics, culture, or economics.

College, as student and teacher

Despite his intense dislike of traditional education, Dewey attended the University of Vermont. While a student there, Dewey was exposed to various philosophers and their schools of thought. Having graduated in 1879, he spent the next two years teaching high school. During this time, Dewey considered his future, fully aware that he did not want to teach high school for the rest of his life. He entertained the idea of pursuing a career in philosophy. When the *Journal of Speculative Philosophy* published one of his philosophical essays, the budding writer took that as a sign that he should continue his studies. He enrolled as a graduate student at Johns Hopkins University in Baltimore, Maryland.

Dewey's experience at Johns Hopkins was a positive one. There, he studied under two professors who would help the young philosopher develop his own ideas about education. George Sylvester Morris (1840–1889) exposed Dewey to idealism (the concept that one can never know objects, but only the representation, image, or sensation of those objects), a philosophy Dewey would embrace for years. G. Stanley Hall (1844–1924), one of the most respected experimental psychologists of his time, showed Dewey the importance of scientific methodology (the techniques and strategy one uses to gather information) as it applies to human sciences (such as psychology, political science, and sociology).

After earning his Ph.D. in 1884, Dewey was hired to teach at the University of Michigan, a position he would keep for nearly ten years. He did leave in 1888 to teach at the University of Minnesota, but he returned to his post at Michigan after one year. In 1886, he married one of his students, Harriet Alice Chipman. They eventually had six of their own children and adopted another. Two of his sons died in childhood. During his tenure at Michigan, Dewey wrote and published two books, the first of dozens of books on various aspects of philosophy.

Dewey the pragmatist

In 1894, Dewey accepted a professorship at a new school, the University of Chicago. He remained there for another decade. It would be one of the most productive periods of his life.

While at the University of Chicago, Dewey's idealism was replaced with another school of thought. Pragmatism was, at the time, still in its development stages in America. The shift to pragmatism was a major one for Dewey because idealism was a philosophy in which results cannot be measured. Pragmatism, on the other hand, is a theory in which results can be easily measured by their practicality. With a curriculum based on each student's real life, lessons of the student's choosing could be incorporated. How those lessons were applied and the results of that application were the measurement of one's success or failure. Dewey's exploration of pragmatism resulted in a series of four essays he published under the collective title "Thought and Its Subject-Matter." The essay collection was published in 1903, along with essays written by his colleagues and students, in *Studies in Logical Theory*.

Establishes experimental school

Two years into his teaching position at Chicago, Dewey established what he called a laboratory school. This school would be the testing ground for his philosophical ideas and their implementation. The school was a laboratory in two ways: Dewey's primary intention was to use the school to facilitate research into new methods of learning and teaching. His second purpose was to allow children to experiment with their own unique approaches to learning.

Dewey envisioned his lab school as a place where children could experiment, find answers to questions that intrigued them, and create. No rows of wooden desks filled his school. Rooms were designed for movement and group activities. Furniture was designed to help students in their approach to learning, not to keep them in one position for hours at a time. Dewey felt traditional classroom furniture was built more for listening than for actual working, so he filled his school rooms with comfortable seating that could be easily moved, either to be pushed aside or gathered into groupings. But perhaps what set apart the lab school from the traditional American schools was Dewey's overall expectation that students would generally learn things for themselves. The teacher was there only to guide and direct, not to lecture, dictate, and test.

Students in the lab school were not under the authority of their teachers. It was not the teachers' responsibility to impose ideas on their students. Instead, their job was to help students find methods and styles of learning that were most effective for each student's unique personality or character. The student was at the center of education as an active, involved learner. The goal of education at the lab school was not to simply gather knowledge, but to reach a level of self-realization in which the knowledge learned truly helped each student function in his or her world.

Three principles Dewey based his experimental school on three principles. These principles formed the foundation of his educational philosophy. The first principle involved the role of the school. Its job was to train children to help them live and grow within a community. Dewey believed education should help children develop an awareness of their role within a larger group so that they can successfully operate in real-life settings such as towns, neighborhoods, workplaces, and even families.

The second principle placed the children at the center of their own education and gave them the responsibility of navigating where that education would go. Dewey did not believe children learned if the presentation and application of knowledge was structured. His philosophy was that learning must come from a natural desire to know more about a particular subject. Dewey saw this principle as directly related to the idea of community. He argued that a child was social and that a community was made up of individuals. He believed that if one takes away social interaction, what the child or individual has learned is useless because the knowledge gained is not being used effectively to support or add to the community.

Dewey's third principle was that learning must promote a child's unique tendencies and activities. Under the proper guidance and influence (which the teacher would provide), these tendencies and activities would be organized to encourage the individual to thrive in a cooperative setting.

Dewey's school became famous throughout the country for its groundbreaking research. He published his first work on education based on his experiences with the school. *The School and Society* was published in 1899 to much critical acclaim.

Moving on

Dewey fell into disagreement with administrators at the University of Chicago over how the school should be run. Since he had achieved a level of fame, there was no shortage of job offers. He left the Laboratory School in 1904 and accepted a job as professor of philosophy at Columbia University in New York. He remained at this school until his retirement in 1930.

Teaching at Columbia gave Dewey the perfect arena in which to spread his ideas about education as he had experienced them at the Laboratory School. Here he came into contact with the most brilliant philosophical minds of his time. He secured a reputation as a progressive, brilliant mind himself. His first decade at Columbia was one of his most productive periods as a writer. He published several books and countless articles on the theory of knowledge. As a professor, he lectured and traveled the world during his years at Columbia, which gave him further opportunity to share his ideas. He came to be perceived as an important commentator on current events. This perception was supported by his contributions to popular magazines and his involvement with important political issues of the day, such as women's suffrage (the right to vote).

Alice Dewey died in 1927; Dewey retired from active teaching in 1930 but continued to teach as professor emeritus (a professor who has officially retired) for another nine years. He continued to write and publish books and articles until shortly before his death. At the age of eighty-seven, he remarried, this time to a widow named Roberta Grant. Dewey died of pneumonia in his New York home on June 1, 1952, at the age of ninety-two. By the time of his death, he had published more than twenty books.

Not without his critics

Not everyone hailed Dewey as a great thinker. His educational theory had its opponents during his lifetime, most of them traditionalists who believed children needed to be controlled or they would go wild. More modern critics of Dewey credit him with the general failure of the public school system in America. To these critics, Dewey's theories had a harmful and lasting influence on education.

Other critics claimed to disagree with him when they simply could not understand him. According to an article on Dewey, written by Spencer J. Maxcy of Louisiana State University and posted on the *Thoemmes Continuum,* Dewey was "notorious for his terrible writing style, boring and meandering [wandering] lectures . . . by nature his writing style was difficult to penetrate and almost impossible to interpret." Being misunderstood did not bother Dewey; he knew what he meant and it was everyone else's responsibility to figure it out.

The most common misunderstanding about Dewey is that he was a proponent of progressive education. The early twentieth century was known as the Progressive Era, and generally this means American society was experiencing reform and change on every level, including education. There are similarities between pragmatism and progressive education, but one major difference separates the philosophies. Progressive education revolves around the idea of giving students total freedom in their learning methods. Dewey was against this absolute freedom because he believed it was not a solution to the problems presented by the strict structure of traditional education methods. He believed some structure and order was necessary. That structure needed to be based on a theory of experience (how humans have the experiences they do) and not developed on the whim of teachers or students.

Although many general aspects of Dewey's educational philosophy were incorporated into the progressive education movement, Dewey never considered himself a supporter of the progressive education movement. The movement lasted until the 1950s, when people finally grew weary of the endless debates about the nature of education in general and the administration of progressive education in particular.

Another reason some philosophers and educators criticized—and continue to criticize—Dewey was his tendency to change the essential meaning of common words such as "experience" and "democracy." Dewey would define such words in his own terms, then comment on the work of others using his personal definition rather than the common interpretation of the words. This habit made it difficult to critique his work, and it made it pointless for him to accurately assess others' work at times.

Without argument, Dewey's theories and research had a major impact on America's school systems. Simultaneously praised for his vision and criticized for his influence on education, Dewey is looked upon as a revolutionary (one who fights the system). Whether the results of his philosophy of education were positive or negative is up to individual interpretation.

For More Information

BOOKS

Casil, Amy Sterling. *John Dewey: The Founder of American Liberalism.* New York: Rosen, 2006.

Edmondson III, Henry T. *John Dewey & the Decline of American Education: How the Patron Saint of Schools Has Corrupted Teaching & Learning.* Wilmington, DE: Intercollegiate Studies Institute, 2006.

Jackson, Philip W. *John Dewey and the Lessons of Art.* New Haven, CT: Yale University Press, 1998.

Maxcy, Spencer J., ed. *John Dewey and American Education.* Bristol, England: Thoemmes Continuum, 2002.

WEB SITES

Flanagan, Frank M. "John Dewey." *University of Limerick.* http://www.ul.ie/tilde_accs/philos/www/vol1/dewey.html (accessed on August 21, 2006).

JohnDewey.Org. http://www.johndewey.org/ (accessed on August 21, 2006).

"John Dewey (1859–1952)." *The Internet Encyclopedia of Philosophy.* http://www.iep.utm.edu/d/dewey.htm (accessed on August 21, 2006).

Thomas Edison

BORN: February 11, 1847 • Milan, Ohio

DIED: October 18, 1931 • Llewellyn Park, New Jersey

Inventor

Thomas Edison.
© HULTON ARCHIVE/
GETTY IMAGES.

"It's obvious that we don't know one millionth of one percent about anything."

Thomas Edison was one of the most productive inventors in American history. With 1,093 U.S. patents (documents granting rights of ownership and design to a specific person) and more in the United Kingdom, France, and Germany, no other inventor has come close to Edison's output. Edison's accomplishments were not always complete inventions but improvements made on technology already in place. Edison is best remembered as the inventor of the incandescent lightbulb (a lightbulb powered by heat). In addition, he was an intelligent businessman and a successful manufacturer.

A restless student

Thomas Alva Edison was born to Samuel and Nancy Edison in Milan, Ohio, on February 11, 1847. Young Al, as he was called, was the last of seven children, and he suffered from ill health throughout most of his childhood. As a result, he began school later than most children. Within three months, it became clear that he was not going to find success in a formal classroom setting. Edison's mother pulled him from school and homeschooled him. Edison always credited his mother for putting him in an educational environment that was better suited for him.

In 1854, the Edison family moved to Port Huron, Michigan, where Sam found work in the lumber business. Five years later, Edison began selling newspapers and candy on the Grand Trunk Railroad in Detroit. By the age of twelve, Edison was almost completely deaf. Despite several theories as to how his deafness developed, Edison himself claimed he lost his hearing because someone pulled him off the ground and into a train car by his ears.

The young salesman used the train's baggage car to set up a laboratory for chemistry experiments, but a resulting fire put a halt to mixing pleasure with work. Edison also had a printing press set up in the train. He published the *Grand Trunk Herald,* the first newspaper ever to be published on board a train.

Becomes an inventor

In 1862, at the age of fifteen, Edison saved a three-year-old boy from being run over by a boxcar. The boy's father, J. U. MacKenzie, was the station agent in Mount Clemens, Michigan. Grateful to Edison for his bravery, MacKenzie trained Edison as a telegraph operator. (The telegraph is a communication system used to send messages from one location to another via electric wires, usually using a code of dots and dashes to represent letters.) Edison took a job as a telegraph operator in Port Huron that winter and continued working on scientific experiments in his free time. For the next five years, Edison traveled across the country, taking telegraph jobs in various cities.

Edison moved to Boston, Massachusetts, in 1868, where he worked for Western Union (a company that sends money and messages electronically). He applied for his first patent that year, for an electric vote recorder. Always at work on at least one invention, Edison quit his job in 1869 to devote all his time to inventing. His first patent was awarded to him that year, but his joy was soon overshadowed by disappointment. Politicians were reluctant to use the machine for fear of inaccuracy.

In the summer of that year, Edison moved to New York City. A friend and telegraph engineer, Franklin L. Pope (1840–1895), worked at Samuel Laws' Gold Indicator Company and let Edison sleep in a room there. When Edison fixed a broken machine on the premises, he was hired to manage the maintenance of the company's printing machines.

Forms his first company

In October 1869, Edison teamed with Pope and another businessman, James Ashley, to establish Pope, Edison and Co. The businessmen promoted themselves as electrical engineers and builders of electrical devices. Edison was granted several patents to improve the telegraph. Not only could his machine send messages electrically, it could now print as well. The company merged with Gold and Stock Telegraph Company in 1870. Next, Edison invented a simple copier machine, an early version of the modern facsimile (fax) machine.

That same year, Edison joined forces with mechanic William Unger. They founded the Newark Telegraph Works in Newark, New Jersey, where the company manufactured printers. Edison used the facility to conduct his many other sideline experiments. He would never be without a workshop again.

Edison was devoted to his inventions, but he found time to marry in 1871. Though he had known her for only two months, Edison married sixteen-year-old Mary Stilwell. The couple eventually had one daughter and two sons. That year was not entirely full of joy, however. Just before his wedding, Edison mourned the death of his mother. The loss of the person he loved most in the world may have influenced his decision to marry so quickly. His marriage, though based in love, was often difficult. Edison spent most of his time working in the lab, even sleeping there.

Gets a reputation

Edison quietly established himself as the leading American inventor throughout the first half of the 1870s. In 1873, he sold a British company the rights to his automatic telegraph. He had an oral agreement with Western Union to develop multiple telegraphy systems throughout 1873 and 1874. In that last year, Edison invented the four-message telegraph, which landed him a contract with Western Union. From that point on, all his work in multiple telegraphy would solely benefit Western Union. The contract brought Edison his first major financial success of $10,000.

Although recognized as a genius by others in the telegraph industry, international fame would not come to Edison until 1877, when he earned the title, "Wizard of Menlo Park."

Thomas Edison stands in his laboratory in Menlo Park, New Jersey. © BETTMANN/CORBIS.

Menlo Park

Edison bought a parcel of rural land in Menlo Park, New Jersey, in 1876 and set about building the laboratory of his dreams. According to *The Edison Papers,* the lab became known as the "invention factory." Edison employed a team of expert experimenters and machinists to turn ideas and theories into useful machines and products. At just twenty-nine, Edison already had one hundred U.S. patents in his name.

As America's telegraph expert, Edison was asked by Western Union to look into the possibility of a speaking telegraph. Such a machine had already been invented by Alexander Graham Bell (1847–1922), but it left much room for improvement. Sound traveled clearly but could not be transmitted at a great distance or in a noisy environment, as businesses tended to be. In 1878, Edison unveiled his transmitter, a device that allowed telephones to transmit voices over long distances. That transmitter was used for almost one hundred years.

Invents the phonograph Edison invented the phonograph somewhat by accident, yet it is the invention that thrust him into the spotlight and made him something of a celebrity. While working on the telephone, which was supposed to be used by telegraph companies to transmit messages between operators, Edison noticed a problem. Speech was too fast to be written down, so there was no written record of messages. To remedy that, he figured out a way to record the vibrations of the receiving instrument. His recording method enabled them to be played back at a slower speed, thus allowing operators to write down the words.

Edison kept notebooks full of notes and ideas and outcomes of all his inventions. When he reread what he had written about the telephone, he realized he had found a way to record not just messages, but sound. In December 1877, Edison and his employees unveiled their "talking machine" at the offices of *Scientific American* magazine in New York. Newspapers immediately published reports of the amazing invention. Because it was impractical for anyone but trained technicians to operate it, however, the invention did not catch on with the public as anything but a novelty (something of interest, but not necessary). Still, Edison's name made headlines.

The Edison Electric Light Co.

Since there was little interest in the phonograph, Edison turned his attention to the electric light system. With financial backing from several investors, he founded the Edison Electric Light Company on November 15, 1878. Edison agreed to give the company all his patents in exchange for a large share of stock in the company. The inventor's experiments began as a search for a lamp that could replace gas lighting. Work on this project continued into 1879. Edison wanted to develop not only an incandescent lightbulb but a complete electrical lighting system that cities across the country could support.

The answer to the search for a long-lasting bulb lay in a tiny filament (a threadlike fiber inside the bulb) made of carbon. His first incandescent lamp burned for two days. With the discovery of the carbon filament, Edison was able to provide America with lightbulbs that were practical for home use. He did not invent the electric bulb; he improved upon it and made it available for homes. He did invent the electric light system, which made electric light safe, practical, and economical. Because of his system, America's cities forever changed. Businesses could stay open longer, and nighttime no longer put an end to production in factories.

Edison demonstrated his incandescent lighting on December 31, 1879, in Menlo Park. Approximately sixty lamps were installed around the grounds of the lab, and the public was invited to view the spectacle that night. Americans saw, for the first time, the power of electric light.

On January 27, 1880, Edison filed for a U.S. patent for his lamp. The patent office ruled that Edison's patent was based on the work of another inventor, William Sawyer, and was invalid. Finally, on October 6, 1889, Edison's patent was ruled valid by a judge who declared that Edison's improvement of the filament was based on his own work, not that of someone else.

Lights up the world

Edison established a light factory in East Newark in 1881. The following year, he and his family moved to New York, where he set up another laboratory. In 1882, the first commercial electric light system was installed on Pearl Street in Manhattan. Four hundred lamps were lit. Within a year's time, more than ten thousand lamps were being used by 513 customers. The lighting system was exhibited at the Paris Lighting Exposition in France in 1881 and elsewhere throughout Europe. Soon, Edison established several companies to manufacture and operate these electrical systems, both in America and abroad.

In 1884, Edison's wife died, and for a short while, his work suffered. The thirty-nine-year-old inventor married nineteen-year-old Mina Miller in 1886, and her support of his work allowed him to return full-time to his research. The couple would have three children. By the time of his second marriage, he had moved back to New Jersey. In 1887, he decided to build another laboratory. This new lab was larger than his first at Menlo Park, and it served as the research and development center for his many companies.

In 1889, Edison brought all his companies together to form Edison General Electric. His company merged with its main competitor, Thompson-Houston, in 1892, and became known simply as General Electric. With that merger, Edison left the electric light industry and used his profits from the deal to fund research on a piece of equipment that still interested him: the phonograph.

New and improved

Edison's 1887 lab included a phonograph department, and he had been trying to improve the apparatus since the lab was built. In 1896, Edison established the National Phonograph Company in the hopes of attracting customers to buy his invention for home entertainment.

Since first introducing the phonograph, Edison had worked to make necessary improvements. The phonograph initially played cylinders, not discs. The early cylinders were made of wax and did not last longer than two or three plays. Around the turn of the century, Edison and his staff developed the disc phonograph. Discs were longer lasting, easier to play and store, and more economical. Edison went into the disc-making business in 1912. His discs were designed for use with Edison phonographs only. His success in this venture was seriously hampered by Edison putting himself in charge of choosing which musical groups his company would record. The nearly deaf Edison saw his discs earn the reputation of featuring low-quality musicians. Because of the choice of music and the competition provided by the newly invented radio, Edison's disc business came to an end in 1929.

Although unsuccessful as a disc recorder, Edison was a leader in the disc-duplicating industry. He used the profits from that business to finance two more innovations: a cement manufacturing process, and an electrical storage battery. The battery was intended to be used to power electric automobiles, but it found more use in various industries. Within a few years, the battery became the most profitable invention of Edison's various businesses.

Makes movies In 1888, Edison began working on a motion-picture camera in his lab. As pointed out by the Library of Congress's Web site on the inventor, *American Memories,* Edison wrote, "I am experimenting upon an instrument which does for the eye what the phonograph does for the ear."

Edison was not the actual inventor of the motion-picture camera. One of the researchers who worked in his lab, William K. L. Dickson (1860–1935), invented the camera in October 1889. After Edison further

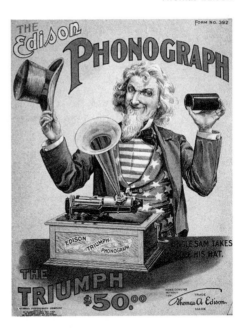

A poster advertising the Edison Triumph phonograph, c. 1901. © BETTMANN/ CORBIS.

refined the camera, he applied for a patent in 1891 for a device called a Kinetograph (which would take photos for his next invention), and a motion-picture peephole viewer called a Kinetoscope.

The Kinetoscope's popularity was immediate, and Kinetoscope parlors opened up throughout New York and other major cities in 1894. In these establishments, customers could view short films featuring various singers, dancers, and other performers through the new Kinetoscope machines. It was a profitable business for Edison.

Dickson eventually helped Edison's competitors develop a different peephole device and was fired for his actions. Dickson went on to form a company with three other men. Edison worked with two other inventors in his lab to develop the Vitascope, a movie projector. The Vitascope, like the Kinetoscope, was immediately popular when it debuted on April 23, 1896.

Despite his success in films, it was never an industry that was as close to the inventor's heart as the phonograph inventions and innovations he had developed. In 1913, he merged the two industries when he developed the Kinetophone (*kineto* means "movement"), a device that synchronized sound on a phonograph to the picture shown through the movie projector. It was a flawed system, though, used for just two years before technicians gave up trying to get it to work properly. Within three years, Edison removed himself from the movie business.

Final years

As he aged, Edison had less to do with the day-to-day operation of his many companies. In 1911, he reorganized all of them into one large company, Thomas A. Edison, Incorporated. Unlike in the earlier years, his mission was not to invent as many useful devices as possible but to remain on the market with the inventions he had already developed.

During World War I (1914–18), Edison was involved in naval research and believed technology would be the future of war. Although he was appointed head of the Naval Consulting Board in 1915, he was frustrated by his position. He felt that the U.S. Navy was not open to many of his ideas and suggestions.

Edison's health began to fail in the 1920s. The highlight of the decade for him came on the fiftieth anniversary of the electric lamp, in 1929. Automobile manufacturer Henry Ford (1863–1947) hosted a huge celebration attended by such dignitaries as President Herbert Hoover (1874–1964; served 1929–33), aviation pioneer Orville Wright (1871–1948), and chemist Madame Curie (1867–1934). Edison reenacted the invention of his incandescent lamp at the gathering.

Edison died at age eighty-four on October 18, 1931. His remains, along with those of his second wife, are buried on his New Jersey estate, known as Glenmont. It is maintained by the National Park Service and is called the Edison National Historic Site.

For More Information

BOOKS

Baldwin, Neil. *Edison: Inventing the Century.* New York: Hyperion, 1995. Reprint, Chicago: University of Chicago, 2001.

Cousins, Margaret. *The Story of Thomas Alva Edison.* New York: Random House, 1965. Reprint, 1993.

Delano, Marfe Ferguson. *Inventing the Future: A Photobiography of Thomas Alva Edison.* Washington, DC: National Geographic Children's Books, 2002.

TIME for Kids Editors. *Thomas Edison: A Brilliant Inventor.* New York: HarperCollins, 2005.

WEB SITES

Beals, Gerald. *Thomas Edison's Home Page.* http://www.thomasedison.com/ (accessed on September 1, 2006).

"Edison National Historic Site." *National Park Service.* http://www.nps.gov/edis/home.htm (accessed on September 1, 2006).

"The Edison Papers." *Rutgers University.* http://edison.rutgers.edu/ (accessed on September 1, 2006).

Library of Congress. "Inventing Entertainment: The Motion Pictures and Sound Recordings of the Edison Companies." *American Memory.* http://memory.loc.gov/ammem/edhtml/edhome.html (accessed on September 1, 2006).

Menlo Park Museum. http://www.menloparkmuseum.com/ (accessed on September 1, 2006).

PBS. "Edison's Miracle of Light." *American Experience.* http://www.pbs.org/wgbh/amex/edison/ (accessed on September 1, 2006).

Emma Goldman

BORN: June 27, 1869 • Kovno, Russia
DIED: May 14, 1940 • Toronto, Ontario, Canada

Anarchist; political activist

"Those in authority have and always will abuse their power."

Emma Goldman was an anarchist. She believed in the political theory known as anarchy, which holds all forms of governmental authority to be unnecessary and undesirable and advocates a society based on voluntary cooperation and free association of individuals and groups. She believed in the independence of women, sexual freedom and birth control, freedom of expression, and the right to form labor unions. Her willingness to fight for these causes—at all costs—resulted in her deportation (permanent exile) from America. But her advocacy of such causes made her one of the most hated and feared figures of the Gilded Age and the Progressive Era. (The Gilded Age was the period in history following the Civil War and Reconstruction [roughly the final twenty-three years of the nineteenth century], characterized by a ruthless pursuit of profit, an exterior of showiness and grandeur, and immeasurable political corruption. The Progressive Era was the period that followed the Gilded Age [approximately the first twenty years of the

Emma Goldman.
THE LIBRARY OF
CONGRESS.

53

twentieth century]; it was marked by reform and the development of a national cultural identity.)

Simple beginnings

Emma Goldman was born on June 27, 1869, in the small town of Kovno, Russia (modern-day Lithuania). Being a Jew, she and her family suffered under the anti-Semitic (anti-Jewish) laws of the day, which included being forced to live in Jewish ghettos (impoverished areas) and frequently moving to escape oppression. It was a difficult life.

Her father reacted to society's hatred of his race by taking out his anger on his family, often through violence. As explained on the *Jewish Women's Archive* Web site, Goldman considered her father "the nightmare of my childhood." Young Goldman was acutely aware of the injustice done to the Russian Jews, but she thought her father's anger would be more productive if directed toward their persecutors. By age twelve, she was already thinking in terms of political organization and action.

Goldman left Russia in her early teens to obtain what she believed would be a modern education in Germany. She was sorely disappointed to realize that her schooling there would be nothing but lectures, memorization, and authoritarian teaching. Her rebellious attitude toward such schooling led her to fights with her German relatives with whom she was living. After just six months, she returned to Russia.

Her father forced her to work in a factory and informed her that she would be entering into an arranged marriage. (In an arranged marriage, parents pick their child's spouse.) He refused to hear her ideas of furthering her education, insisting that Jewish women need only know how to prepare fish and give their husbands many children. Goldman, at sixteen, would have nothing to do with such plans. In 1885, she set sail for America with her half-sister, Helena.

Disappointment with America

Despite her anticipation of living in freedom, Goldman quickly realized that only the wealthy enjoyed true freedom in her new homeland. In Rochester, New York, factory work was even harder than it had been in Russia; for a ten-and-a-half-hour day, she was paid a meager $2.50. Goldman experienced firsthand the inequality of America's social classes; she knew all too well of the inhuman working conditions of industrial society.

Within four months of arriving in America, Goldman accepted a marriage proposal from Jacob Kershner, another immigrant factory worker. The two shared interests in reading, dancing, and traveling, and Kershner offered Goldman an escape from the drudgery of her home life living with relatives. Though hesitant, she married Kershner in February 1887.

Discovers anarchism

Goldman found marriage, like America, disappointing. The couple began having marital problems. A depressed Kershner turned to cards and gambling, wasting the little money the newlyweds had. This strained relationship, now void of any dancing or happiness, made Goldman feel isolated and lonely. She had left her job out of respect for her husband's wishes to uphold the societal norm that proper married women do not work outside the home. Money troubles became a major concern.

In the midst of this great personal sadness, Goldman took special interest in the resolution of national controversy. On May 4, 1886, labor activists held a rally in Chicago's Haymarket Square to protest the police brutality of strikers (employees refusing to work) at the local McCormick Harvester Company the day before. The rally was peaceful until someone threw a bomb at the police after they tried to shut down the demonstration. People in the crowd were injured, and one police officer was killed.

In the chaos that ensued, an uncertain number of demonstrators were killed, as were six police officers (though evidence indicates they were killed by friendly fire, for the most part). Some of the officers lingered for several weeks before they died from their injuries. America followed their fate in newspaper accounts.

The press and the police blamed Chicago's anarchist leaders for the bombing, and the public agreed with that assumption. In keeping with the general panic surrounding the event, eight anarchists were arrested. Despite plenty of evidence to suggest their innocence, all eight were found guilty of the crime. Seven were sentenced to death; one was to serve fifteen years in prison. Of the seven who were given the death penalty, one committed suicide the night before the execution, and two had their sentences commuted to life in prison. The remaining four were executed on November 11, 1887, despite international protest at the apparent injustice of the rulings.

Goldman followed the situation in the news and was convinced of the innocence of the eight men. Empowered by this sense of righteousness, she took up the anarchist cause and became its most outspoken activist. According to *SunSITE,* a University of California at Berkeley digital library Web site, anarchism is a political philosophy that embraces the concept of a society based on shared ownership and voluntary agreements among individuals and groups. It further poses that without the consent and involvement of each individual in the social order, any form of government gets its power from the threat of force. Some anarchists believe in the use of violence to further their cause; others do not. In anarchy, there is no single source of power or authority, no leader. This is not to be interpreted to mean that anarchy means chaos or disorder; rather, it favors order based on cooperation and voluntary participation.

Anarchism was especially appealing to the working class in the Gilded Age. As America evolved from a society based on agriculture to one based on industry, members of the lower classes were controlled and exploited by their wealthier peers. Business owners and managers were unconcerned about the health and safety of their workers; they did as little for them as possible. The Gilded Age was the time period in history when capitalism (an economic philosophy based on private ownership of business and competition) first made Americans aware that, because of its belief in private ownership and willful competition, the poor would get poorer while the rich would get richer. Anarchism was seen as a solution, or an alternative, to a capitalist society. In theory, it would allow everyone to live equally.

Begins a life of political activism

As Goldman's political philosophies became clearer to her, so too did her personal beliefs. She left Kershman and chose to live with the shame divorce brought to a woman of her era rather than remain in an empty and oppressive relationship. She also left Rochester in favor of New York City, where she could live among other passionate anarchists. She immediately immersed herself in the anarchists' world and spent her time attending meetings, organizing labor demonstrations and strikes, and engaging in philosophical and political discussions.

For Goldman and her fellow activists, the State—meaning any form of government—was restrictive (limiting) and not in the best interests of the individual. They promoted the idea that the State should be destroyed. Goldman herself was not in favor of violence; part of her definition of anarchism was a belief in the basic goodness of each individual human. She believed anarchy could work because, without the provocation of capitalism and government force, people would not live in fear.

No one would have anything the next person did not have, so there would be no need for crimes such as robbery and murder.

Every cause Goldman believed in and fought for was an extension of her basic belief in absolute freedom. She found a soul mate in 1889 in fellow Russian immigrant Alexander Berkman (1870–1936), who would become the great love of her life as well as a lifelong comrade in the quest for anarchism. The two made the agreement that they would dedicate their lives to their cause and willingly give their lives if necessary, either together or apart.

With passion and eloquence, Goldman quickly established herself as a gifted speaker in the anarchist community. She was popular among her fellow anarchists but feared and loathed for her commitment by most of American society. What happened in 1892 only served to cement her reputation as a rabble-rouser (someone who stirs up large groups of people in anger or violence) and a radical (someone with extreme views who wants change).

Homestead Strike of 1892

Homestead, Pennsylvania, was a steel-mill town with a population of more than ten thousand people. Of those inhabitants, just over thirty-four hundred were employed by Carnegie Steel Company. Of those employees, eight hundred were skilled and earned an average of $2.43 for a twelve-hour shift, or roughly twenty cents an hour. Unskilled laborers earned fourteen cents an hour.

In 1889, these wages were paid on a sliding scale that was dependent on the market price (the price paid to the steel companies by other businesses who bought their product) being paid for steel. The higher the market price, the higher the wages would be. If the market price dropped, so did wages. Twenty and fourteen cents an hour was the average.

This agreement between management and labor was due to expire on June 30, 1892. Of the eight hundred skilled workers, all but twenty were members of the Amalgamated Association of Iron, Steel and Tin Workers. These union members were expecting better terms upon expiration of the old contract. Their expectations did not seem unrealistic. Andrew Carnegie (1835–1919), owner of the mill, had publicly empathized with (claimed to understand the feelings of) strikers in other industries. He even implied that he understood how their frustration led to violence.

Carnegie was out of the country in 1892, visiting his homeland of Scotland. Negotiations were in the hands of Henry Clay Frick (1849–1919), chairman of Carnegie Steel. Frick was known for his hard-hearted, antiunion attitude. He had no patience for workers who complained and would not tolerate rebellion in any form.

The union would not accept the new contract proposed by Carnegie Steel because it required workers to accept an 18- to 26-percent decrease in wages. Union leader Hugh O'Donnell met with Frick throughout June in the hopes of reaching a compromise that both sides could accept. Frick refused to consider any negotiations. Instead, he ordered the construction of a solid-wood fence topped with barbed wire built around the mill. Workers soon called it "Fort Frick."

As meetings continued to be held without progress, frustrated workers made dummies that looked like Frick and superintendent J. A. Potter and hung them on mill property. Potter sent men to tear down the dummies, but Carnegie employees turned powerful water hoses on them. Frick used this event as an excuse to order a lockout (an event in which workers are forbidden to work and are refused pay). In addition to the 3 miles of fencing he had built, Frick contacted Pinkerton National Detective Agency. He paid $5 a day to each of three hundred detectives to act as guards at the mill. The detectives arrived on July 6. By this time, workers had already barricaded themselves inside the steel plant.

Frick never had the chance to carry out his plan to hire strikebreakers. Citizens of the town joined Carnegie Steel's displaced workers and confronted the Pinkerton detectives just outside the mill. With both sides armed, they fought from 4 AM on July 6 until 5 PM. It is not clear who fired the first shot, but when gunfire had ceased, seven strikers and three detectives were dead, with numerous others injured. The strikers surrendered that same day. Although there was no more violence, workers had made it clear that no one would run the Carnegie plant but themselves. This attitude worried the sheriff of Homestead, who contacted Governor Robert Pattison (1850–1904) in hopes of getting some help. On July 12, eight thousand state troops marched into Homestead under the governor's orders and took control. They evicted workers from their homes, repeatedly arrested others just so that they could charge them bail, and generally harassed those who had been involved in the strike.

When news accounts of the slaughter reached Goldman and Berkman, who had been following the unfolding of events through newspaper reports, a feeling of desperation took over. Goldman wrote in her autobiography, *Living My Life,* "Sasha [Alexander Berkman] broke the silence. 'Frick is the responsible factor in this crime, he must be made to stand the consequences.'" Berkman went to Homestead and shot Frick. He failed to kill him, however, and spent the next fourteen years in prison. Goldman was not arrested because of insufficient evidence to prove her involvement.

Carnegie's Homestead plant reopened on July 27 with a thousand new workers under the protection of the military. The company pressed charges against O'Donnell and the strikers, but no jury would find them guilty. Both sides decided to drop the matter. The strike officially ended on November 20, 1892. Three hundred locked-out employees were rehired and joined the newly hired workers in the mill. Under their new contract, former employees worked longer hours at a lower hourly wage than they had before the strike. Most of the strikers who were not rehired were blacklisted (their names were put on a list that circulated throughout the industry, warning potential employers not to hire the troublemakers). This resulted in them being unable to get jobs in the steel industry. The strike did nothing but hurt the reputation of labor unions throughout the country.

Although Carnegie privately wrote letters to Frick in support of Frick's handling of the affair, Carnegie publicly implied that Frick was responsible for the tragic events stemming from the strike and asked him to resign as chairman. In spite of his departure from the steel firm, Frick was rewarded handsomely when Carnegie bought Frick's stocks in the company for $15 million.

Spends a year in jail

In August 1893, Goldman led a march of one thousand people in Union Square in New York City. Speaking in English and German, she encouraged the working-class poor to steal bread if they needed it, telling them they were entitled to at least that much. In October of that year, she was found guilty of trying to start a riot and sentenced to one year in prison. Upon her release in 1894, she published an account of her experience in the *New York World* newspaper.

While awaiting sentencing, famous journalist Nellie Bly (1864–1922) interviewed Goldman. In the interview, published in the September 17, 1893, issue of the *New York World* and available on the Berkeley Digital Library SunSITE Web site, Goldman revealed that she spoke four languages and wrote and read two. When Bly inquired as to the prisoner's future, Goldman replied, "I shall certainly get a year or a year and a half, not because my offense deserves it, but because I am an Anarchist."

Free speech for all

In 1901, President **William McKinley** (1843–1901; served 1897–1901; see entry) was assassinated by anarchist Leon Czolgosz (1873–1901). When he told police he had been influenced by Goldman's many public speeches, Goldman was arrested on charges that she was somehow involved in McKinley's assassination. Authorities released her due to lack of evidence, but the anarchist avoided appearing in public for a few years to avoid charges of harassment.

When Goldman returned to the spotlight, she embarked on the most politically active period of her lifetime. From 1906 to 1917, she edited her magazine *Mother Earth,* a political and literary periodical devoted to publishing anarchist essays and other writings by radical writers. In 1910, she gave 120 speeches, in thirty-seven cities and twenty-five states. Topics of her speeches focused on free speech, a concept that was not well tolerated by authorities since the assassination of McKinley. Goldman's speeches, however, attracted not only the common laborer but men and women of the middle class who believed her ideas were necessary to keep the government under control. That same year, Goldman published the first of what would be many collections of essays.

Goldman on other issues

Although Goldman's beliefs had their roots in Jewish tradition and the search for universal justice, her personal opinion was that religion was repressive because of its many rules and the submissive role she believed it required of women. She criticized not only Christianity but also traditional Jewish religion. She considered it narrow-minded and made it a point to take part in public activities on Jewish holidays to show her rejection of Judaism as a religion.

Goldman also rejected the idea of marriage in its Progressive Era form. She did not believe women should be submissive to men, nor did she believe they were put on earth solely to have children and raise families. Although she was not a firm supporter of women's suffrage (the right to vote) because she did not believe it would bring women the status they deserved, she did believe in the equality of women. She played a pioneering role in the birth control movement.

American anarchist Emma Goldman speaks about birth control in 1916. © BETTMANN/CORBIS.

Having worked as a nurse and midwife (someone who helps deliver babies) in New York's Lower East Side in the 1890s, she saw what happened to women and children when birth control was not permitted. She fought for its legality on the basis of women's freedom as well as social and economic freedom.

The matter of war

Goldman was not a pacifist (a person completely against war and violence), but she did not believe the government had the right to make war. In her eyes, war was fought only to improve the conditions of life for the wealthy, and the cost usually came at the expense of the working class.

When it became apparent that the United States would participate in World War I (1914–18) in 1916, Goldman used her magazine as a forum to discuss the wrongness of such an action. She was merely part of a much larger antiwar movement. Despite its size, the government crushed the movement in an almost panic-stricken effort. *Mother Earth* was

Anarchists—and wife and husband—Emma Goldman and Alexander Berkman. NATIONAL ARCHIVES AND RECORDS ADMINISTRATION.

banned, as were any other periodicals opposing the war. Under the direction of President Woodrow Wilson (1856–1924; served 1913–21), hundreds of immigrant activists were deported.

Just weeks after America entered the war, Goldman launched the No-Conscription League. Conscription is also known as the draft, in which the government orders all male citizens age eighteen and over who are physically and mentally able to serve in the military. The League encouraged people to speak out against the draft. When it became clear that Goldman and her peers were having an effect on Americans (more than eight thousand people attended just one meeting), the government arrested both Goldman and Berkman in 1917 and charged them with conspiring against the draft. They were found guilty, and each served a two-year prison sentence.

Goldman was released in 1919, only to be almost immediately rearrested by J. Edgar Hoover (1895–1972), head of the Justice Department's General Intelligence Division. Eager to advance his career, Hoover pushed to the limit the government's plan to deport all immigrant radical activists. Goldman was a main target of his efforts. On December 21, 1919, more than two hundred immigrant activists, including Goldman and Berkman, were exiled to the Soviet Union.

Goldman spent the remaining twenty-one years of her life in exile. During that time, she lived in several countries, including Russia, Sweden, Germany, France, England, and Canada. She remained politically active. In 1934, a ninety-day lecture tour brought her back to the United States. During her visit, Hoover had his men follow her to ensure she would not incite riots. Exile was hard for Goldman, who considered America her home.

Spanish Civil War

Goldman's beloved Berkman committed suicide in 1936; his death devastated her. In July of that year, the Spanish Civil War (1936–39) broke out, and the idea of an anarchist revolution in Spain brought Goldman some comfort. She worked endlessly to help her fellow anarchists in Spain by writing hundreds of letters to supporters and editors in the United States. When the anarchist revolution failed in 1939, she spent the last year of her life trying to raise money and find homes for the women and children refugees of the Spanish war.

Goldman suffered a stroke in February 1940, and she lost her ability to speak. She died in Toronto, Ontario, Canada, on May 14, 1940. Goldman's body was buried next to the demonstrators killed in the Haymarket Riot. Her friend and lawyer Harry Weinberger spoke at her funeral and memorialized her with these words, as published on *The Emma Goldman Papers Project* Web site: "You will live forever in the hearts of your friends and the story of your life will live as long as the stories are told of women and men of courage and idealism."

For More Information

BOOKS

Chalberg, John. *Emma Goldman: American Individualist.* New York: HarperCollins, 1991.

Falk, Candace, Lyn Reese, and Mary Agnes Dougherty. *The Life and Times of Emma Goldman: A Curriculum for Middle and High School Students.* 2nd ed. Berkeley: University of California, 1992.

Glassgold, Peter, ed. *Anarchy!: An Anthology of Emma Goldman's Mother Earth.* Washington, DC: Counterpoint Press, 2001.

Goldman, Emma. *Living My Life.* New York: Alfred Knopf, 1931. Reprint, New York: Penguin Books, 2006.

Goldman, Emma. *Red Emma Speaks: Selected Writings and Speeches.* 3rd ed. Edited by Alix Kates Shulman. Amherst, NY: Humanity Books, 1998.

PERIODICALS

Bly, Nellie. "Nelly [sic] Bly Again: She Interviews Emma Goldman and Other Anarchists." *New York World* (September 17, 1893). Available at http://sunsite.berkeley.edu/Goldman/Samples/bly.html (accessed on September 2, 2006).

Goldman, Emma. "Was My Life Worth Living?" *Harper's Magazine* (May 1, 2000).

Goldman, Emma. "What Is There in Anarchy for Women?" *St. Louis Post Dispatch Sunday Magazine* (October 24, 1897). Available at http://sunsite.berkeley.edu/Goldman/Samples/whatis.html (accessed on September 2, 2006).

WEB SITES

Berkeley Digital Library Site. *The Emma Goldman Papers.* http://sunsite.berkeley.edu/Goldman/ (accessed on September 2, 2006).

"Exhibit: Women of Valor: Emma Goldman." *Jewish Women's Archive.* http://www.jwa.org/exhibits/wov/goldman/ (accessed on September 2, 2006).

Goldman, Emma. "I Will Kill Frick." *History Matters.* http://historymatters.gmu.edu/d/99/ (accessed on September 2, 2006).

PBS. *American Experience: Emma Goldman.* http://www.pbs.org/wgbh/amex/goldman/ (accessed on September 2, 2006).

Wehling, Jason. "Anarchy in Interpretation: The Life of Emma Goldman." *Spunk Library.* http://www.spunk.org/texts/people/goldman/sp001520/emmabio.html (accessed on September 2, 2006).

Jay Gould

BORN: May 27, 1836 • Roxbury, New York
DIED: December 2, 1892 • New York, New York

Financier

Jay Gould.
© BETTMANN/CORBIS.

"I can hire one-half of the working class to kill the other half."

Jay Gould was a financier (someone who finances business ventures) during a time when business was largely unregulated by federal law. He earned a reputation as a corrupt businessman. His unethical dealings with the railroads made him one of the wealthiest men in America during the Gilded Age. The Gilded Age was the period in history following the Civil War and Reconstruction (roughly the final twenty-three years of the nineteenth century), characterized by a ruthless pursuit of profit, an exterior of showiness and grandeur, and immeasurable political corruption. Gould ruined the financial standing of thousands of people when a business scheme failed. He is remembered as one of the men responsible for the infamous economic failure known as Black Friday.

Born into a life of struggle

Jason "Jay" Gould was born on May 27, 1836, into a New York family of farmers. Gould watched his parents work themselves from dawn till dusk and still have very little to show for their efforts. By the age of thirteen, he knew he wanted more out of life than farming would ever bring him. He began taking odd jobs that would allow him to try out other careers. He learned blacksmithing and worked as a general store clerk. Gould discontinued his education at the age of sixteen, when he decided to work for his father, who had entered the hardware business. He would continue private study, however, with a particular interest in mathematics and surveying (measuring angles and distances for the purpose of mapping).

At eighteen, Gould became a land surveyor in his home state of New York as well as in Ohio and Michigan. By the time he was twenty-one, he had mapped six counties and saved $5,000, an impressive sum in the mid-1800s. Having never enjoyed robust health, Gould was small in size but made up for any perceived physical deficiencies with his intense motivation to succeed in business. Even at that young age, he proved himself willing to do whatever it took—even if it meant crossing the line between right and wrong—to become a success.

Becomes a business partner

Using the money he had saved, twenty-two-year-old Gould joined forces with a New York politician named Zadock Pratt (1790–1871). The two men opened a tannery (a factory where animals hides, or skins, are made into leather) in Pennsylvania. Gould's approach to managing his new company was an indication of how he would conduct business for the rest of his life.

Without Pratt's consent, Gould stole small, unnoticeable amounts of his partner's share of business funds and stashed them in a bank in Stroudsburg, Pennsylvania. Pratt eventually discovered his partner's illegal activity and chose to sell his share of the business rather than prosecute Gould. Gould became a millionaire, but lost nearly all of it when the market for hides collapsed in 1857. By that time, Gould had a new partner, a New York leather merchant named Charles Leupp. Although the business was nearly bankrupt (without funds and near closing down), Gould used the tannery's funds illegally to speculate (to make risky investments while hoping for large profits as a result of ups and downs in the stock market) in other businesses. Leupp was dismayed at his partner's lack of ethics and willingness to risk Leupp's money. He committed suicide in 1859; at the time, Gould was blamed for contributing to Leupp's suicide, but some historians point to Leupp's history of depression as the cause of his death. As chaos erupted within the company, Gould took advantage of the situation and quietly took control. This sneaky move enraged some of the outside investors, who proceeded to file a lawsuit. As the case dragged on, Gould used that time to rid the company of most of its assets. He left it, and Pennsylvania, in 1859. He spent the next year in New York, selling leather.

While in New York City, Gould met Helen Day Miller, daughter of a local businessman. The two married in 1863, when Gould was twenty-seven years old. They would eventually have three sons and two daughters. Historians often remark that although Gould was ruthless as a business-man, he was a devoted husband and father who placed family high on his list of priorities.

Enters the railroad industry

Gould entered the railroad business when his father-in-law appointed him manager of the Rensselaer & Saratoga line. This particular railroad was not doing well, but Gould bought and skillfully reorganized the line. Encouraged by his success, he repeated the process with the Rutland & Washington railway. As soon as that railway was in good condition, he sold it and made a large profit.

In 1867, Gould made a business move that would officially put him in the ranks of the robber barons. He joined the board of directors of the Erie Railroad, one of the largest railways in the East. By becoming a director, he had more power than if he had simply remained an investor. As a director, he was privileged to information that would allow him to control more of the railroad. He used this information to fight with another robber baron, **Cornelius Vanderbilt** (1794–1877; see entry), for complete control of the Erie line.

Gould did not act alone. Daniel Drew (1797–1879) and James Fisk (1834–1872; see box), two other Erie directors, joined Gould in his scheme to keep Vanderbilt from taking control of the railroad. Vanderbilt owned the New York Central railway. His goal was to control as much of the railroad industry as possible. Gould found a loophole in the law that allowed him, Drew, and Fisk to convert newly printed bonds (certificates of debt) into stock, which they then sold to the public on the open market. In selling fifty thousand shares of illegal stock, they diluted Van-derbilt's power in the company.

Vanderbilt attempted to fight Gould and his men in court, but Gould and Fisk developed a relationship with William Marcy Tweed (1823–1878), a corrupt New York politician who used his power to in-fluence politics and legislation. Tweed, also known as Boss Tweed,

Jim Fisk: Man of Many Names

Railroad tycoon Jim Fisk. © BETTMANN/CORBIS.

James Fisk was born on April 1, 1834, in Bennington, Vermont. Having little interest in education, Fisk attended school only periodically. While in his early teens, he ran away from home and joined the circus. From there, he held a series of odd jobs, including waiter and salesman. As a salesman, he was able to make some money; his shrewd business sense earned him stock in the company.

During the Civil War (1861–65), Fisk used his position as a salesman to smuggle Southern cotton across the Union (North) blockade. This brought him a small fortune, but he soon lost that money in failed speculation ventures.

Fisk, known by such nicknames as Big Jim, Diamond Jim, and Jubilee Jim, became a stockbroker in 1864. His boss was Daniel Drew. Through his association with Drew, he developed a relationship with Jay Gould. The friendship would last throughout Fisk's lifetime, but it did not make him popular in society. His attempt to corner the gold market with Gould in 1869 led to the financial ruin of thousands of people. The event became known as Black Friday.

As unlucky as he was in money, Fisk was even unluckier in love. Although married, he engaged in numerous extramarital affairs throughout his short life. His affair with showgirl Josie Mansfield led to his murder on January 6, 1872, when a jealous rival for Mansfield's affections shot Fisk.

Fisk's funeral was a major event and featured a 200-piece band. By all accounts, it was a fitting end for a man who lived his life with little care of what others thought of him. Fisk's life was the subject of a 1937 film titled "The Toast of New York."

controlled most of the Democratic nominations in New York. He illegally placed his men in positions of great control in the state legislature and in judgeships, for example. Tweed changed the laws to benefit his friends Gould and Fisk. In return, he was made a director of the Erie Railroad and received cash payments as part of the deal. The men were soon known as the "Erie Ring." Their underhanded dealings became the subject of newspaper articles and political cartoons.

Because of Tweed's influence and Gould's bribery of New York legislators, Vanderbilt lost his case. He sold Gould his shares in the Erie line for $9 million, an amount that nearly bankrupted the railroad. Through skill and illegal manipulation, Gould saved the railroad. But the board of directors had had enough of Gould's antics. They voted him out in 1872 and demanded he pay the line $7.5 million, the approximate amount he cost the company in fraudulent (fake) stock. The Erie Ring had been broken. Although the Erie did not ever become the most used line in the East, Gould did manage to expand it, and his own personal wealth increased in doing so.

Black Friday

Despite the amount of time Gould spent trying to swindle Erie Railroad funds into his own pockets, he managed to get himself involved in another financial disaster in 1869. As before, Fisk was his partner in crime.

The two schemers set their sights on the U.S. gold market. At the time, Ulysses S. Grant (1822–1885; served 1869–77) was America's president. During the Civil War, the government attempted to keep the economy steady by issuing a large sum of money backed by nothing but credit. The American public understood that the plan after the war was to have the government buy back the "greenbacks," as they were called, with gold. The greenbacks that the government would buy back would be replaced with currency backed by gold.

Fisk and Gould did not want the government to rid itself of the gold. They hoped to buy up as much gold as possible and hold onto it while its value rose. When they could sell it at a profit, they would. Grant's plan would ruin their scheme because it would put more gold on the market, which would force the value down.

Gould was smart enough to know he could not convince the president to do what he wanted on his own, so he and Fisk befriended financier Abel Rathbone Corbin (1808–1881), Grant's brother-in-law. Together, the three men approached the president, who gave no clear response to their proposal. Gould and Fisk were encouraged that the president even took time to speak with them, so they kept at their plan. Corbin knew the assistant treasurer of the United States, and he agreed to let Fisk and Gould know when the government was ready to sell gold.

All seemed to be going according to plan, when Grant became suspicious of his brother-in-law's unusual interest in the gold market.

Political cartoon showing the corruption and control of the railroad monopoly during the Gilded Age, as represented by railroad tycoon Jay Gould.
© BETTMANN/CORBIS.

He happened upon a letter written by his sister to his wife, and in the letter was an explanation of Gould's scheme. Grant, furious that he had been conned by family, contacted Corbin and ordered him to stop the plan. He then ordered the sale of $4 million in government gold.

Gould and Fisk began buying as much gold as they could on September 20, 1869. They watched gleefully as the value soared. On September 24, the price of an ounce of gold peaked at $162.50. But when the $4 million worth of government gold hit the market, people panicked. Within fifteen minutes, the price of gold dropped to $133 per ounce. Investors could not get rid of their gold fast enough, and many men lost their fortunes in what became known as Black Friday. Railway stocks lost nearly all their value, and businesses across the nation were left paralyzed.

As perilous as Black Friday was for thousands of Americans, it had little effect on Jay Gould.

Takes his money west

After leaving the Erie Railroad under less-than-favorable circumstances, Gould set his sights on the new railroads running in the West. By 1874, he was director of the Union Pacific Railroad and took control of its operations. He drove up the value of the company's stock by lying to the public about the company's future. When stocks were at an all-time high in 1879, he sold his shares and used the money to buy out several smaller railroads in the West. By 1880, he owned 10,000 miles (16,000 kilometers) of railway, which was equal to roughly one-ninth of the country's railway mileage. It was, by far, more than any other one person owned in America.

Gould had expanded his investment interests beyond railroads by that time. He bought the *New York World* newspaper in 1879 and used it for his own purposes by publicly doubting the financial security of the Western Union Telegraph Company. He did the same to the Manhattan Elevated Rail Company. When the stock prices of both companies plummeted, Gould quickly bought them.

Great Southwest Strike

Gould was disliked not only by other businessmen but also by his employees. They both feared and despised him. Gould's attitude toward his workers was that he hired them to do a job and they should be grateful he did. Gould was against labor unions because they challenged his unfair work practices. For example, in 1885 Gould fired all the shopmen who belonged to the labor union known as the Knights of Labor (KOL). In response, workers on the Gould-owned Wabash Railroad walked off the job and went on strike (refused to work until specific conditions are agreed to between workers and management).

Without the Wabash line, trains could not run throughout the Southwest. Even Gould understood the financial loss involved in a strike of this magnitude, and he agreed to quit discriminating against KOL members. Gould's promise shocked everyone. The union victory led to an increase in membership the following year, from one hundred thousand to more than seven hundred thousand.

In 1886, Gould fired another KOL member who was an employee of his Texas & Pacific Railway company. Again, the Knights went on strike. This time, the conflict spread to other lines in the region, and soon violence occurred among the strikers. As reported on *The Institute for Labor* Web site, Gould hired scabs (strikebreakers), saying, "I can hire one-half of the workers to kill the other half." He also hired security services and successfully requested state militia (troops). It soon became apparent to the KOL that his agreement the prior year was nothing more than a way to get his employees back to work. It seemed he was now focused on dismantling the union.

Negotiations between the labor union and Gould were unsuccessful; he would not compromise with the workers on any level. Frustrated with this response, workers continued to commit acts of violence in the railyards by destroying property. Soon, public sentiment was against them.

Congress ordered an investigation into the strike, but the appointed committee made little progress. Management would not cooperate; the public had made up its collective mind that the strikers were in the wrong. Terence Powderly (1849–1929), head of the KOL, decided that the strike was hopeless.

The Great Southwest Strike was not so great after all for the workers. It was a dismal defeat. It showed America that powerful industrialists would beat the downtrodden worker at every opportunity.

Legacy

Altogether, Gould was a director of seventeen major railroad lines and president of five between 1873 and 1893. Although he had endured his share of failed business ventures, his worth upon his death of tuberculosis (lung disease) at the age of fifty-seven was estimated to be between $72 million and $77 million, all of which he left to his family.

His fortune allowed him to purchase an impressive estate known as Lyndhurst, along New York's Hudson River, in 1880. At the time of his acquisition, the estate's interior was falling apart, yet the exterior had remained managed and beautiful. Gould's money, along with his wife's interior decorating sense, allowed for the renovation and rejuvenation of the mansion's rooms. Lyndhurst is a national historic trust in the twenty-first century and hosts hundreds of thousands of tourists each year.

For More Information

BOOKS

"Jay Gould." *Business Leader Profiles for Students.* Vol. 1. Detroit: Gale, 1999.

Klein, Maury. *The Life and Legend of Jay Gould.* Baltimore: Johns Hopkins University Press, 1997.

Morris, Charles R. *The Tycoons: How Andrew Carnegie, John D. Rockefeller, Jay Gould, and J. P. Morgan Invented the American Supereconomy.* New York: Holt and Co., 2005.

Renehan, Edward J. Jr. *The Dark Genius of Wall Street: The Misunderstood Life of Jay Gould, King of the Robber Barons.* New York: Basic Books, 2005.

WEB SITES

"The Great Southwest Strike—1886." *The Institute for Labor Studies.* http://www.umkc.edu/labor-ed/history6.htm (accessed on September 2, 2006).

"Hazardous Business: The Fight for the Commission." *Texas State Library and Archives Commission.* http://www.tsl.state.tx.us/exhibits/railroad/fight/page4.html (accessed on September 2, 2006).

"James Fisk." *U-S-History.com.* http://www.u-s-history.com/pages/h865.html (accessed on September 2, 2006).

Klein, Maury. "The Robber Barons' Bum Rap." *City Journal.* http://www.city-journal.org/html/5_1_a2.html (accessed on September 2, 2006).

Lyndhurst: A National Trust Historic Site. http://www.lyndhurst.org/home.html (accessed on September 2, 2006).

Maroney, James C. "Great Southwest Strike." *The Handbook of Texas Online.* http://www.tsha.utexas.edu/handbook/online/articles/GG/oeg1.html (accessed on September 2, 2006).

PBS. "People & Events: Black Friday, September 24, 1869." *American Experience: Ulysses S. Grant.* http://www.pbs.org/wgbh/amex/grant/peopleevents/e_friday.html (accessed on September 2, 2006).

Trumbore, Brian. "Homestake Gold Mine, Part 3." *BUYandHOLD.* http://www.buyandhold.com/bh/en/education/history/2001/homestake3.html (accessed on September 2, 2006).

Edward Harriman

BORN: February 20, 1848 • Hempstead, New York
DIED: September 9, 1909 • Long Island, New York

Railroad tycoon

"I never cared for money except as power for work."

Edward Harriman built a fortune investing in failing railroad companies and nurturing them back to life. He also had an adventurous streak and set sail on a scientific expedition to Alaska in 1899. Harriman is remembered as much for his even temper and ability to maintain his composure under stress as he is for his business sense and massive fortune.

Ambitious youth

Edward Henry Harriman was born on February 20, 1848, to Cornelia and Orlando Harriman, residents of Hempstead, New York. His mother came from the upper-class society of New Jersey, but she had married a man of lower social status. Harriman's father was an ordained deacon (church leader) in the Presbyterian church. Harriman looked upon his father with dismay as an example of a man who, despite his extensive studies and knowledge, had done very little with his life.

Never a strong or an interested student, Harriman dropped out of school at the age of fourteen to find for himself the financial security

Edward Harriman.

he had never known but always wished for. What he lacked in interest in school, he made up for in ambition. The usual procedure for learning about business was to secure a job in a store or to apprentice (study alongside an experienced professional) in a trade and progress to better positions. Instead, Harriman went straight to the center of business: Wall Street, home of the stock exchange, where men invested money in businesses and either expanded their wealth or lost their savings.

From Wall Street to railroads

Harriman began his business education as an office boy in a brokerage firm (a business that buys and sells stock in companies). From there, he became a messenger boy and carried securities (stocks) between firms on Wall Street. After that, he was promoted to the position of "pad shover." In the days before electricity, all stock prices and buy-or-sell orders were recorded on paper. Pad shovers ran these price and order records between buildings and companies on Wall Street. This experience allowed them to learn every aspect of the stock-market industry. Harriman, with an eye for detail and an excellent memory, quickly became recognized as an asset to Wall Street brokers. He was trustworthy and dependable, two qualities not easy to come by in a cut-throat industry. Before long, he was promoted to managing clerk.

By the time he was twenty-one, Harriman knew he wanted to get involved in Wall Street on an investment level, but he had little money to invest. He approached his uncles—all successful businessmen—and was given a loan by one of them. On August 13, 1870, at just twenty-two years of age, Harriman bought a seat on the New York Stock Exchange. Memberships that year cost between $4,000 and $4,500, plus a one-time $500 initiation fee. He was officially a stockbroker.

In 1879, Harriman married Mary Williamson Averell, daughter of the president of the Ogdensburg & Lake Champlain Railroad Company. Harriman's new relationship with his father-in-law stimulated the stockbroker's interest in the railroad industry. Within two years, he began his career as a reviver of failing railroads. His first acquisition was a 34-mile (54.7-kilometer), broken-down line called the Lake Ontario Southern, which he renamed Sodus Bay & Southern and sold for a profit to the Pennsylvania Railroad. From that point on, Harriman's name was linked to railroads.

Takes over the Union Pacific

Harriman continued to buy, fix, and sell smaller railroads, but it was not until 1883 that he got involved with a major line. He took a seat on the board of directors of the Illinois Central (IC) line that year. Within a few years, he left his brokerage firm and became vice president of the IC. He spent the next decade expanding the IC line into the west. Harriman would maintain control of it the rest of his life.

Harriman became a director of the Union Pacific (UP) Railroad in 1897. By 1898, he was chairman of the executive committee. As such, he traveled the railroad from the Missouri River to the Pacific Ocean, inspecting every train car and station. In an effort not to miss any small problems, he traveled only during daylight. He paid attention to the tiniest details, down to the railroad ties and bolts. Everything that needed fixing got fixed. After several months and $25 million in repairs, the UP was running smoothly. Harriman's insistence on safety made him well liked among the railroad's superintendents and workers.

The Harriman Expedition Such intense work in a short time period took its toll on Harriman's health, and he was ordered by his doctor to take a relaxing vacation. Harriman followed the doctor's suggestion and decided to take his family to Alaska. Before plans were made, he broadened his scope and decided to turn the vacation into a full-blown scientific expedition. No one except Harriman knows for certain why he chose to take a two-month cruise to Alaska. Some historians believe he planned to build a railway into Alaskan territory; others believe he was hoping to supplement his inadequate formal education. Harriman himself had always wanted to hunt grizzly bear, so perhaps this was his motivation toward an Alaskan destination.

Whatever the reason for his decision, 126 passengers and crew joined Harriman on the ship *George W. Elder*. The group, which included famous scientists (see box) and had enjoyed newspaper coverage since the planning stages, took a train to Seattle, Washington, and left the dock shortly after 6:00 PM, May 31, 1899. The ship included newly renovated staterooms, a library stocked with more than five hundred books about Alaska, research spaces, and even livestock stalls.

The two months spent traveling 9,000 miles (14,481 kilometers) along the coast of British Columbia and Alaska proved invaluable to scientists and researchers interested in that region. They made more than fifty stops along the way so that the research team could go ashore to collect and study animal life and plant specimens. The information they collected filled thirteen volumes and took them twelve years to compile and publish.

On Board the *Elder*

Edward Harriman could afford to make his expedition the largest of its kind, and he spared no expense. Cargo on the ship even included an organ and piano for relaxation and entertainment on the long voyage.

Although the trip was a mere vacation for Harriman and his family, he made sure a team of the era's finest scientists was assembled for the expedition. The team itself was unusual for the time in that it comprised scientists from several areas of study rather than several scientists from the same field. The twenty-member team included:

C. Hart Merriam (1855–1942): As a Yale- and Columbia-educated scientist, Merriam revolutionized the study of biological specimens. Merriam was given the responsibility of organizing the scientific team. After the voyage, he took charge of assembling the collected data. Harriman felt so indebted to Merriam that he set him up with a $12,000 annual allowance for life.

John Burroughs (1837–1921): The most famous nature writer of his time, Burroughs wrote and published twenty-seven books, which sold more than two million copies. In addition, he wrote and published hundreds of magazine articles on birds, flowers, and other natural wonders.

John Muir (1838–1914): Chosen for his previous experiences on Alaska expeditions, Muir was recognized as an authority on glaciers in that region. Muir and Harriman developed a friendship based on mutual admiration and respect.

Charles Augustus Keeler (1871–1937): Director of the Natural History Museum at the California Academy of Sciences, Keeler joined the team as an ornithologist (one who studies and watches birds).

George Bird Grinnell (1849–1938): Editor of the era's leading natural history magazine, *Forest and Stream,* Grinnell helped establish several nature organizations, including the Audubon Society. Glacier National Park was founded primarily through his efforts.

Edward Curtis (1868–1952): This photographer snapped more than five thousand pictures of the voyage, often risking his life to do so.

Harriman found the expedition immensely satisfying, as he shot a grizzly bear mother and cub. Naturalist **John Muir** (1838–1914; see entry) and ornithologist Charles Keeler took issue against the hundreds of animal specimens that were killed on the expedition, including Harriman's grizzlies.

From a scientific standpoint, the expedition was most successful in its discovery of information on glaciers. From the photographs and observations gathered, scientists were able to develop theories about glacial climates and topography. Prior to the expedition, very little was known to Americans of the Alaska-British Columbia coastline, its environment, or its people. Harriman himself was responsible for a major

A photograph of a canoeist near the Muir Glacier in Alaska, taken by Edward Curtis during the Edward Harriman expedition of 1899. THE LIBRARY OF CONGRESS.

discovery of a fiord (glacier valley between steep cliffs), which was mapped and named "Harriman Fjord." Its largest glacier was called "Harriman Glacier."

Goes up against James Hill

Harriman's motivation to own a large portion of American railways was not unlike the ambitions of other railroad tycoons of the Gilded Age and the Progressive Era. (The Gilded Age was the period in history following the Civil War and Reconstruction [roughly the final twenty-three years of the nineteenth century], characterized by a ruthless pursuit of profit, an exterior of showiness and grandeur, and immeasurable political corruption. The Progressive Era was the period that followed the Gilded Age [approximately the first twenty years of the twentieth century]; it

An editorial cartoon showing the head of railroad tycoon Edward H. Harriman as a tunnel, with all of the railroads of America going through him © CORBIS.

was marked by reform and the development of a national cultural identity.) One such tycoon was James J. Hill (1838–1916), who owned several large and important railroads. Harriman bested Hill in one area: He was willing to take risks. One of the risks Harriman took was to begin a policy of shipping large-volume freight for long distances at a reduced rate. Both men maintained high standards within their railroads, but Harriman's consolidated lines of the Union Pacific and the Southern Pacific, which he acquired in 1901, made his the largest transportation system in the world.

In 1900, Hill owned the Northern Pacific and the Great Northern, two profitable lines. He wanted to own more, however, and went after the Chicago, Burlington & Quincy (commonly referred to as the Burlington or the Q), the last independent railroad in Iowa. If he owned that line, Hill could compete with Harriman. The owner of the Burlington knew he could not survive in the railroad industry without merging with either Harriman or Hill. In 1901, Harriman tried to gain control of the Burlington by buying up as much stock as possible. This caused a panic on the stock market, but it did not win him control of the Burlington. That victory went to Hill.

All was not lost, however, as Hill and Harriman—along with financier J. P. Morgan (1837–1913)—established Northern Securities, a holding company (a firm that owns enough shares in another company to secure voting control). The men joined forces so that they could control shipping rates. Between them they had total control of all railroad traffic between Chicago and the Northwest. This control made them a trust (company with total control without fear of competition), which was not legal because such power often led to unfair practices and rates. Northern Securities was ordered disbanded as a result of the 1904 U.S. Supreme Court ruling in *Northern Securities Co. v. United States*.

Death comes early

Harriman died in 1909, at the age of sixty-two, at the family estate known as Arden. At the time of his death, he controlled the Union Pacific, Southern Pacific, Illinois Central, Central of Georgia, Saint Joseph, and Grand

Island lines; the Pacific Mail Steamship Company; and the Wells Fargo Express Company. He died an incredibly wealthy man. Estimates of his estate ranged from $200 million to $600 million. In 2006, Forbes.com ranked Harriman the eighteenth most influential businessman of all time.

Harriman left his entire fortune to his wife. In 1910, she donated $1 million and 10,000 acres of land to the state of New York to start Harriman State Park. In the twenty-first century, that park claims 42,500 acres (172 square kilometers) and boasts thirty-one lakes and reservoirs as well as 200 miles (321.8 kilometers) of hiking trails. It is the second-largest park in New York's state park system. In his lifetime, Harriman was a financial sponsor of boys' clubs (organizations to keep teenagers off the streets and involved in productive pastimes). In his honor, Harriman's widow created the E. H. Harriman Award in 1913, to be given out each year in recognition of outstanding achievements in railway safety.

In 1912, John Muir wrote a short book titled *Edward Henry Harriman*. Available online at *SierraClub.org,* Muir's recollection recalled his friend's explanation of his views of money. "I never cared for money except as power for work.... What I most enjoy is the power of creation, getting into partnership with nature in doing good, helping to feed man and beast, and making everybody and everything a little better and happier."

For More Information

BOOKS

Klein, Maury. *The Life & Legend of E. H. Harriman.* Chapel Hill: University of North Carolina Press, 2000.

Mercer, Lloyd. *E. H. Harriman: Master Railroader.* Boston: Twayne, 1985. Reprint, Washington, DC: Beard Books, 2003.

Muir, John. *Edward Henry Harriman.* New York: Doubleday, Page and Company, 1911. Also available at *Sierra Club: John Muir Exhibit.* http://www.sierraclub. org/john_muir_exhibit/frameindex.html?http://www.sierraclub.org/john_ Muir_exhibit/writings/edward_henry_harriman.html (accessed on September 2, 2006).

WEB SITES

"A Brief Historical Sketch of the Illinois Central Railroad." *Illinois Central Historical Society.* http://icrrhistorical.org/icrr.history.html (accessed on September 2, 2006).

"Edward H. Harriman (1848–1909)." *Forbes.com.* http://www.forbes.com/business/ 2005/07/06/harriman-railroads–northern-securities-cx_0706harriman.html (accessed on September 2, 2006).

Moody, John. "The Life Work of Edward H. Harriman." In *The Railroad Builders: A Chronicle of the Welding of the States*. New Haven, CT: Yale University Press, 1919. Reprint, Washington, DC: Ross & Perry, 2003. Also available at http://www.cprr.org/Museum/Railroad_Builders/Railroad_Builders_11.html (accessed on September 2, 2006).

PBS. *Harriman Expedition Retraced: A Century of Change.* http://www.pbs.org/harriman/1899/1899_part/participantharriman.html (accessed on September 2, 2006).

PBS. "People & Events: James J. Hill, 1838–1916." *American Experience: Streamliners: America's Lost Trains.* http://www.pbs.org/wgbh/amex/streamliners/peopleevents/p_hill.html (accessed on September 2, 2006).

Benjamin Harrison

BORN: August 20, 1833 • North Bend, Ohio
DIED: March 13, 1901 • Indianapolis, Indiana

U.S. president

Benjamin Harrison.
© HULTON-DEUTSCH
COLLECTION/CORBIS.

"I do the same thing every day. I eat three meals, sleep six hours and read dusty old books the rest of the time. My life is about as devoid of anything funny as the great desert is of grass."

Benjamin Harrison was America's twenty-third president. He was also the grandson of the nation's ninth president, William Henry Harrison (1773–1841; served 1841), and the great-grandson of Colonel Benjamin Harrison (1750–1808), one of the signers of the Declaration of Independence. His time in the White House was largely uneventful, and historians generally consider Harrison a mediocre president. He was not the best or most active president, but he was not the worst, either.

From farm to war

Benjamin Harrison was born on August 20, 1833, in the house belonging to his grandfather, William Henry Harrison. He spent his childhood on The Point, the Harrison family farm, located in North Bend, Ohio. Harrison received his education in a one-room schoolhouse as well as from a tutor at home. Between 1847 and 1850, he attended a preparatory school (a school that prepares students for college) in Cincinnati. In 1852, he graduated from Miami University in Oxford, Ohio.

Harrison loved to read, and it was no secret he preferred the company of books to people. He became an effective public speaker over the span of two years, when he studied law from 1852 to 1854. In 1853, he married Caroline Scott, and the couple moved to Indianapolis, Indiana. There, Harrison quickly became active in the Republican Party. (One of the oldest political parties in the United States, the Republican Party was founded as an antislavery party in the mid-1800s; it transformed into one associated with conservative fiscal and social policies.) In 1862, he joined the Union (North) Army by way of the Seventieth Regiment of the Indiana volunteers during the Civil War (1861–65). He would leave the war as a brigadier general.

Gains political experience

Harrison returned to political activism upon returning home from the war. He was heavily involved in supporting the presidential campaigns of Rutherford B. Hayes (1822–93; served 1877–81) and James A. Garfield (1831–81; served 1881). Both men won their elections. Harrison was named to the U.S. Senate in 1880 (senators were appointed by state legislature until 1913, when they began to be elected by popular vote). As a senator, Harrison supported pensions for Civil War veterans, high tariffs (taxes), and a modern navy.

The Indiana state legislature was taken over by Democrats in 1887, and Harrison was not returned to the Senate. The following year, he ran in the presidential election. In addition to the issues he chose to support as a senator, he upheld conservation of wilderness regions and a limited reform of civil service (government jobs). Harrison broke from traditional Republican viewpoint in his opposition to the Chinese Exclusion Act (1882), which ended Chinese immigration to the United States.

The main issue of the 1888 race was tariffs. These were taxes imposed on goods imported from other countries. Republicans generally favored high taxes because that money went into the government budget and would give the government more spending money. Democrats generally favored lower tariffs because they believed overseas competition was healthy for the American economy.

Becomes twenty-third president

Harrison's campaign was unique. He was the first candidate to participate in what became known as "front-porch speeches." Rather than tour the country giving speeches in formal settings, Harrison would stand on the front porch of his home in Indiana and speak to the public. This folksy atmosphere helped people to consider the president a regular man with a regular family and life. They felt that what mattered to them, mattered to him. Harrison got favorable press coverage from these speeches. His opponent, President **Grover Cleveland** (1837–1908; served 1885–89 and 1893–97; see entry), gave just one speech during the 1888 campaign.

Although Cleveland won 90,000 more popular votes (votes from citizens) than Harrison, Harrison won the election with 233 of the electoral votes (compared with Cleveland's 168). Electoral votes are the votes a candidate receives for winning the majority of popular votes of a particular state. If a candidate wins the most popular votes in a state, he wins all of that state's electoral votes. Not all states are worth the same number of electoral votes. That number is determined by how many U.S. representatives a state has in the House plus two, one for each of the state's U.S. senators. In order to win a presidential election, a candidate must have more than 50 percent of electoral votes. It is very rare that a presidential candidate would win more popular votes than his opponent, yet fail to win the election. In Harrison's case, a Republican president was back in the White House. Not only that, the Republicans controlled the Senate and the House of Representatives.

Life and law on the homefront

The most important piece of legislation to cross Harrison's desk was the McKinley Tariff of 1890. Named after U.S. representative **William McKinley** (1843–1901; see entry) of Ohio, the law raised protective tariffs an average of 49.5 percent, to make them the highest rates in the nation's history. That same bill also expanded the powers of the president in regard to foreign trade. For example, under the McKinley Tariff, Harrison could negotiate agreements with overseas manufacturers without getting approval from Congress. If he wanted to, the president could offer lower import rates for specific products in exchange for lower rates on American exports. The new law also allowed him to establish a federal committee to authorize and oversee the many details and functions of foreign trade.

Sherman Antitrust Act The Harrison administration also passed the Sherman Antitrust Act in 1890. By the late nineteenth century, big businesses and giant corporations had taken over the economy. American consumers were forced into paying high prices for things they needed, and Republicans and Democrats alike called for reform of regulations in industry. The loudest outcry was against monopolies, businesses that have total control over a sector of the economy, including prices. With a monopoly, there is no competition.

As a result of the public's fury, Harrison passed the Sherman Antitrust Act, which was named after Republican U.S. senator John Sherman (1823–1900) of Ohio. Some states had already passed laws restricting the use of trusts (companies working together to take total control of production and distribution of a product or service). Those laws applied only to business conducted within those states, however. Under the Sherman Act, trusts and monopolies were illegal both within states and when dealing with foreign trade.

The passing of the act was a step in the right direction, but like many other laws passed during the Gilded Age, it had little effect on reality. (The Gilded Age was the period in history following the Civil War and Reconstruction [roughly the final twenty-three years of the nineteenth century], characterized by a ruthless pursuit of profit, an exterior of showiness and grandeur, and immeasurable political corruption.) Disobeying the terms of the Sherman Antitrust Act brought a maximum fine of $5,000 and a one-year prison term. Those who were inclined to break the law were not put off by a fine they could easily pay. For these industrialists, the benefits of a trust far outweighed the punishment for building it.

The federal government had the power to dissolve trusts, but the Supreme Court kept them from implementing the act for years. The Sherman Act had little effect until **Theodore Roosevelt** (1858–1919; served 1901–9; see entry) took office in 1901. Known as the "trust-busting" president, Roosevelt sought prosecutions of trusts he thought were ignoring the law.

Sherman Silver Purchase Act Senator Sherman sponsored another important bill that Harrison passed, again in 1890. The Sherman Silver Purchase Act had the U.S. Treasury purchase 4.5 million ounces of silver at market price each month. The silver was bought with Treasury notes that could be redeemed in either gold or silver. Citizens who held notes turned them in for gold because they got more money for each note that way. In doing so, they nearly emptied the Treasury's gold supply. Silver production increased as a result. Silver prices then went down, rather than up, which was the original intent of the act.

The act was repealed in 1893, when America was experiencing the worst economic decline in its history up to that time. Historians cite a number of factors that contributed to the panic, but the Sherman Silver Purchase Act is the most responsible. In addition to depleting the nation's gold reserves and the decrease in silver prices, railroads went bankrupt (ran out of money and could not repay their debts) and hundreds of banks failed. The results of the financial crisis were high unemployment rates and a shortage of money circulating in the economy.

U.S. senator John Sherman of Ohio, sponsor of the Sherman Silver Purchase Act. THE LIBRARY OF CONGRESS.

Land Revision Act of 1891 Harrison, always a supporter of conservation, passed the Land Revision Act of 1891. This law gave the president the authority to set aside public lands for the sake of preservation. Harrison authorized the first forest reserve in Yellowstone, Wyoming.

Active overseas

Harrison was protective of American interests overseas, and worked hard to maintain that protection. He threatened war with Chile when American sailors were injured in the country's port city of Valparaiso. After discussing the incident with Chile's leaders, Harrison received an apology and the United States was paid $75,000 in reparations (compensation for wrongdoing).

Harrison believed in modernizing and expanding the U.S. Navy. Under his direction, the navy was reorganized and developed into a fleet of seven armored ships.

Pan-Americanism Since the early 1800s, Latin American countries had struggled for independence. They looked to the United States as a model, and President Harrison accepted that responsibility. Working

James Blaine: Persistent Politician

BLAINE'S GRANDEST ACHIEVEMENT.
The Commercial Unity of the Americas.

An illustration celebrating the successful role of U.S. secretary of state James Blaine in the 1889 Pan-American Conference. © BETTMANN/CORBIS.

James G. Blaine was born in Pennsylvania in 1830. He spent his entire childhood there and did not leave the state until he moved to Maine in 1854. There, he worked as a newspaper editor. He also was a founder of the Republican Party in Maine.

Respected for his tireless activism and commitment to his party, Blaine was elected to the state legislature for four years (1859–62). He served the last two as speaker (leader) of the state House of Representatives. In 1862, he was elected to the U.S. House of Representatives, where he would serve for thirteen years. He was Speaker of the House (leader of the entire U.S. House of Representatives; a highly powerful position) for the last six years of his tenure.

Blaine was appointed U.S. senator in 1876 to fill a vacancy and quickly became a leading candidate for the Republican presidential nomination. His reputation suffered when the press publicized a scandal over an Arkansas railroad that

closely with Secretary of State James Blaine (1830–1893; see box), Harrison organized the first Pan-American Conference (the first conference of or relating to North, South, and Central America) in Washington, D.C., in December 1889. Every nation from these regions except the Dominican Republic was represented at the meeting. The mission of the conference was to promote peace throughout the world. Delegates worked together to develop treaties and guidelines for nations to refer to in times of international conflict and dispute.

An offshoot of the Pan-American Conference was the formation of the Commercial Bureau of American Republics. This group was renamed the Pan-American Union at the fourth conference in 1910. With membership from all three Americas, the Union strove to maintain peace through what they called collective security, which meant that they agreed to help each other in times of trouble. Maintaining and storing

Blaine supposedly aided by using his power as speaker. His accusers claimed he used his stature to obtain a land grant for the railroad and then sold the railroad's bonds for a profit. Blaine lost the nomination to Rutherford B. Hayes. Blaine sought the presidential nomination again in 1880, but lost to James A. Garfield. When Garfield won the presidency, he appointed Blaine secretary of state. Garfield was assassinated shortly after taking office, however, and Blaine resigned only a few months after Garfield's successor, Chester A. Arthur, took office. He retired for a brief time.

Although finally nominated as the Republican presidential candidate in 1884, Blaine's scandalous past interfered with his efforts, and he could not beat Democrat Grover Cleveland. He used the next four years to give strong vocal support to the tariff and continued to work within the Republican Party.

Blaine surprised everyone in the presidential election of 1888 by not seeking the nomination and supporting Benjamin Harrison instead. The following year, Blaine became secretary of state once again. As part of the Harrison administration, he helped the president develop and maintain improved foreign relations with Latin America. His relationship with Harrison worsened over the year. Harrison, long known as being a cold man who did not listen to or enjoy being around people, often felt overshadowed by his charming and friendly secretary of state. Many people believed Blaine made most of Harrison's decisions for him, but a more modern analysis of the Harrison administration shows that this was not the case. Regardless, the two men had less to say to one another as Harrison's term progressed. In 1892, Blaine resigned his position and once more sought the Republican nomination for the next presidential election. He failed, as the incumbent Harrison again won the nomination in 1892.

Blaine died in Washington, D.C., just four days before his sixty-third birthday, in 1893. He had been suffering from several health problems for years.

official documents was the responsibility of the Union, and it provided useful technical and informational services to the Americas. In 1948, a meeting was held with the single purpose of banding together to fight communism (economic theory of public ownership and control over all production and distribution) in the Americas. The Union was again renamed; as the Organization of American States, it remains active in the twenty-first century. Its members come from all thirty-five independent nations of the Americas.

Territorial expansion Harrison believed in territorial expansion, or adding more land to the United States. He felt strongly that Hawaii should become a U.S. territory. Hawaii was important to the United States for a variety of reasons. It was a key spot for America's whaling ships, and hundreds of missionaries traveled to the islands every year. Sugar was an important export of Hawaii's, and the region's economy and politics soon relied heavily on the United States. Furthermore, Harrison did not want Hawaii to become annexed (taken over) by any European country. Such control would have given Europe even more power than it already had.

Sugar cane farmers in Hawaii also wanted the annexation of their homeland to America. They believed that such a move would end the threat of a high export tariff on their product. Harrison tried to convince the Senate to approve the annexation, but he failed. Eventually, Hawaii was annexed in 1898 under President William McKinley. Because of his early efforts, however, Harrison is often credited as being the president who put America on the path to becoming an empire.

More states were admitted to the Union during Harrison's term than during any other presidential administration: North Dakota and South Dakota (November 2, 1889), Montana (November 8, 1889), Washington (November 11, 1889), Idaho (July 3, 1890), and Wyoming (July 10, 1890). On January 1, 1892, Ellis Island in New York Harbor became the official entry point for the millions of immigrants coming to America's shores. America's population increased by more than five million in the years 1888 to 1892; half of the new people were immigrants.

The 1892 election

The election of 1892 was of great historic importance: It was the first election in which both candidates had been president. Harrison beat President Cleveland in the 1888 election, but he did not beat him again.

Harrison had done well for himself and his country with his foreign agenda, but his handling of domestic issues (situations within the country) was not looked upon so favorably. Never a personable fellow, his cold manner and his refusal to listen to advice turned even his own party against him. The president's popularity suffered over three major issues: his support of the McKinley Tariff, which millions of Americans took as a sign that he had forgotten the average citizen and was siding with big business; his lack of response to the plight of farmers in the South and West, who were suffering from the fallout of high tariffs and so were financially in danger; and the fact that throughout his administration, American workers participated in a series of violent labor strikes (when workers refuse to work until negotiations for improvements are made), which again linked the president to monopoly industrialists and unethical bankers.

In addition to these perceptions, many Americans were not in favor of how easily Harrison spent federal dollars. Early in Harrison's administration, Congress was nicknamed the "Billion Dollar Congress" because of all the money that was appropriated. No president before him had so freely spent money in peacetime. According to Harrison's biography on the Web site *The White House,* Thomas B. Reed (1839–1902), twice Speaker of the House of Representatives, answered critics by saying, "This is a billion dollar country."

Cleveland won the election with 277 electoral votes, as compared with Harrison's 145. Cleveland also won nearly 373,000 more popular votes than his opponent. It was the most decisive victory of any presidential election in twenty years.

His last years

Harrison's wife Caroline had died in 1892 from tuberculosis (lung disease). Together, they had three children, one of whom died in infancy. In 1896, he married again, this time to a widow named Mary Scott Lord Dimmick; she was his first wife's niece. They had one daughter.

Although he was stiff and formal with the public, Harrison was a loving father and husband. His grandchildren were especially dear to him, and he often quit working at noon so that he could have time to play with them.

By the time of his defeat, Harrison was ready to leave the White House. His feelings toward the public were about the same as theirs were for him. Upon learning of his defeat, he told his family he felt as if he had been freed from prison. He spent his last years active in law.

In February 1901, Harrison came down with a cold that eventually turned into pneumonia. He died in his Indianapolis home on March 13, 1901.

For More Information

BOOKS

American Presidents in World History. Vol. 3. Westport, CT: Greenwood Press, 2003.

Cherny, Robert W. *American Politics in the Gilded Age: 1868–1900.* Wheeling, IL: Harlan Davidson, 1997.

Sievers, Harry J. *Benjamin Harrison: Hoosier President.* Newtown, CT: American Political Biography Press, 1997.

Stevens, Rita. *Benjamin Harrison, 23rd President of the United States.* Ada, OK: Garrett Educational Corp., 1989.

Williams, Jean Kinney. *Benjamin Harrison: America's 23rd President.* New York: Children's Press, 2004.

WEB SITES

"Benjamin Harrison." *American President.org.* http://americanpresident.org/history/benjaminharrison/biography (accessed on September 2, 2006).

"Benjamin Harrison." *The White House.* http://www.whitehouse.gov/history/presidents/bh23.html (accessed on September 2, 2006).

The President Benjamin Harrison Home. http://www.presidentbenjaminharrison.org/ (accessed on September 2, 2006).

"Who Was James Blaine?" *Blaine Amendments.* http://www.blaineamendments.org/Intro/JGB.html (accessed on September 2, 2006).

Lewis Hine

BORN: September 26, 1874 • Oshkosh, Wisconsin

DIED: November 3, 1940 • Hastings-on-Hudson, New York

Photographer; social reformer

Lewis Hine.
THE GRANGER
COLLECTION, NEW YORK.

"I wanted to show things that had to be corrected."

Lewis Wickes Hine was a teacher-turned-reformer who exchanged his classroom for a camera and set about changing the world, one child at a time. Hine's most famous photos featured children at work—in fields, factories, mills, and anywhere else young children were forced to work. His photographs were not effective because he was expertly skilled, but because the raw quality of his work reinforced the tone of harshness and despair that accompanied child labor. He was a pioneer in the field of photography as art.

Hine also used his talent to document relief efforts after World War I (1914–18), the construction of the Empire State Building, and the plight of women workers in the 1930s. Because of Hine's work, America has a recording of its evolution throughout the Gilded Age and the Progressive Era. The Gilded Age was the period in history following the Civil War and Reconstruction (roughly the final twenty-three years of the nineteenth century), characterized by a ruthless pursuit of profit, an exterior of showiness and grandeur, and immeasurable political corruption. The Progressive Era was the period that followed the Gilded Age (approximately the first twenty years of the twentieth century); it was marked by reform and the development of a national cultural identity.

The student becomes the teacher

Lewis Hine was born in Oshkosh, Wisconsin, on September 26, 1874. His father, Douglas Hull Hine, was a veteran of the Civil War (1861–65). Hine's mother, Sarah Hayes Hine, was a teacher. Douglas Hine died in an accident in 1892, forcing Hine to find his first job at the age of eighteen. He found work in a furniture upholstery factory and worked thirteen hours a day, six days a week. This exhausting schedule (seventy-eight hours weekly) earned him $4 a week.

Over the course of the decade, Hine worked several odd jobs. Every job was virtually the same: long hours and little pay. These frustrating experiences gave Hine firsthand knowledge of the world of the working-class poor. He worked alongside child laborers; he knew their lives intimately. This knowledge motivated him to want to make a positive change for children.

Hine wanted something better for himself as well, so he enrolled in extension courses at the University of Chicago while still living in Oshkosh. During this time, he met Frank Manny, a professor at the State Normal School in Oshkosh. Manny saw in Hine ability fueled by motivation, and he encouraged Hine to pursue his education. Hine became a teacher and had the great fortune to study with two of the most famous educators of the era: Ella Flagg Young (1845–1918), who became the first female superintendent of an American school in 1909; and **John Dewey** (1859–1952; see entry), an education reformer.

When Manny took a job as superintendent of New York's Ethical Culture School in 1901, he hired Hine to be the nature study and geography teacher. Manny unknowingly set Hine on a path that would change his life when, in 1903, he gave Hine a camera to use as an experimental teaching tool. Hine was immediately fascinated with the camera and taught himself how to use it. Almost instantly, Hine realized the power of a photograph to tell a story. Throughout his life, he would improve his picture-taking technique and experiment with various styles of photography.

Creates first photo documentary

Hine designed a project for his students, most of whom were immigrants (people who permanently moved from one country to another) from

Eastern Europe. The purpose of the project was to teach the children respect for the multicultural atmosphere that filled New York during the early 1900s. In an effort to help his students understand the impact immigration was having not only on the immigrants themselves but also on American culture, Hine made several trips with his camera to Ellis Island, the port of entry for immigrants who crossed the Atlantic Ocean. The first of these trips took place in 1904; the last, in 1909.

With each visit to Ellis Island, Hine instinctively knew he was embarking on a journey that would seriously affect his life. By the time the documentary was completed, Hine had gathered together a large collection of photographs related to the immigrant experience. These photos were eventually published in various books.

Hine married Sarah Rich in 1904 (they would have one son, Corydon, in 1912) and continued teaching at the Ethical Culture School until 1908. In 1905, he completed work on his master's degree in pedagogy (the study of strategies, techniques, and approaches used in the classroom) and graduated from New York University. Despite this busy schedule, Hine managed to establish a sideline income by submitting photos on a regular basis to educational magazines, including *Elementary School Teacher* and the *Photographic Times*. He wanted to encourage other educators to use photography as an educational tool.

During this time, Hine attended the Columbia School of Social Work, where he met Arthur Kellogg (1878–1934), business manager of a social commentary magazine called *Charities and the Commons*. Establishing a friendship with Kellogg was a turning point in Hine's career. In 1907, he was hired to photograph various aspects of Pittsburgh, Pennsylvania, a major industrial city with a focus on the steel industry. The magazine was investigating social and working conditions in Pittsburgh as part of a survey; Hine would supply the photos. His participation in this project, which encompassed two years, led him to capture the worklife of laborers and the issues surrounding them, such as industrial accidents, work conditions, and industrial employment of women. Hine also documented the health, recreational, and educational aspects of the lives of these residents of Pittsburgh.

The results of this investigative report were published in three special issues of *Charities and the Commons* throughout the spring of 1909. The completed Pittsburgh Survey, published in six volumes, became the model of "modern" social research. That same year, Hine left the world of teaching when he accepted a paid position on the staff of the magazine, as its photographer.

Joins the National Child Labor Committee

In 1908, Hine joined the National Child Labor Committee (NCLC), an organization dedicated to regulating child labor. The NCLC was not popular among the big businesses of America's industrial society. Companies depended on child labor to maximize their profits. For pennies a day, managers and owners could—and did—squeeze ten or more hours of work out of a child. If forced to hire adults to do the same jobs children were capable of doing, companies would make less money. The bonus of hiring child laborers was that they were less likely to complain about poor working conditions, and even less likely to strike (refuse to work unless specific conditions were met).

Child labor was common in the late nineteenth and early twentieth centuries. In 1900, nearly 20 percent of all children in the country between the ages of ten and fifteen worked. Some industries, such as coal mining and agricultural-based businesses (for instance, orchards and other farms), hired children as young as five to do simple, repetitive tasks. The workday began before dawn and did not end until sundown. During busy seasons, the hours were even longer. In addition to the jobs held inside factories and mills, thousands of very young children performed work at home, such as sewing and cigar-rolling, in their tenements (run-down apartments). Most child laborers gave up their schooling for the mere pennies they earned; they were forced to exchange their futures for dismal, miserable childhoods.

By the second decade of the twentieth century, some states had their own child-labor laws. Because the practice of using children as laborers was a cornerstone of big business, however, industrialists and other businessmen refused to adhere to the laws. Unfortunately, many child laborers could not count on protection from their parents, either. Parents often lied about their children's ages and looked the other way when employers expected children to work longer hours than permitted by law. What was needed was federal regulation, which would not be enacted until the 1930s.

In the meantime, Hine helped child-labor reform move forward by traveling throughout America, photographing children working under unimaginable conditions. Usually he would disguise himself in order to gain entry to the factories, mines, fields, and mills where he found the children. Had his identity been discovered, his life would have been in danger. Social reform was going to occur only at the cost of big-business profits, and no company owner was going to let that happen without a fight. To get into a company, Hine would pose as a Bible salesman or an equipment and machinery inspector.

Once inside the business, Hine would engage children in conversation and quickly note their ages, jobs, and any other information he felt was important. In those instances when he could not gain entry to the

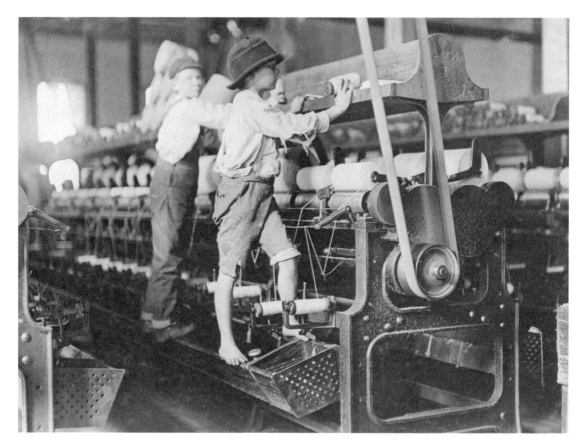

Two young boys replace bobbins on a spinning machine at the Bibb Cotton Mill in Macon, Georgia, in 1909. Photograph by Lewis Wickes Hine. © CORBIS.

workplace, he would wait outside—sometimes all day or night—for the children to leave. As they did so, he would try to gather information, but more importantly, he would photograph them, with or without knowing his subjects' information.

A mere glimpse at the children featured in Hine's photographs told the story of their lives. Hine understood the power of perspective, light, and position in photography, and he used a combination that left no doubt in viewers' minds that the children they were looking at led lives of misery and neglect. Going against the common photography style of the day, which had subjects gazing past the camera so as to appear as if they were not actually posing for a portrait, Hine would tell the children to look directly at the camera. In doing so, Hine made sure that when viewers looked at the children, the children were looking back at the viewers. The impact of these photos on the child-labor cause was intense.

Hine had his photos published in magazines throughout the country, but he also published them in books and pamphlets, on posters and in bulletins. He traveled the country presenting them in slide lectures and exhibitions. In doing so, the reformer made sure to reach audiences at every level, whether their interests lie in reading or attending cultural events. Hine knew he had to appeal to the segment of the public that wielded the power to implement change.

Hine was not alone in his attempts to promote reform via a camera lens. Immigrant reporter Jacob Riis (1849–1914; see box) had done for tenement housing what Hine eventually achieved for child labor. Riis's photographs of immigrant slums in New York City brought to the public the plight of the city's poor. Although they were of two different generations, both Riis and Hine dedicated their lives toward eliminating poverty and improving the lives of America's lower class.

A child works at a mine in the Scotts Run area of West Virginia in 1936. Photograph by Lewis Wickes Hine. NATIONAL ARCHIVES AND RECORDS ADMINISTRATION.

Becomes an interpretive photographer

Hine's photographs helped the NCLC achieve its goals. When the public pressured lawmakers into passing protective legislation for child laborers, the NCLC no longer needed Hine. More and more states began passing not only child-labor laws but also mandatory education laws. Although federal protection would not be in place until the 1930s, the NCLC knew they were on the road to serious reform, and their star photographer's contribution had paved the way. Hine left the NCLC in 1917 to pursue a freelance (self-employed) career.

Hine worked with the Red Cross in 1918 to document the postwar relief efforts in Europe. In 1919, he organized exhibitions for the American Red Cross Museum. For the next six years, Hine was hired by various organizations to help their cause. Among them were the Boy and Girl Scouts, the National Tuberculosis Commission, and the

Jacob Riis: Reporter Turned Reformer

Jacob Riis emigrated from Denmark to America in 1870, at the age of twenty-one. He immediately loved his new country but was concerned about conditions in the cities. He became a reporter for the *New York Evening Sun* and quickly became known as a pioneer of photojournalism. Riis took his own photos to accompany stories he wrote about situations he saw in his new country.

Riis began photographing and documenting conditions in the city's slums. He collected his work in a groundbreaking book entitled *How the Other Half Lives*. The book, published in 1890, brought Riis to the attention of an influential man who would one day be the twenty-sixth president of the United States. **Theodore Roosevelt** (1858–1919; see entry), then New York Police Board of Commissioners president, and Riis became fast friends. Together, they spearheaded the housing-reform movement.

Riis is credited with bringing to the forefront the plight of America's urban poor. His two other photojournalism books are *Children of the Poor* (1892) and *Children of the Tenements* (1903).

Riis's photojournalism efforts matched a new type of journalism called muckraking. Muckrakers exposed scandalous and unethical practices among established institutions in America. Some of the more famous muckrakers were Ida Tarbell (1857–1954), for her series on the Standard Oil Company; **Upton Sinclair** (1878–1968; see entry), for exposing the dangers and poor working conditions of the meatpacking industry in Chicago; and Lincoln Steffens (1866–1936), for his investigation of the scandals among city and state politicians. Muckrakers worked side by side with reformers throughout the Gilded Age and the Progressive Era.

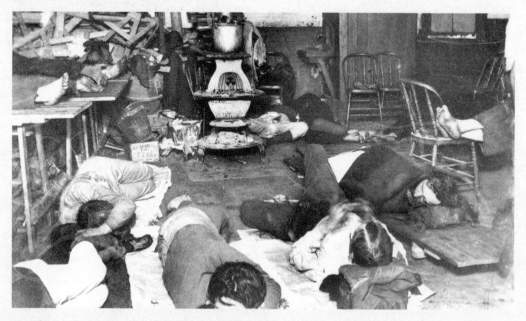

Homeless people sleep in a New York City shelter in 1886. The fee for sleeping indoors was five cents a night. Photograph by Jacob August Riis. © BETTMANN/CORBIS.

Tenement House Commission. For his photography achievements, Hine was awarded the Art Directors Club of New York Medal in 1924.

Hine promoted himself as an "interpretive" photographer throughout the 1920s. He organized traveling exhibitions of his photograph collections for much of the decade. As the era's most popular photographer, his exhibitions were in demand, especially in New York City.

Beginning in the 1920s, Hine used his camera to depict the working conditions for women across the country. He photographed women in the workplace as part of a famous series called the Shelton Loom Series. Hine's photos for that project were published on the cover of *Western Electric News*. As part of his efforts, and with a clarity that indicates he was a man ahead of his times, Hine included photographs of homemakers (women who did not work outside the home) because he believed they deserved the same recognition as their workplace counterparts.

Climbs the Empire State Building

Hine received one of his most prestigious commissions in 1930, when he was hired to document the construction of New York's Empire State Building. From May to November of that year, the fifty-six-year-old photographer climbed stairs, balanced himself on beams suspended hundreds of feet in the air, and dangled himself over the bustling city streets—all in search of the perfect photo.

Hine thought nothing of hanging one hundred stories above the ground to capture just the right angle on any one of hundreds of riveters, welders, and bricklayers. The building was constructed in record time. Over the course of just one year and forty-five days, at a rate of four-and-one-half stories a week, the Empire State Building was completed. Its official opening was on May 1, 1931. Many of Hine's photos from that project were published in 1932. The book, *Men at Work,* received great acclaim by reviewers and readers alike.

Hine photographed other major events in the 1930s, including the 1933 Chicago World's Fair. That same year, he was hired by the Tennessee Valley Authority (TVA) to photograph the construction of some dam sites. (The TVA was a government-controlled operation that provided flood control, electricity, and economic development in the Tennessee River Valley.) That assignment ended when Hine's photos were published without giving him credit.

A worker sits on a steel beam, high atop New York City, as the construction of the Empire State Building continues in 1931. The ornate Chrysler Building can be seen in the background. Photograph by Lewis Wickes Hine. © LEWIS W. HINE/GEORGE EASTMAN HOUSE/GETTY IMAGES.

The end of the road

After the problem he encountered with the TVA, Hine sought out photographer Roy Stryker (1893–1975) in 1935 to seek advice about getting control of the rights to his photos. At the time, Stryker was head of the historical section of the Farm Security Administration (FSA). As America was experiencing its worst economic situation in history throughout the 1930s, the FSA was organized to assist farmers whose livelihoods had been devastated by the Great Depression (1929–41). Stryker told Hine to keep the negatives to all his photos as proof that he indeed owned them.

At the same time, Stryker was asked by President Franklin D. Roosevelt (1882–1945; served 1933–45) to select a handful of photographers to travel to America's rural heartland and document the struggles of its people during the Depression. Although Stryker told Hine about the job and Hine expressed deep interest in the project, Stryker kept coming up with excuses as to why he would not select Hine. Stryker never had any intentions of sending Hine on the mission; he told a friend that Hine was past his prime. The new, modern photography was of places and buildings, not of people. His encouragement of his fellow photographer was only out of pity.

Perhaps in response to Stryker's suggestion that he try photographing urban and rural subjects without people, Hine spent the next couple years photographing machines. This change in subject matter allowed Hine to experiment with his style. The result was a collection of prints that perfectly reflected industrial America: Man had been replaced by machinery.

Hine was lead photographer of the National Research Project of the Works Project Administration (WPA) in 1936 and 1937. The WPA had been established in 1935 to continue providing relief for those Americans hit hardest by the Depression. It provided jobs to the unemployed at a time when work was hard to find. In 1939, Hine arranged for a small exhibition of his work at New York City's Riverside Museum. Although the show was a success, it did not bring Hine the work he so desperately wanted. He was a portrait photographer without work. He died, penniless, in New York on November 3, 1940. Hine was a man whose work had outlived its usefulness: his photos were meant to inspire social reform, but by the 1930s, that reform had happened. Therefore, his particular form of photography no longer had any use. Yet his work provides detailed insight into a country that was changing by leaps and bounds, often at the expense of its people.

For More Information

BOOKS

Dimock, George. "Hine, Lewis (1874–1940)." In *Encyclopedia of Children and Childhood: In History and Society*. Edited by Paula S. Fass. New York: Macmillan, 2004.

Freedman, Russell, and Lewis Hine. *Kids at Work: Lewis Hine and the Crusade Against Child Labor*. New York: Clarion Books, 1994.

Goldberg, Vicki. *Lewis W. Hine: Children at Work*. New York: Prestel Publishing, 1999.

Hine, Lewis. *The Empire State Building*. New York: Prestel Publishing, 1998.

Panzer, Mary. *Lewis Hine*. New York: Phaidon Press, 2002.

PERIODICALS

Martinez Wright, Lee. "Spiders in the Sky." *Smithsonian* (January 2002): p. 17.

Millstein, Barbara Head. "Lewis Wickes Hine: The Final Years." *Magazine Antiques* (November 1998): p. 714.

WEB SITES

"Child Labor in America 1908–1912: Photographs of Lewis W. Hines." *The History Place.* http://www.historyplace.com/unitedstates/childlabor/index.html (accessed on September 3, 2006).

Davis, Kay. "Lewis Hine." *Documenting "The Other Half": The Social Reform Photography of Jacob Riis and Lewis Hine.* http://xroads.virginia.edu/~MA01/davis/photography/hine/hine.html (accessed on September 3, 2006).

Hall, Maureen P. *Lewis Hine's Men at Work.* http://xroads.virginia.edu/~1930s/Print/document/men/coverpage.html (accessed on September 3, 2006).

Leggat, Robert. "Hine, Lewis Wickes." *A History of Photography.* http://www.rleggat.com/photohistory/history/hine.htm (accessed on September 3, 2006).

"Lewis Wickes Hine: The Construction of the Empire State Building, 1930–1931." *The New York Public Library.* http://www.nypl.org/research/chss/spe/art/photo/hinex/empire/empire.html (accessed on September 3, 2006).

"Lewis Wickes Hine." *Getty Museum.* http://www.getty.edu/art/gettyguide/artMakerDetails?maker=1601&page=1 (accessed on September 3, 2006).

Library of Congress. "National Child Labor Committee Collection Photographs by Lewis Hine." *Prints and Photographs Reading Room.* http://www.loc.gov/rr/print/coll/207-b.html (accessed on September 3, 2006).

Oden, Lori. "Lewis Hine (1874–1940): Photography for Social Reform." *International Photography Hall of Fame & Museum.* http://www.iphf.org/inductees/LHine.htm (accessed on June 2, 2006).

Scott Joplin

BORN: November 24, 1868 • Linden, Texas

DIED: April 1, 1917 • New York, New York

Composer

"When I'm dead twenty-five years, people are going to begin to recognize me."

Scott Joplin was once one of America's most popular composers. By his death at the age of forty-nine, he had spent years as the "King of Ragtime." Rag is a style of music based on complicated rhythms. The fast-paced music has its roots in African American folk traditions, but Joplin created a craze for ragtime when he played it publicly in bars and honky-tonks (rundown dance halls). More than mere music, Joplin's compositions came to represent the African American heritage and experiences during the late nineteenth and early twentieth centuries.

Develops musical ability

Scott Joplin was born to Jiles and Florence Joplin on November 24, 1868. His father, a former slave, was a laborer. Scott inherited his musical ability from his father. Around the age of seven, Joplin's family moved to Texarkana, Arkansas (on the Texas-Arkansas border). During this time, Joplin had already proved himself a natural talent on the banjo and had

Scott Joplin.
© HULTON ARCHIVE/
GETTY IMAGES.

begun experimenting on the piano. The instrument was owned by a law-yer for whom Joplin's mother cleaned house. Joplin began taking piano lessons at the age of eleven from a tutor named Julius Weiss (1814–1898). The German music teacher worked as a tutor for the same family that employed Joplin's mother.

Details of Joplin's teen years are not completely known. He left home in his early teens and attended high school in Sedalia, Missouri. Why he moved or if he graduated is unknown and among the mysteries that characterize the composer's life as a young adult. In 1891, Joplin returned to Texarkana and joined a minstrel troupe (a band of traveling musicians). One of the highlights of his early career was his participation in a band that played at the popular Columbian Exposition in 1893 in Chicago, Illinois. While performing at the fair, where countries and cultures from all over the world exhibited their best, Joplin first heard the unique sounds of ragtime.

He spent the early 1890s traveling with his minstrel troupe, the Texas Medley Quartette. His travels took him back to Sedalia, where he played two honky-tonks on a regular basis: The Maple Leaf and the Black 400 Club. During those years, Joplin studied music formally at George R. Smith College in Sedalia.

Becomes a published composer

Joplin's first published compositions appeared in 1895. His first two pieces were waltzes entitled "Please Say You Will" and "A Picture of Her Face." "Combination March," "Harmony Club Waltz," and "Great Collision March," all published in 1896, were not rags, but they helped cement his reputation as a solid composer.

Joplin's first rag, "Original Rags," was published in 1898. The following year, he published the most famous rag of all time. Named after a favorite honky-tonk at which he liked to play, "Maple Leaf Rag" sold four hundred copies in its first year of publication. Joplin hired a lawyer to help him negotiate a deal with music publisher John Stilwell Stark (1841–1927). The final contract gave Joplin one penny for each copy of "Maple Leaf Rag" sold. This arrangement was in effect for all of the composer's life and was one of the earliest examples of a musician being paid royalties, or particular amounts of money for each product sold. The usual contract during that time paid composers $25 or less per published piece. By the end of the first decade of the twentieth century, Joplin had sold almost half a million copies of the popular rag. Healthy sales of the song continued throughout the next twenty years.

That same year, Joplin wrote what can only be described as a ragtime ballet that incorporated folk dances choreographed by him as well as a narrative written by him. *Rag Time Dance* was performed at the Black Club 400 in 1899, but it was not published until 1902. It proved Joplin's ability to write longer pieces. The ballet never caught on with the public, however, and Joplin returned to writing rags.

The entertainer

Joplin married Belle Hayden in 1901 and the newlyweds moved to St. Louis, Missouri. There the composer established the Scott Joplin Opera Company, a business that reflected Joplin's lifelong fascination with breaking into opera. Despite his instant success with ragtime, Joplin was forever dismayed by the perception of upper-class, white society that ragtime was a tasteless form of "black" music. Joplin believed that if he could find success in opera, a music form long respected by upper-class whites, he would be taken seriously as a composer. He had single-handedly put ragtime on the map of American music, but that success was never enough for him.

Sheet music cover of Scott Joplin's "Maple Leaf Rag," 1899. © HULTON ARCHIVE/ GETTY IMAGES.

Joplin composed twenty-seven rags within the first decade of the twentieth century. One of those rags, "The Entertainer," eventually became the theme song for a 1973 film called *The Sting,* starring Robert Redford (1936–) and Paul Newman (1925–). The movie was a box-office success, and Joplin's rag became one of the nation's most popular tunes. For many younger Americans, it was their introduction to Joplin's music. The tune was heard everywhere from radios to rock concerts, as artists performed their own versions of the fast-moving song. In 1976, the Pulitzer Committee awarded Joplin a posthumous (post-death) award for his contribution to American music.

In 1903, Joplin's unhappy marriage to Belle ended as his first opera, *A Guest of Honor,* was published. In order for the opera to receive national attention, Joplin's company put together a troupe of thirty performers and scheduled a tour that included performances in Iowa,

Nebraska, Kansas, Missouri, and Illinois. According to Edward Berlin, who wrote a Joplin biography for the *Scott Joplin International Ragtime Foundation* Web site, someone working for the touring company stole a great deal of money, leaving Joplin unable to pay the performers for their work or the boarding house for its hospitality. In addition to money, the score (sheet music) of the opera was stolen, and the opera never enjoyed more than a rehearsal. The score never was recovered and remains a lost piece of music in the twenty-first century.

Another opera

After the opera failed, Joplin took a few months off to travel. In Chicago, he met and fell in love with nineteen-year-old Freddie Alexander. Joplin wrote and published a rag titled "Chrysanthemum" in his new love's honor in 1904. He married her that same year. The marriage was doomed, however, when Joplin's new wife succumbed to pneumonia at the age of twenty. The two had been married for only ten weeks, and those weeks had been spent traveling so that Joplin could perform concerts. Ironically, the couple was in Sedalia, where Joplin had gotten his first big break in music, when Freddie died. The broken-hearted composer never returned to Sedalia again.

Never having fully recovered from the extensive financial loss of his opera, Joplin spent the next few years mostly in St. Louis, playing piano in bars and saloons. These jobs paid very little money, and his financial situation worsened. He continued to publish rags, but it was the hope of publishing yet another opera—in his continuing attempt to be accepted into white society—that inspired Joplin to work.

He traveled to New York that year, hoping to secure financial backing for a new opera he had written. This one was called *Treemonisha,* and it was not a ragtime opera. It was a folk tale about a young orphan girl named Treemonisha. Because she is educated, she is chosen to move her people beyond ignorance and into enlightenment. Joplin wrote the music and words as well as choreographed the dance.

Although some music historians consider *Treemonisha* to be the first great American opera because of its blend of American music with conventional opera techniques, society at the time did not share that opinion. Joplin's name was associated with ragtime, and that kind of music no longer enjoyed the popularity it once had. A few songs from the opera were performed in separate productions in 1913 and 1915, but the opera as a whole performance never materialized except for one production, which

Joplin produced. Owing to a lack of funding, the opera was performed without scenery, costumes, or a symphony. Joplin accompanied the actors on the piano.

Final curtain call

Joplin married for the third and final time in 1907. Having settled in New York, Lottie Stokes and Joplin formed a husband-and-wife publishing company in 1913. Over the next two years, Joplin wrote several more musical pieces, including rags, a symphony, and even a vaudeville (song-and-dance) act. None of these pieces were ever published, and the manuscripts disappeared.

Joplin began feeling ill. By 1916, he suffered from the physical and mental deterioration of syphilis, a sexually transmitted disease that can gradually rob its victims of their sight, hearing, and memory loss. It also can lead to mental illness and other neurological disorders. At the time, there was no effective treatment for syphilis. Joplin died in a mental hospital on April 1, 1917.

According to Berlin's biography of the composer, Joplin was intelligent and quiet, willing to volunteer his time to help aspiring musicians. His interests outside music were few. Despite his great popularity during ragtime's heyday, he was never satisfied because he believed he had not been allowed to reach his full potential. As a pianist, he was considered to be of average talent. Although he played other instruments and sang, he did so with little enthusiasm. Joplin had perfect pitch, meaning he could sing musical notes with perfect accuracy even without musical accompaniment. This talent held little interest for him; Joplin was, above all else, a composer.

For More Information

BOOKS

Bankston, John. *The Life and Times of Scott Joplin.* Hockessin, DE: Mitchell Lane Publishers, 2005.

Berlin, Edward A. *King of Ragtime: Scott Joplin and His Era.* New York: Oxford University Press, 1994.

Curtis, Susan. *Dancing to a Black Man's Tune: A Life of Scott Joplin.* Columbia: University of Missouri Press, 1994.

Joplin, Scott. *Joplin Gold.* London, England: Chester Music, 2004.

Rosen, Isaac. "Scott Joplin." In *Contemporary Black Biography.* Vol. 6. Detroit: Gale, 1994.

WEB SITES

Albrecht, Theodore. "Joplin, Scott." *The Handbook of Texas Online.* http://www.tsha.utexas.edu/handbook/online/articles/JJ/fjo70.html (accessed on September 3, 2006).

Berlin, Edward A. "A Biography of Scott Joplin." *The Scott Joplin International Ragtime Foundation.* http://www.scottjoplin.org/biography.htm (accessed on September 3, 2006).

Due, Tananarive. "Excerpt: 'Joplin's Ghost.'" *National Public Radio.* http://www.npr.org/templates/story/story.php?storyId=5346117 (accessed on September 3, 2006).

Levang, Rex. "100 Years of the Maple Leaf Rag." *Minnesota Public Radio.* http://music.minnesota.publicradio.org/features/9905_ragtime/index.shtml (accessed on September 3, 2006).

Moss, Charles K. "Scott Joplin: King of Ragtime." *Charles K. Moss Piano Studio.* http://www.carolinaclassical.com/joplin/index.html (accessed on September 3, 2006).

"The Music of Scott Joplin." *Geocities.com.* http://www.geocities.com/BourbonStreet/Bayou/9694/music.html (accessed on September 3, 2006).

"Scott Joplin." *Essentials of Music.* http://www.essentialsofmusic.com/composer/joplin.html (accessed on September 3, 2006).

Jack London

BORN: January 12, 1876 • San Francisco, California
DIED: November 22, 1916 • Glen Ellen, California

Writer

Jack London.
THE LIBRARY
OF CONGRESS.

"I write for no other purpose than to add to the beauty that now belongs to me."

Jack London was a writer whose style was in direct opposition of the popular writing of the Gilded Age. The Gilded Age was the period in history following the Civil War and Reconstruction (roughly the final twenty-three years of the nineteenth century), characterized by a ruthless pursuit of profit, an exterior of showiness and grandeur, and immeasurable political corruption. While most authors were writing long-winded, detailed paragraphs, London filled page after page with crisp, clean sentences. His many articles and novels gave readers adventure and insight without bogging them down in endless description. He wrote on themes of struggle and survival, and the messages of his stories brought him international renown. London was one of the most publicized figures of his time, equal in status to celebrities and the wealthy elite (upper class).

Born to the working class

John Griffith London was born on January 12, 1876, in San Francisco, California. His unmarried mother, Flora Wellman, came from a wealthy

111

family, and many historians believe London's biological father was William Henry Chaney (1821–1903). Chaney was a journalist and lawyer, but he made a name for himself in the developing world of American astrology (the study of planets and how they may affect human behavior and characteristics). No one knows without doubt about who fathered London. His birth certificate was destroyed in the fires of the great San Francisco earthquake in 1906 (see box). That tragic earthquake would be covered in a magazine article by London, and would be considered one of the most moving accounts of the earthquake.

London's mother was sick often, so he was raised mostly by a former slave named Virginia Prentiss. Later in 1876, his mother married John London, a veteran of the Civil War (1861–65). The family moved to West Oakland, where London completed grade school. He would later write of being poor as a child, but his family was actually of the working class.

London's teenaged years were spent working at various jobs, many of them involved with the sea. For a time, he served on a patrol in the San Francisco Bay that scouted out and captured poachers (men who fished illegally). He also sailed the Pacific Ocean on a sealing ship. Once he became accustomed to the traveling life, London traversed the country. He enjoyed moving around. At nineteen, he returned home to attend high school.

Through his travels and experiences with various individuals and cultures, London came to consider himself a socialist, someone who believes in the public ownership of the means of production and distribution of wealth. In comparison, a capitalist believes in an economic system based on private ownership of business and the ability for businesses to compete; America's economic system is capitalistic. Socialists view capitalism as the root of poverty and believe that equal distribution of wealth would put an end to the divisions of social class. London unsuccessfully ran for mayor of Oakland, California, on the Socialist Party ticket several times.

Becomes a writer

Many writers cannot recall a time when they did not write. For them, writing is something they felt they were born to do. This was not the case with London. He saw writing as a means to make money. He studied other writers and practiced mimicking their style as he began to submit jokes, poems, and short stories for publications. Most of these early attempts failed.

The San Francisco Earthquake of 1906

San Francisco residents sit on Russian Hill watching the fires from the 1906 earthquake. © BETTMANN/ CORBIS.

At 5:15 on the morning of Wednesday, April 18, 1906, the quiet slumber of San Francisco's hundreds of thousands of residents was interrupted by a rumble such as they had never heard before. Although the powerful earthquake was over in one minute, the fires it caused raged for three days, destroying much of the West Coast's most densely populated and economically developed city.

That earthquake was not the most powerful ever experienced in the state or country, but it was the closest to a highly populated metropolitan area. City streets rolled up and down as if they were waves on the ocean. Tall buildings collapsed, killing and trapping not only pedestrians but occupants as well. In all, the great quake destroyed 28,000 buildings over 490 city blocks. More than 250,000 residents were left homeless. Estimates of those killed reach 3,000. Estimates of total damage to the city peaked at $350 million.

According to eyewitness Adolphus Busch, whose words are recorded on *Eyewitnessto-History.com,* "The most terrible thing I saw was the futile [pointless] struggle of a policeman and others to rescue a man who was pinned down in the burning wreckage. The helpless man watched it in silence till the fire began burning his feet. Then he screamed and begged to be killed. The policeman took his name and address and shot him through the head."

In London's report of the tragedy, the first night after the earthquake found San Francisco not riotous, but absolutely calm and still. Wrote London, "There was no hysteria [panic], no disorder. . . . In all those terrible hours I saw not one woman who wept, not one man who was excited, not one person who was in the slightest degree panic stricken."

The same could not be reported about what happened as the fires continued to ravage the city. Evacuation efforts via ferries were made, and complete chaos took over. Men and women fought for seats on the escaping ferry boats; children had their clothing torn from their backs as people tried to pull them to the ground in order to get on the boat in front of them.

Finally, the flames died out on Friday. Firefighters had given all they had—mostly in vain— to put out the fire. In the end, the flames had to run their course and burn themselves out.

Jack London writing in the outdoors. © BETTMANN/ CORBIS.

London spent the winter of 1897 in the Yukon, at the time part of the Northwest Territories in the northwest region of Canada (a year later, it became its own territory). There, he joined thousands of others in the search for gold. The Yukon Gold Rush began in July 1897 when two ships docked in San Francisco Bay and Seattle, Washington. Onboard both ships were miners, carrying the gold they had found in the Yukon territory. Suddenly, America was immersed in the gold rush craze, and London was among the hopeful gold prospectors seeking the gold deposits found naturally in the earth and in rivers and streams.

Although not successful as a gold prospector, London did manage to write about his adventures. Those exploits were first published in the magazine *Overland Monthly* in 1899. From that point on, America could not get enough of London's stories. He met the demand: Rarely a day passed that he did not write something. Between 1900 and 1916, he wrote more than fifty novels and hundreds of short stories and articles. His routine was to write no fewer than one thousand words a day, early in the morning.

Rises to celebrity status

The first decade of the twentieth century was busy for London. In 1900, he married his friend, Bess Maddern. Based on deep friendship rather than love, the union was one of many of its kind during that era, when men of importance chose women of good breeding for their wives. London and Maddern had two daughters, but the marriage did not last. In 1903, London and his wife divorced, and he married his secretary, Charmian Kittredge, in 1905. Throughout their lives, the two would call each other "mate," and their marriage lasted until London's death at the age of forty. The couple's only child, Joy, died just thirty-eight hours after birth.

London had written his first novel, *The Son of the Wolf,* in 1900. In 1903, London wrote what would become one of his most famous novels, an adventure tale titled *The Call of the Wild.* It was quickly followed by the books *The Sea-Wolf* (1904) and *White Fang* (1906). In between writing and researching his novels, London continued to write magazine features, both fiction and nonfiction. He maintained a heavy correspondence with readers, who wrote about ten thousand letters to him each year.

London's writing appealed to readers across the globe; he was the highest paid writer of his time. His critics, however, called him a hack, someone who churns out writing that is popular with the public but has little literary merit. They accused him of sensationalism (writing to gain attention) because he often used his power as a popular author to discuss topics he believed were important, such as socialism and women's suffrage (the right to vote). The accusation of being a sensationalist, modern critics recognize, may stem more from London's choice of words—he preferred strong words over precise words—than his choice of topics.

Beauty Ranch

Open space was important to London. As an adventurer, he had developed a strong connection to both land and sea. In June 1905, he and Charmian were living in Glen Ellen, California. For $7,000, London bought the Hill Ranch in Sonoma Valley: 130 acres (0.53 square kilometers) of trees, fields, streams and springs, canyons, hills, and a variety of wildlife. By 1913, he had made six more land purchases and was the proud owner of Beauty Ranch, an estate comprising 1,400 acres (5.67 square kilometers).

The ranch was actually an experimental farm, where London promoted the concept of scientific breeding (for the best and strongest features) of animals and even imported European purebreds to improve the quality of his stock. He was a pioneer in soil conservation, and used tilling (overturning many layers of soil) and terracing (shaping a slope into steps to prevent soil erosion) to improve the quality of soil on the hillsides. In addition to growing grapes, London planted vegetables, fruit trees, grass for hay, and even cacti.

In 1911, London and his wife began building their dream home. The sprawling Wolf House was built of redwood trees, the roof made of imported Spanish tiles. By 1913, London had invested approximately $80,000 in the house, and it was nearly complete. On August 22, final cleanup began, and the couple made plans for moving their custom-built furniture into the house. At 2:00 AM, London got word that his house was on fire. Nothing could be done to save the building, and the writer was crushed as he watched his dreams go up in smoke.

Worse yet, he felt that someone had deliberately set fire to the Wolf House. Investigations into the tragedy showed that the fire probably started because someone had left oil-soaked rags at the scene. The mystery was never solved, and the house was never rebuilt.

Cruises on the *Snark*

The Londons were determined to sail around the world in a yacht designed by Jack. The plan was to take seven years for the voyage, but the reality of the trip was far different. After spending $30,000 to build the yacht, which he named *Snark,* the Londons traveled to Hawaii, Tahiti, Samoa, and the Solomon Islands. A severe case of sun poisoning forced the couple and their small crew to sail for land in Australia, where doctors told London he could not spend any more time in the sun. The voyage, which began in 1907, lasted just a little over two years, and the Londons returned home, heartbroken.

Immerses self in work

After two great disappointments (the fire and interrupted voyage), London was a depressed man. He traveled to New York as well as to San Francisco and Los Angeles on business, and he spent much of his writing time on his boat, the *Roamer.* His wife coaxed him into returning to Hawaii in 1915 and again in 1916. Each time, he spent months there, writing and relaxing. London could never relax for long, however, when he thought about life at Beauty Ranch and all that he wanted to get done there. Because he was forever trying to expand his property and ranch, London was constantly in debt and under pressure to write.

London's doctors were concerned about his health and urged him to cut back on the use of alcohol and improve his diet. London refused and remained focused on writing so that he could fund his interests. He pushed himself to the limit, and on November 22, 1916, London died of uremia (toxins in the bloodstream). He was just forty years old. For years, he had suffered from a painful kidney disorder, which could have only been made worse by his drinking alcohol. There has been speculation that London killed himself by overdosing on the painkiller morphine, but no evidence has ever been found to support that claim.

The world was in shock. As reported on the *Jack London Online Collection* Web site, London's good friend, George Sterling (1869–1926), remarked upon hearing of his friend's passing, "His greatness will surge triumphantly above race and time."

London's novels and books have been translated into several dozen languages, and his works remain popular overseas. For those readers, London's books give them insight into the American character and all its contradictions. They provide understandable commentaries on key historic movements and events as well.

In 1959, London's nephew gave the state of California 39 acres (0.16 square kilometers) of London's beloved Beauty Ranch. On October 1, 1960, the state held a dedication ceremony marking the opening of the Jack London State Historic Park. Between 1977 and 1979, the state purchased another 756 acres (3.06 square kilometers) from the family and enlarged the park to nearly 800 acres (3.24 square kilometers).

For More Information

BOOKS

Dyer, Daniel. *Jack London: A Biography*. New York: Scholastic Press, 1997.

Kershaw, Alex. *Jack London: A Life*. New York: St. Martin's Press, 1998.

London, Jack. *The Best Short Stories of Jack London*. Garden City, NY: Sun Dial Press, 1945. Reprint, Greenwich, CT: Fawcett, 1992.

London, Jack. *The Call of the Wild*. Philadelphia: D. McKay, 1914. Multiple reprints.

London, Jack. *The Cruise of the Snark*. New York: Macmillan, 1911. Reprint, New York: Penguin Books, 2004.

London, Jack. *The Iron Heel*. New York: Macmillan, 1907. Reprint, New York: Mondial, 2006.

Wilson, Margie, ed. *The Wit and Wisdom of Jack London: A Collection of Quotations from His Writing and Letters*. Santa Rosa, CA: Wordsworth Pub. Co., 1995.

PERIODICALS

London, Jack. "The Story of an Eyewitness." *Collier's* (May 5, 1906). Also available at http://www.jacklondons.net/Journalism/san_francisco_earthquake. html (accessed on September 3, 2006).

Nolte, Carl. "Jack London's Lens on 1906 Quake." *San Francisco Chronicle* (January 6, 2006): B-1. Also available at http://www.sfgate.com/cgi-bin/article.cgi?f=/c/a/2006/01/06/BAGN3GI4NU1.DTL (accessed on September 3, 2006).

WEB SITES

"Jack London—His Life and Books." *Jack London State Historic Park*. http://www.parks.sonoma.net/JLStory.html (accessed on September 3, 2006).

The Jack London Online Collection. http://london.sonoma.edu/ (accessed on September 3, 2006).

"Jack London's Ranch Album." *The World of Jack London*. http://www.jacklondons. net/intro.html (accessed on September 3, 2006).

"The 1906 San Francisco Earthquake and Fire." *The Bancroft Library.* http://bancroft.berkeley.edu/collections/earthquakeandfire/index2.html (accessed on September 3, 2006).

"The San Francisco Earthquake, 1906." *Eyewitness to History.* http://www.eyewitnesstohistory.com/sfeq.htm (accessed on September 3, 2006).

Stasz, Clarice. "Jack [John Griffith] London." *The Jack London Online Collection.* http://london.sonoma.edu/jackbio.html (accessed on September 3, 2006).

"Who Was Jack London?" *Get Your Words' Worth.* http://www.getyourwordsworth.com/WORDSWORTH-JackLondon.html (accessed on September 3, 2006).

William McKinley

BORN: January 29, 1843 • Niles, Ohio

DIED: September 14, 1901 • Buffalo, New York

U.S. president

William McKinley.
THE LIBRARY OF
CONGRESS.

"War should never be entered upon until every agency of peace has failed."

William McKinley was once considered by historians to be a weak president who was controlled by his own administration. More recent scholars have revised that point of view and generally see McKinley as a politician who tried to avoid war but who remained firm in his commitment once it was made. As the last president of the Gilded Age, McKinley paved the way for the twentieth-century leaders who would guide America through the constantly changing times of the Progressive Era. The Gilded Age was the period in history following the Civil War and Reconstruction (roughly the final twenty-three years of the nineteenth century), characterized by a ruthless pursuit of profit, an exterior of showiness and grandeur, and immeasurable political corruption. The Progressive Era was the period that followed the Gilded Age (approximately the first twenty years of the twentieth century); it was marked by reform and the development of a national cultural identity.

119

Born shy

William McKinley was born on January 29, 1843, the seventh of eight children. He spent the first ten years of his life in the small town of Niles, Ohio, where father William owned an iron foundry. At age ten, McKinley and his family moved to a nearby town called Poland. McKinley's childhood was typical of boys during that time. He went fishing, hunting, swimming, and horseback riding. From his mother, he learned the value of honesty, while his father instilled in him a strong work ethic.

After finishing his basic education, McKinley attended Allegheny College in Meadville, Pennsylvania. He never graduated, though, because of financial hardships and illness. McKinley joined the Twenty-third Ohio Volunteer Infantry at the start of the Civil War (1861–65). He repeatedly showed courage on the battlefield. As a second lieutenant, McKinley served under Rutherford B. Hayes (1822–93), a man who would be president of the United States one day. After the war, McKinley went home to Ohio and studied law at Albany Law School.

After passing the bar exam in 1867, McKinley opened his legal firm in Canton, Ohio. In 1869, he met Ida Saxton. The two married in January 1871 and had two daughters, Katherine and Ida. Katherine, born on Christmas Day 1871, lived only until 1875. Her sister, born in 1873, died at the age of four months.

Enters politics

McKinley earned a living as a lawyer, but he was passionate about politics. He was elected county prosecutor in 1869, and he won a Republican seat in Congress in 1876, where he served until 1891. (During that time, he lost only one election, in 1882.) McKinley was appointed chair of the House Ways and Means Committee in 1889, a powerful position. He used his power to help pass the McKinley Tariff of 1890. The bill increased the cost of imported goods by almost 49.5 percent, an increase that was reflected in the prices consumers were forced to pay for products. The monumental increase angered voters, and McKinley was defeated in the 1890 election.

McKinley was elected governor of Ohio in 1891. He spent his first term trying to improve relations between management and labor in industry. He developed an arbitration (negotiation) program and managed to convince the state's Republicans to support it. Traditionally, Republicans refused to recognize the rights of labor, but McKinley changed their position with his gifted public speaking.

Although he publicly acknowledged the rights of workers, he refused to give in to them if he believed their requests were not rational. In 1894, he called in the National Guard to break up a strike (formal protest of workers who refuse to work until negotiations are made) of the United Mine Workers.

America suffered an economic depression (a long-term economic state characterized by high unemployment, minimal investment and spending, and low prices) in 1893. This depression was one of the worst in American history. The unemployment rate (percentage of the total working population that was out of a job) exceeded 10 percent for half a decade, something that had never happened before and would not happen again until the Great Depression of the 1930s. No city or region was left unscarred. One of every four workers in Pennsylvania was unemployed; in Chicago, Illinois, one hundred thousand people were sleeping on the streets.

McKinley himself suffered financial hardship through the depression. He had cosigned a loan for a friend, and then the friend went bankrupt, leaving McKinley to pay off the debt. That he suffered right along with millions of other Americans only increased his popularity, and he was reelected for another term.

Election of 1896

The presidential campaign and election of 1896 was one of the most complicated and interesting in history. McKinley was the Republican candidate. Although Democrat **Grover Cleveland** (1837–1908; served 1885–89 and 1893–97; see entry) was the president at the time, he had angered America so much with his lack of response to the Panic of 1893 that his party did not nominate him as its candidate, but instead chose William Jennings Bryan (1860–1925; see box).

Party platforms In addition to the Democrats and Republicans, the 1896 election involved the Populist Party. Displeased farmers and laborers who believed their interests and concerns were not fairly represented or considered by either major political party formed this party in 1892. The Populists wanted public ownership of railroads so that prices could be controlled. They wanted the government to issue more silver and paper currency in the hope that the increase of money in circulation would raise prices and help farmers pay off their debts. Populists campaigned for the graduated income tax (where the more money people

William Jennings Bryan: Popular Presidential Candidate

Political poster for 1900 Democratic presidential candidate William Jennings Bryan. © CORBIS.

William Jennings Bryan was born in Salem, Illinois, on March 19, 1860. He practiced law in his home state until 1887, when he moved to Lincoln, Nebraska. From 1891 to 1895, Bryan held a seat in the U.S. House of Representatives.

A gifted public speaker, Bryan used his skill to defend and champion the small farmer and laborer, two factions of America that the Democrats and Republicans often overlooked. His efforts included supporting the Free Silver movement, which would require the government to use silver to back the dollar at a value that would increase the prices farmers received for their crops. This, in turn, would help them pay their debts, which were considerable.

At the Democratic convention in 1896, Bryan gave his most famous speech, known as the "Cross of Gold" speech. In the address, Bryan dramatically compared the gold standard (at the time, the government's policy of backing paper money with equal amounts of gold) to crucifixion (death by being hung on a cross). As reported on Vassar College's *1896* Web site, Bryan closed his heartfelt speech with these words:

If they say bimetallism is good, but that we cannot have it until other nations help us, we reply, that instead of having a gold standard because England has, we will restore bimetallism, and then let England have bimetallism because the United States has it. If they

made, the more taxes they paid). The graduated tax would redistribute wealth by taxing the rich more heavily than the poor. Populists wanted postal savings banks, which would give the poor a safe place to deposit their money because the banks would be government-owned. This new party supported the direct election of U.S. senators (rather than having them appointed by state legislatures). Populists wanted a reduction in tariffs and called for an eight-hour workday. Unlike the Republicans and the Democrats, corporate America did not influence the Populists. The Populists represented the working class and tried to give these voters a voice.

dare to come out in the open field and defend the gold standard as a good thing, we will fight them to the uttermost. Having behind us the producing masses of this nation and the world, supported by the commercial interests, the laboring interests and the toilers everywhere, we will answer their demand for a gold standard by saying to them: You shall not press down upon the brow of labor this crown of thorns, you shall not crucify mankind upon a cross of gold.

Bryan did not win the 1896 election, nor did he win the presidential elections of 1900 and 1908. America never elected the man as president, but many of the causes he supported eventually came to be upheld: a woman's right to vote; the graduated income tax, in which the amount of one's taxes is linked to the amount of one's income; the establishment of the U.S. Department of Labor; and the popular election of senators.

When Woodrow Wilson (1856–1924; served 1913–21) was elected president in 1912, he appointed Bryan his secretary of state, a position he held until his resignation on June 9,

1915. His fame intensified in 1925, when he took on the role of prosecutor in the Scopes Trial. Tennessee high school teacher John T. Scopes (1900–1970) was on trial because he dared to teach his students the theory of evolution, which suggests that humankind descended from a lower order of animals. At the time, a Tennessee state law called the Butler Act forbid the teaching of any theory that did not include the creation of human beings by God, as taught in the Bible.

Bryan was pitted against famous attorney Clarence Darrow (1857–1938). Bryan's own personal devotion to and belief in religious fundamentalism fueled his prosecution of Scopes, and he won a guilty verdict. Scopes was ordered to pay $100 by the judge, but the sentence was later overruled because the jury, not the judge, should have chosen the amount the defendant was ordered to pay. The Butler Act was upheld until 1967.

Bryan's beliefs were ridiculed in the courtroom by Darrow, who called the lawyer to the stand as an expert on the Bible. Once there, Bryan faltered in his answers to Darrow's questions. On June 26, 1925, five days after the grueling trial ended, Bryan died.

In an effort to increase the party's appeal, the Populists decided in January 1895 to downplay some of the more radical reforms of their platform (for example, transportation and land reforms, for which some party members wanted government ownership of all railroads and a portion of public lands to be set aside for settlers). Instead, they focused on the money issue. Party leaders promoted free silver as a way to gain control of the federal government. Many Populists balked at the change in campaign strategy. They wanted the whole Populist platform or nothing at all and feared a change in focus would distract the movement from issues they considered equally important.

The Populists approached the election of 1896 as a split party. Those in favor of focusing on the issue of bimetallism (the use of both gold and silver coins) to the exclusion of all other issues were also in favor of blending their platform with the Democrats, who shared their perspective on the money issue. Those who preferred to stay with the original platform established in 1892 remained committed to participating in the election as an independent political party. They were against free silver (another term for bimetallism) because they did not believe it would change the existing system of commerce and banking. This faction of Populists felt the issue of industrial monopolies was more important than free silver.

In comparison to the Populists, the Republican platform favored high tariffs and the gold standard. Since the mid-1700s, the U.S. monetary system had been based on bimetallism. But the California Gold Rush in 1849 resulted in the discovery of such large quantities of gold that its value decreased. Before 1849, gold had been sixteen times more valuable than silver.

People soon began melting their silver dollars and using the metal for other purposes, such as jewelry. In 1873, Congress ceased making silver coins, and America was placed on a gold standard. A series of silver strikes beginning in 1875 and continuing throughout the 1880s in the San Juan Mountains of Colorado and nearby regions caused the price of silver to fall even further. In spite of this decrease in value, silver mining as an industry continued to grow. Farmers, however, were going further into debt as prices per bushel of their crops continued to decrease quickly due to increased foreign competition and supply. In order to remain competitive, farmers had to continue lowering their prices, yet they still had monthly payments to make on expensive farm equipment and mortgages.

Although most Republicans were in favor of the gold standard, some were not. These Silver Republicans would eventually side with the Democrats and Bryan. Bryan spoke out against the gold standard in his famous "Cross of Gold" speech in which he portrayed gold supporters as crucifiers of Christ and silver supporters as true Christians. In other words, he portrayed the gold standard as the downfall of the American economy.

Early in the campaign, the Populist Party realized it could not win; it simply could not compete against the two major parties. Given that the gold standard was driving them into poverty, the Populist voters supported Bryan. The Populists were aware that although Bryan shared their concerns about gold versus silver, he showed little interest in other issues that mattered to them. Still, the silver issue was important enough to give him their vote.

Campaign, election

The Republicans raised $4 million for their campaign, an unheard-of amount in 1896. Most of that money came from big business and bankers, all of whom wanted to keep tariffs high. Republican campaigners used the money to print and distribute 200 million pamphlets. McKinley delivered 350 speeches from his front porch in Canton, Ohio. Campaigners traveled the nation rallying support for their candidate.

Bryan was much more active in his campaigning. He traveled 18,000 miles (28,962 kilometers) in three months. An even more engaging speaker than McKinley, Bryan painted McKinley as a puppet of big business. His speeches were moralistic in tone, almost as if he were a church preacher. This turned some of his more progressive supporters against him.

McKinley beat Bryan with 271 electoral votes compared with Bryan's 176. Electoral votes are the votes a candidate receives for winning the majority of popular votes in a particular state. If a candidate wins the most popular votes in a state, he wins all of that state's electoral votes. Not all states are worth the same number of electoral votes. That number is determined by how many U.S. representatives it has in the House plus two, one for each of the state's U.S. senators. In order to win a presidential election, a candidate must have more than 50 percent of electoral votes. McKinley also took 52.2 percent of the popular vote (citizens' votes). His victory marked the beginning of what would be a Republican White House until Democrat Woodrow Wilson's inauguration in 1913.

Domestic and foreign issues

By the time McKinley took office, the depression was all but over. People's fear was subsiding, and so was the uproar over bimetallism versus the gold standard. Although McKinley had supported the gold standard, he spent most of 1897 pursuing an international agreement to bimetallism with Italy, Russia, England, and France. When negotiations failed late in the year, McKinley endorsed a gold-based currency and signed

Campaign poster for William McKinley. © CORBIS.

the Gold Standard Act in 1900. With that legislation, all currency was backed by gold at a fixed price of $20.67 per ounce.

Among McKinley's campaign promises was the one to raise tariffs. In 1896, taxes on certain products used in the United States brought in fairly large amounts of money. Alcohol taxes brought in $114.5 million, tobacco another $30.7 million. McKinley wanted to increase tariff levels so that internal taxes could be reduced; this, in turn, would allow taxpayers to spend less on those items they used more often. A raise in tariff rates would also encourage the expansion of American industry and increase the number of jobs because people would not want to buy from abroad when doing so would cost more.

In 1897, U.S. congressman Nelson R. Dingley (1832–1899) of Maine sponsored the Dingley Tariff Act, which raised rates to an average of 49 percent. The bill also gave the president authority to negotiate reductions of up to 20 percent. He also could move items to what was called a "free list," which meant those items would not be subject to the tariff. Other items could be dropped completely if all those in positions of authority agreed upon it. McKinley remained a committed supporter of high tariffs until the end of his life. Just days prior to his death, he announced his shift in attitude and gave his support to reciprocal trade treaties (trade agreements in which both countries benefit).

For McKinley, the issue of trusts (a group of companies who band together to form an organization that limits the competition by controlling the production and distribution of a product or service) was not one that could be easily categorized. He believed trusts were useful in terms of international competition, where Americans could compete against foreign businesses. But he thought they were not so desirable within the American market, where they curbed competition between American businesses. He limited his support of legal suits against trusts that hurt interstate (within the nation) commerce only.

McKinley was a supporter of the labor movement, and his time in the White House increased his popularity among workers throughout the nation. He endorsed the Erdman Act of 1898, which developed a means for negotiating wage disputes involving international railroad companies. McKinley also favored the Chinese Exclusion Act, which prohibited Chinese immigrants from settling in America and taking jobs that Americans could fill. He had strong professional relationships with a number of leaders in the labor movement as well. Despite his support of America's workers, McKinley sent in federal troops to keep order at a mining strike in Coeur d'Alene, Idaho, in 1899. The incident ended in the arrest of about five hundred miners, who were kept in a large pen from the time of their arrest in April until September. This five-month detention of miners was the one incident during his presidency in which McKinley angered the organized-labor voting population.

President McKinley put little effort into improving race relations while in office. He spoke against lynching (illegal hanging) in his first presidential address in 1897 but did not condemn the practice formally with legislation or any other efforts. Nor did he take measures to limit the racial violence in the South. For the most part, McKinley's reaction to the race issue was to appear as if he was doing something about it. For example, he appointed thirty African Americans to official positions in diplomatic and records offices. This seemed to whites to be enough, but it fell far short of what African American voters had expected. McKinley also allowed African American soldiers to fight in the Spanish-American War (1898), which went against the wishes of the majority of the military. Still, these measures did little to help African Americans.

McKinley undid much of the reform work Cleveland had done within the civil service. The civil service is the system in which civilians work for various government agencies and departments. Cleveland reformed the system so that appointment to positions was based on a person's qualifications rather than on favors done or political party affiliation only. As a result, Republicans were unhappy that many of the most influential positions within the civil service were filled with Democrats. McKinley bowed to Republican pressure and removed about four thousand positions from the list. This satisfied Republican congressmen but led many of his citizen supporters to change their minds about him. It now looked as though the president was being controlled by, rather than in charge of, the Republican Party.

Territorial expansion As the twentieth century drew closer, many Americans believed that to increase the greatness of the nation, the nation ought to increase its size and power. Others believed just as strongly that expansionism would cost too much money and bring too many non-white people into the country. Their stance was called "anti-imperialism." Some of its better-known supporters were former president **Benjamin Harrison** (1833–1901; served 1889–93; see entry); William Jennings Bryan; industrialist Andrew Carnegie (1835–1919); and writer **Mark Twain** (1835–1910; see entry).

In 1897, McKinley negotiated a treaty with Hawaii that would annex it (make it a U.S. territory). He not only recognized the island's value as a military strategic point but also realized other world powers would want to lay claim to the land if the United States did not. Anti-imperialists and Democrats were against the annexation and delayed it until 1900. At that point, Congress successfully petitioned McKinley to pass the resolution for annexation with a simple majority (more than 50 percent) vote, rather than the usual two-thirds majority vote. In 1959, Hawaii became the fiftieth state admitted to the Union.

The Spanish-American War During this period of imperialism versus anti-imperialism, President McKinley had to deal with a problem he had inherited from the Cleveland administration: Cuba. Spanish rule in Cuba was based on repression (put down or controlled with force), and Cubans revolted in 1895. Spain's response was to round up three hundred thousand Cubans and put them in camps where they could not help the rebels. Spain's behavior angered many Americans, who believed Cuba should be independent of Spain's rule.

Throughout 1897, McKinley tried to convince Spain to give Cuba its independence. In November of that year, Spain gave Cuba limited independence (regarding political matters within Cuba, it could govern itself; Spain would still handle international matters). Spain then closed the camps. The peace was short lived, when in January 1898, pro-Spanish demonstrators rioted in the streets of Havana, Cuba. McKinley sent the U.S. battleship *Maine* to the Havana harbor to protect American citizens who had arrived to help Cuba. His move showed Spain that America still valued its relationship with Cuba.

Spanish minister to the United States Enrique Dupuy de Lome (1851–1904) wrote a private letter to a friend in Spain that was stolen from the post office by the Cubans. The Cubans, in turn, leaked the letter to the U.S. media. The letter described McKinley as weak and indicated that the Spanish were not negotiating in good faith with the United States. The letter was published in the *New York Journal*. Americans, who saw it as an attack on the honor of both their president and their nation, were furious.

Things got worse when the *Maine* exploded and sank on February 15, 1898. The explosion killed 266 crew members. A Navy investigation concluded that the explosion had been caused by an outside source, presumably a Spanish mine. (More recent scholarship has speculated, however, that the explosion more likely occurred because of problems in the ship itself.) Although McKinley did not want to go to war, he saw no alternative at this point. He ordered U.S. ships to block Cuba's ports; America and its president wanted an end to the Cuban crisis. On April 23, 1898, Spain declared war on the United States. Two days later, America declared war on Spain. The war lasted just over three months, and fewer than four hundred American soldiers died in battle. Many more died from disease.

The Spanish-American War ended with the signing of the Paris Peace Treaty on December 10, 1898. The treaty gave Guam and Puerto Rico to the United States and allowed America to buy the Philippine Islands for $20 million. Spain gave up its hold on Cuba, which would be a protectorate (under the protection and partial control) of the United States until 1934. The United States, under McKinley's leadership, had become one of the world's great colonial powers.

War in the Philippines The war with Spain left America with a global influence it had not previously enjoyed. Filipinos, at first, viewed American troops as liberators. It became clear to the U.S. government almost immediately that the Philippines were not ready to govern themselves. McKinley disagreed with American anti-Imperialists and decided that the islands were too strategically valuable to be left to the inexperienced rule of the Filipinos themselves. The president took it upon himself to educate the islanders and bring them to Christianity, which he believed would make them more capable of self-rule.

McKinley sent twenty thousand troops to the Philippines, but the islanders proved more adept at defending themselves than the United States had predicted. They revolted, and the conflict there lasted until 1902, as American troops fought battle after battle against island rebels who employed tactics of guerrilla warfare, a strategy the United States was little prepared to combat. In guerrilla warfare, soldiers gain the support of local citizens, who help them carry out plans of deception, assassination, and sabotage, often behind enemy lines. Although McKinley predicted the war would be rather bloodless as far as war goes, it cost more than five thousand American lives and two hundred thousand Filipino lives.

The Boxer Rebellion China soon became a concern to McKinley as well. He knew that other world powers, such as Japan, Germany, and France, were also trying to establish influence throughout the world. In an effort to guarantee that Chinese ports would remain open to U.S. business, the president authorized an "Open Door" policy to China. This policy put China on an equal status with America in terms of trade and business. There would be no restrictions or tariffs, and the United States would support an independent China. The policy became useless at the end of World War II (1939–45), when China was recognized as a sovereign (self-governing) nation. As such, no country had the right to influence or attempt to exclude it from trade. By 1949, China had become a Communist country, and the Open Door Policy was rejected. The government did not wish to promote foreign trade or investment. Despite its demise, the Open Door policy remains one of the most important ever issued by the federal government.

In June 1900, a group of Chinese rebels known as Boxers killed a number of western missionaries and Chinese converts to Christianity. The Boxers did not want foreign influences in their country or on their national identity. The group also invaded foreign populations in the city of Peking. McKinley sent over twenty-five hundred troops and several gunboats to China without first getting congressional approval. In addition to U.S. military support, Russia, Britain, Germany, and Japan assisted China. The allied (combined) troops put down the Boxer Rebellion by August. China was forced to pay reparations (costs of war) of more than $300 million, $25 million of which went to America.

Death comes early

In 1900, the Republicans once again spent several million dollars on the presidential campaign. They printed 125 million campaign documents, including millions of inserts that were sent to more than 5,000 newspapers every week. They hired 600 speakers and poll watchers. As was the case the first time, McKinley stayed home and delivered his speeches from his front porch. His running mate was **Theodore Roosevelt** (1858–1919; see entry), who had recently returned home from the Spanish-American War a hero. (McKinley's vice president during his first term, Garret A. Hobart [1844–1899], had died in office.)

McKinley's opponent was a familiar face: William Jennings Bryan. Again, McKinley won both the popular and the electoral vote. He won by an even greater margin this time, receiving 114,000 more votes than in the 1896 election. In addition, the Republicans also held the power in Congress (197 House seats compared with the Democrats' 151, and 55 Senate seats compared with 31).

On September 5, 1901, McKinley delivered a speech at the Pan-American Exposition in Buffalo, New York. At its conclusion, he attended a reception where he got to meet and greet the public. Just after 4:00 PM, McKinley was shot by a twenty-eight-year-old Polish immigrant named Leon Czolgosz (1873–1901). The bullet hit McKinley in the chest and knocked him to the ground. The president was rushed to a hospital, where doctors expected him to recover. Gangrene (decay of skin tissue due to blood loss) set in around his wounds, however, and the president died on September 14, 1901, just six months after his second term had begun. His assassin died in the electric chair on October 29, 1901.

McKinley did not have the charm of some of the earlier presidents. Nor was he as outgoing and outspoken as his successor, Theodore Roosevelt. He did not use his power to convince all Americans to share his beliefs or support his policies. Instead, McKinley was a president whose self-confidence allowed him to make decisions and stand behind them, even when the public did not agree. His successes in territorial expansion took America's power to a new level, and it paved the way for future presidents to carry on in that tradition.

For More Information

BOOKS

American Presidents in World History. Vol. 3. Westport, CT: Greenwood Press, 2003.

Cherny, Robert W. *American Politics in the Gilded Age: 1868–1900.* Wheeling, IL: Harlan Davidson, 1997.

Dolan, Edward F. *The Spanish-American War.* Brookfield, CT: Millbrook Press, 2001.

Gerber, Elizabeth R. *The Populist Paradox.* Princeton, NJ: Princeton University Press, 1999.

Kazin, Michael. *A Godly Hero: The Life of William Jennings Bryan.* New York: Knopf, 2006.

Riehecky, Janet. *William McKinley: America's 25th President.* New York: Children's Press, 2004.

WEB SITES

"William Jennings Bryan." *1896: A Website of Political Cartoons.* http://projects.vassar.edu/1896/bryan.html (accessed on September 4, 2006).

"William McKinley." *American President.org.* http://americanpresident.org/history/williammckinley/biography (accessed on September 4, 2006).

"William McKinley." *1896: A Website of Political Cartoons.* http://projects.vassar.edu/1896/mckinley.html (accessed on September 4, 2006).

"William McKinley: First Inaugural Address." *Bartleby.com: Great Books Online.* http://www.bartelby.net/124/pres40.html (accessed on September 4, 2006).

"William McKinley." *The White House.* http://www.whitehouse.gov/history/presidents/wm25.html (accessed on September 4, 2006).

Wolf, Mari Artzner. "A Home of His Own." *Wm. McKinley Presidential Library & Museum.* http://www.mckinleymuseum.org/mckinleyfeature.html (accessed on September 4, 2006).

John Muir

BORN: April 21, 1838 • Dunbar, Scotland
DIED: December 24, 1914 • Los Angeles, California

Conservationist; environmentalist; writer

"One touch of nature makes the whole world kin."

John Muir was a conservationist at a time when the idea of conserving natural resources was still in its infancy. Muir traveled the globe, exploring nature and recording his observations. His writings heightened his readers' awareness of the world around them. In an effort to organize like-minded people with a concern for the environment, Muir and his supporters founded the Sierra Club in 1892. Muir is mostly remembered for his involvement in the protection of the Yosemite and Sierra Nevada wilderness areas in California. He is considered one of the most influential conservationists in American history.

Of Scottish descent

John Muir.
THE LIBRARY OF
CONGRESS.

John Muir was the third of seven children born to Daniel and Ann Muir. He was born on April 21, 1838, in Dunbar, Scotland. The family moved to Wisconsin in 1849, when Muir was just eleven. His formal schooling ended when he immigrated to America, where he spent most of his time working long hours in the fields of the family farm. When his strict father allowed him time off, Muir and his younger brother liked to explore the woods and hills. Although vastly different from the seacoast of Muir's hometown and the craggy moors (rocky, infertile land) and mountains of the rest of Scotland, America's Midwest helped Muir develop his love for the outdoors.

Muir also enjoyed inventing things. One of his inventions was a device that tipped him out of bed before sunrise each morning. In 1860, Muir attended the state fair in Madison, where he won prizes for his inventions. That same year, he enrolled in the University of Wisconsin at Madison. Although his grades were admirable, Muir's interests lay elsewhere, and he left college after three years to travel through the northern United States and into Canada. He supported himself with odd jobs along the way.

Temporarily loses his sight

Muir was working at a carriage parts shop in 1867 when an accident left him temporarily blind. When he regained his sight a month later, Muir vowed to see as much of the wondrous outdoors as he could and thus began a 1,000-mile (1,609-kilometer) trek across the world. His travels took him from Indianapolis, Indiana, to the Gulf of Mexico. He visited Cuba and eventually, Panama. There, he sailed up the west coast of America and landed in San Francisco, California, in 1868. From that point forward, Muir would consider the state his home.

That same year, Muir's travels took him to California's Sierra Nevada, a 400-mile (650-kilometer) mountain range. After wandering through the San Joaquin Valley, Muir trekked into the high country for the first time. That region would inspire and comfort him for the rest of his life. Muir spent his first summer as a shepherd in what would become Yosemite National Park in 1890. He also ran a sawmill at the base of Yosemite Falls. These jobs gave him the chance to study the nature surrounding him. He became so familiar with the region that he served as a guide for visitors to the area.

In 1871, Muir began studying glacier activity in the Sierra Nevada. He devised a theory that Yosemite Valley had developed from the movement and melting of glaciers, large rivers of ice that slowly "flow" because of their great weight. His theory was in sharp contrast to the idea that was readily accepted at the time, which stated that the valley was formed as a result of an earthquake. As time went by and geologists learned more about glaciers, Muir's theory gained wider acceptance. An earthquake in the valley in 1872 caused many people to fear the valley would deepen even more. When that failed to happen, Muir's theory made even more sense to more people. Muir's discovery of an active glacier within the mountain range further supported his theory.

In 1871, famous poet Ralph Waldo Emerson (1803–1882) visited Yosemite, and Muir acted as his guide. Emerson tried to convince the budding conservationist to leave Yosemite so that he might teach the world the lessons he had learned throughout his travels. Muir could not leave his beloved mountains, however. Another three years would pass before he left the valley.

On December 5, 1871, Muir published his first essay, for which he was paid the then-handsome sum of $200. "Yosemite Glaciers" appeared in the *New York Tribune*. He would spend the next few years writing and publishing essays about his observations in Yosemite. A series of articles titled "Studies in the Sierras" were published in 1874, marking the beginning of a productive writing career. Muir would produce about three hundred magazine articles and ten major books. The articles reflected Muir's lively writing style in which he melded descriptive passages of beauty with basic scientific discussion. His writings appealed to tourists and scientists alike.

Leaves Yosemite

Muir began leaving Yosemite shortly after his series was published. At first, he would leave for just a few months at a time, visiting friends in San Francisco and Oakland. During a visit to Oakland in 1874, Muir met Louise (Louie) Wanda Strentzel, a mutual friend of the family with whom he was staying. The two were married on April 14, 1880. They would eventually have two daughters. The day after the wedding, Muir left on an expedition to Alaska for further glacier exploration. It was his second trip, his first one having been in 1879 and resulting in his discovery of Glacier Bay.

The Muirs moved to the small town of Martinez, California (near San Francisco), the year they were married. Here, Muir partnered with his father-in-law and managed a successful family fruit ranch. During his ten years on the ranch, he continued to travel when time permitted. He went to Alaska several more times as well as to Europe, Africa, Australia, South America, and Asia. His wife accompanied him on a trip to Yosemite in 1884; it was her first and last adventure with her husband. Louie preferred to stay in the familiar confines of her home while her husband traveled. She managed the ranch capably when he did.

Ranch life made Muir a wealthy man but kept him so busy he found little time to write. Domestic life seemed to drain him of his energy. He became depressed whenever he visited the Sierra Nevada. Cattle and sheep were decimating the meadows and forests of the range. Muir knew if he did not take action soon, the region he loved so dearly would be ruined forever. Louie supported her husband, and encouraged him to do what he felt he must, even though it meant leaving the ranch and family. The two kept in touch through letters, and Louie sent Muir money to pay for any traveling expenses.

Creates Yosemite National Park and Sierra Club

In 1890, the family moved to a 14-room Victorian mansion. To lessen her husband's responsibilities, Louie sold some of the fruit ranch. The mansion and the portion of the ranch acreage the Muirs kept is the focal point of the John Muir National Historic Site, a branch of the National Park Service.

Muir drew America's attention through a series of articles he published in *Century* magazine. He wrote about the destruction of the Yosemite area. The magazine's associate editor, Robert Underwood Johnson (1853–1937), worked hard to bring the issue to the attention of Congress. In 1890, Congress created Yosemite National Park. This designation gave federal protection to Yosemite. It was the first of several such endeavors for Muir, who was involved in the formation of the Sequoia, Mount Rainier, Petrified Forest, and Grand Canyon national parks. According to his biography on *SierraClub.org,* Muir is considered the "Father of Our National Park System."

Muir and Johnson joined forces again in 1892 and established the Sierra Club, America's first grassroots environmental organization. Muir served as the group's president until his death. The club's original mission was to make the Sierra Nevada accessible to the public so that everyone could appreciate its natural wonders. By the twenty-first century, the club had developed into a general conservation organization working to protect the wild places of the planet, promote responsible use of natural resources, and educate the public on how to protect and restore the earth's resources.

Growth was slow at first, as people began to learn of the Club's existence. In 1901, the group began hosting annual, month-long "High Trips," in which guides took interested individuals and groups on

John Muir relaxes on a rock in his beloved outdoors. THE LIBRARY OF CONGRESS.

hikes into the Sierra Nevada. By 1938, the High Trip expeditions had become so large that the Club had to devise plans for those hikers who desired more intimate, small-scale experiences. As of 2006, the organization boasted 750,000 members.

The battle for Hetch-Hetchy

Muir published his first book in 1894, but it was not until the 1901 publication of his book *Our National Parks* that President **Theodore Roosevelt** (1858–1919; served 1901–9; see entry) took notice of the conservationist. Roosevelt, himself an enthusiastic outdoorsman, visited Muir in Yosemite in 1903. Muir guided the president through the Sierra Nevada, and together the two men shared ideas about what the president could do to protect the nation's natural resources. Roosevelt eventually created 5 national parks, 150 national forests, 18 national monuments, and the National Forest Service.

By the end of the 1890s, the city of San Francisco had been trying to find a source of municipal water. Although the city looked into several sources, the one it preferred was Hetch-Hetchy, a valley located in Yosemite National Park. The City wanted to dam the Tuolumne (pronounced too-AH-luh-mee) River at the mouth of the Hetch-Hetchy Valley to increase the water supply. The water supply in Hetch-Hetchy was not more abundant or of better quality than anywhere else; the city was interested in it because the valley was situated on public land, which made using it more convenient and affordable.

The Sierra Club immediately began to fight to keep Hetch-Hetchy untouched. The club and other like-minded citizens argued that tapping into the watershed would destroy the integrity of the national park. Soon, the battle for Hetch-Hetchy made front page headlines in newspapers across the country. Muir was an outspoken opponent of the plan. According to the Ecology Hall of Fame, Muir wrote, "These temple destroyers, devotees of ravaging commercialism, seem to have a perfect contempt for Nature, and, instead of lifting their eyes to the God of the mountains, lift them to the Almighty Dollar."

The battle was long and intense, but in the end, Muir and his fellow conservationists lost. In 1913, Congress approved a bill that allowed water supplies within national parks to be used for public purposes. The government never made good on its promise that the reservoir would be used as a recreational center where the public could use the lake for boating and swimming. In reality, the reservoir was closed to public use. As soon as the dam was built, the City of San Francisco decided to raise its height to increase the water supply. More land was used than had been initially planned.

The controversy over the Hetch-Hetchy issue continued into the twenty-first century. The state of California concluded that restoring the Hetch-Hetchy and compensating the city for water loss would cost more than $800 million.

Death comes to a gentle warrior

Losing the battle for Hetch-Hetchy was one of Muir's biggest regrets. He spent his final years traveling the globe and writing articles and books. Muir was still living in the house the family had moved into in 1890 (Louie had died in 1905). After a short bout of pneumonia, Muir died in a hospital in Los Angeles in 1914. Muir had been writing a book about Alaska when he died (it was published in 1915), and in his possession were approximately ten book manuscripts. His writing continued to be published into the 1920s.

In 1915, the Sierra Club convinced the California government to spend $10,000 for the construction of the John Muir Trail. The 211-mile (339.5-kilometer) trail was completed in 1938 and runs through Yosemite, Kings Canyon, and Sequoia national parks.

The U.S. Postal Service has issued two John Muir stamps: one in 1964 and another in 1998. He was inducted into the Conservation Hall of Fame in 1965 and was featured on the new California state quarter, released in January 2005. A minor planet was discovered and named after Muir in 2006.

John Muir Day is celebrated every year in America on April 21. The conservationist was voted the Greatest Californian of All Time in 1976, according to a poll conducted by the California Historical Society.

Muir is remembered for his passion for nature and its beauty. His moving descriptions inspired Americans to acknowledge the importance of protecting and conserving their natural resources.

For More Information

BOOKS

Ehrlich, Gretel. *John Muir: Nature's Visionary.* Washington, DC: National Geographic Society, 2000.

Muir, John. *Meditations of John Muir: Nature's Temple.* Edited by Chris Highland. Berkeley, CA: Wilderness Press, 2001.

Muir, John. *Our National Parks.* Boston: Houghton, Mifflin and Company, 1901. Reprint, Washington, DC: Ross and Perry, 2001.

Muir, John, and Lee Stetson. *The Wild Muir: Twenty-Two of John Muir's Greatest Adventures.* Yosemite National Park, CA: Yosemite Association, 1994.

Wolfe, Linnie Marsh. *Son of the Wilderness: The Life of John Muir.* New York: A. A. Knopf, 1945. Reprint, Madison: University of Wisconsin Press, 1978.

PERIODICALS

Meyer, John M. "Gifford Pinchot, John Muir, and the Boundaries of Politics in American Thought." *Polity* (December 21, 1997).

WEB SITES

Howie, Craig. "John Muir." *Scotsman.com.* http://heritage.scotsman.com/profiles.cfm?cid=1&id=1825412005 (accessed on September 4, 2006).

"John Muir Exhibit." *Sierra Club.* http://www.sierraclub.org/john_muir_exhibit/ (accessed on September 4, 2006).

"John Muir National Historic Site." *National Park Service.* http://www.nps.gov/jomu/ (accessed on September 4, 2006).

John Muir Trust. http://www.jmt.org/ (accessed on September 4, 2006).

Rose, Gene. "The Ghosts of Hetch-Hetchy." *Sierra Club: John Muir Exhibit.* http://www.sierraclub.org/john_muir_exhibit/frameindex.html?http://www.sierraclub.org/john_muir_exhibit/life/ (accessed on September 4, 2006).

Weiss, Don. "John Muir." *Ecology Hall of Fame.* http://www.ecotopia.org/ehof/muir/bio.html (accessed on September 4, 2006).

Thomas Nast

BORN: September 26, 1840 • Landau, Germany
DIED: December 7, 1902 • Guayaquil, Ecuador

Illustrator; political cartoonist

"Nast is often spoken of as the first great American cartoonist. In a very real sense he was the last."

— Writer William Murrell

Thomas Nast's political cartoons and caricatures (cartoon representations of people that emphasize and exaggerate their subjects' most prominent features) influenced American political culture like no art ever had. His art played a key role in bringing to justice a corrupt politician. One cartoon in particular has been credited with helping to reelect Abraham Lincoln (1809–1865; served 1861–65) in 1864. Nast used his pen as if it were a sword to fight for causes he felt were worthy and necessary. By the time of his death at age sixty-two, Nast had spent forty-seven years as a cartoonist and had illustrated more than one hundred books.

Finds his purpose in New York

Thomas Nast.
© BETTMANN/CORBIS.

Thomas Nast was born in Landau, Germany, on September 26, 1840. Germany's political climate during that decade was one of revolution (uprisings by common people against the government). Nast's father wanted to send his family to safety. In 1846, Nast, his mother, and his sister sailed to New York City; Nast's father joined them three years later, after his military service was over.

Nast and his sister were sent to public school in New York. Nast, however, had difficulty adjusting to his new surroundings and culture. Nast did not speak English, which made schoolwork even harder for him. After years of not doing his work and not caring about school, Nast still could not read and write and was in danger of flunking out. Instead of doing his homework, Nast spent time with a neighbor who made crayons and candles for a living. Young Nast would take any rejected crayons and spend hours drawing. It became clear that the twelve-year-old Nast would not ever put forth the effort to read and write, but he did have a natural talent for drawing. His school teacher suggested to his parents that the boy be taken out of regular school and enrolled in art school.

Nast's parents followed the advice. Nast spent the next three years learning drawing techniques. When finances became difficult for the family, Nast quit school and looked for work. Nast, never an athletic boy, experienced weight problems throughout his youth; manual labor was not an option for him. The only skill he had was drawing. Unfortunately, because he was just fifteen years old, no one was willing to risk hiring him outright as an illustrator. In the 1850s, most illustrators began their careers as apprentices, youngsters who work with experts to learn their skills. Apprentices were not always paid, and if they were, the pay was minimal.

Nast could not afford to apprentice to an illustrator. He had faith that his level of drawing ability was high enough to secure a position as an illustrator on his own. Nast tried to make an appointment with the publisher of *Frank Leslie's Illustrated Newspaper,* a popular publication in 1855. After several failed attempts to see Leslie, Nast took matters into his own hands one day and snuck past the receptionist and into Leslie's office. The publisher admired the boy's courage. He gave Nast a test assignment, intended more to make him leave than to encourage him. He instructed Nast to go to a ferry (a boat carrying passengers) dock at rush hour and draw a picture of the crowd.

Nast took this assignment seriously and returned to Leslie's office the following morning, illustration in hand. Leslie was impressed with Nast's talent and hired him. Nast stayed with the publication until 1858, when it developed financial problems and he was laid off.

Finds fame at *Harper's Weekly*

Nast took a job with the *New York Illustrated News,* a competitor of Leslie's *Illustrated Newspaper.* His new job required worldwide travel, and Nast enjoyed his visits to countries such as England and Italy. In 1861, he married Sarah Edwards; the couple would eventually have five children: Julie, Thomas Jr., Edith, Mabel, and Cyril.

While working for the *New York Illustrated News,* Nast began drawing political cartoons as a freelance (self-employed) artist. He sent these cartoons to various publications, including the popular *Harper's Weekly,* the leading illustrated newspaper of the nineteenth century. By the summer of 1862, Nast was a full-time employee of *Harper's.* Assigned to the battlefields of the raging Civil War (1861–65), he drew and sent back sketches of battle scenes. Once in New York, the sketches were given to engravers (skilled artists who cut illustrations into blocks of wood) who transformed them into wood engravings. These engravings included all the tiny details of Nast's large, complex sketches, which were often printed across two pages.

Like his father before him, Nast was a liberal, someone who believes in equality for all people and that change is progress if it is for the betterment of everyone. He was absolutely opposed to slavery, and so supported the Union (North) in the Civil War. Nast, though illiterate (unable to read or write), used his illustrations to communicate his political beliefs. On September 3, 1864, *Harper's Weekly* made Nast famous with its publication of his sketch titled "Compromise with the South." The sketch shows Columbia (symbol for the Americas) crying over the grave of Union heroes. A Northern Union soldier, who has lost one leg in the war, shakes the hand of a well-dressed, uninjured Southern Rebel soldier. At that point in the war, it seemed as if the Union was sure to lose. Nast's illustration reflected his disappointment and sympathy for the side he believed was defending justice. That sketch was reprinted in publications across the country. Many historians credit Nast's drawing with helping to reelect Abraham Lincoln to the U.S. presidency.

Takes on Tammany Hall

Nast's fame brought him a great deal of freelance work after the war. He began illustrating books at this time, work that he would do his entire life. All the while, he continued working at *Harper's.*

In 1868, Nast turned his attention to New York City politics in general, focusing on William "Boss" Tweed (1823–1878) in particular.

"Compromise with the South" cartoon by Thomas Nast; it appeared in the September 3, 1864, issue of Harper's Weekly.
THE LIBRARY OF CONGRESS.

Tweed was an elected Democratic official on New York City's council who had served since 1851. Through the years, Tweed gained a great deal of power, mainly through corrupt business dealings. He and his friends were known as the Tweed Ring. Their headquarters were in a building known as Tammany Hall.

By appointing unqualified but grateful friends to high and powerful positions in city politics, Tweed and his ring managed to have a bill passed in 1870 that gave him complete authority of the city's treasury. He immediately began awarding valuable contracts to his friends, who in turn paid him large sums of money for the work he sent their way.

Tweed's crimes were many. For example, he faked leases on city-owned buildings, padded bills with charges for repairs that never happened, and bought overpriced goods and services from suppliers controlled by the ring. Altogether, the corrupt politicians stole between $30 million and $200 million from the city between 1865 and 1871.

Nast did not approve of Boss Tweed and his ring. He used his public forum to inform readers of Tweed's criminal activity. He regularly caricatured Tweed as a criminal and invented the "Tammany Tiger" to represent Tweed's ring. When Tweed discovered Nast's personal campaign to bring him down, the Boss offered the cartoonist $500,000 to put an end to his scheme. Although it was one hundred times more than his yearly salary, Nast refused the money. Not ready to give up, Tweed went directly to *Harper's Weekly* and tried to force the owners to fire Nast.

As reported in a Thomas Nast biography published on the Ohio State University Libraries: Cartoon Research Library Web site, Tweed sent his cronies to the publishing offices with this sentiment: "Stop them damn pictures. I don't care what the papers write about me. My constituents [people in his voting district] can't read. But, damn it, they can see the pictures." *Harper's* refused to fire its star cartoonist, and he kept his drawing campaign moving forward. In November 1871, Tweed and his ring were voted out of office. Tweed was sued by the City and was sent to debtor's prison since he could not pay the fine. He escaped and fled to Spain in 1876. He was recognized there and arrested by a customs official who had seen Nast's caricatures of the corrupt politician. Tweed died in prison in 1878.

Nast was, by standards of the day, a rich man by 1880. *Harper's Weekly* paid him an annual salary of $20,000. He received an additional $150 for every engraving published. Nast owned property in Harlem, New York, valued at $90,000, and owned another $60,000 in government bonds. His home, which was completely paid for, was valued at $100,000. But the majority of his income came from lectures to art students.

Nast used his popularity to sway public opinion, and *Harper's* knew they had a gold mine in the illustrator. Circulation increased as Nast's popularity grew, and his influence became enormous (see box).

A political cartoon from about 1871 by Thomas Nast showing New York politician William Marcy "Boss" Tweed with a money bag for a head. The original caption read: "The brains that achieved the Tammany victory at the Rochester Democratic Convention." © KEAN COLLECTION/HULTON ARCHIVE/GETTY IMAGES.

Decline of popularity

Times were changing, though, and Nast did not want to change with them. Nast's popularity was declining. One of the primary factors

Political cartoon by Thomas Nast showing the Tammany Tiger controlling New York City. Tammany's leader, New York politician William Marcy "Boss" Tweed, is depicted in the tiger's face, with Tweed's hat and cigar. The original caption read: "I'm monarch of all I survey; my rule there is none to dispute. From Harlem right down to the bay, I'm lord of the man and brute." © BETTMANN/CORBIS.

How Thomas Nast Left His Mark on America

Illustration of Santa Claus, by Thomas Nast. DOVER PUBLICATIONS.

Aside from the obvious influence Nast had on American culture and society, he left legacies he probably never imagined he would:

- Created his first drawing of Santa Claus, an image that for Americans remains the model of this famous figure.

- Used a donkey to represent the Democratic Party in a cartoon. Nast used an elephant to symbolize the Republican Party. Modern politics continues to use the donkey for Democrats, the elephant for Republicans.

- Developed John Chinaman, a sympathetic Chinese immigrant, to symbolize all Chinese immigrants in the United States. John Chinaman was the subject of several songs written during the Gilded Age and was written about by **Mark Twain** (1835–1910; see entry). This caricature eventually came to be perceived as a negative stereotype.

influencing this decline was the change in American society as leisure time increased throughout the 1870s. Readers once relied solely on newspapers for their information on everything from politics to business. Now they expected to find amusement and entertainment in newspapers and magazines as well. They wanted publishers to provide them with information on fashion, family matters, and events happening around town. To do this, newspapers had to either grow in page count, which was costly, or limit the amount of space dedicated to current events and politics.

At that same time, Fletcher Harper (1806–1877), publisher and founder of *Harper's Weekly,* died and left the publication to Joseph W. Harper Jr. (1830–1896). Nast did not enjoy the editorial freedom under his new boss that he had become accustomed to, and he would not draw cartoons that went against his personal politics. His editor refused to allow Nast to publish cartoons that went against the publication's editorial positions. As *Harper's* changed its focus to that of a more general content, Nast found himself without much to say.

Nast's position was also affected by changes in the printing process. Woodblocks were no longer used by 1880, when photochemical processes replaced them. As a result, Nast's sketches looked harsh and angry because lines that had been softened by the engraving process were now more solid. Nast left the newspaper in 1886, after having contributed about twenty-two hundred cartoons, and freelanced for several years. He established his own publication, *Nast's Weekly,* in 1892, but the venture failed within six months.

A tragic end, a lasting legacy

Having gone through his savings, Nast was desperate for work by 1902. His friend, U.S. president **Theodore Roosevelt** (1858–1919; served 1901–9; see entry), offered him an appointment to serve as consul general (diplomat who represents the United States and handles issues related to individuals and businesses within the other country) in Ecuador. Nast accepted the appointment, but died of yellow fever within six months of leaving the United States.

Nast remains an icon (hero) of his profession in the twenty-first century. He was a paradox (a combination of opposites) in many ways. A man who could neither read nor write, he earned wealth and fame by influencing America's politics and readers for decades. Having had very little formal education, he made a fair percentage of his income giving lectures to college students. Throughout some of the most major cultural and societal shifts in American history, he maintained his commitment to his art and beliefs.

Illustrations and cartoons by Nast are worth a great deal of money. His Christmas drawings have been compiled and published in book format. His sketches for *Harper's Weekly* have become collector's items.

For More Information

BOOKS

Pflueger, Lynn. *Thomas Nast: Political Cartoonist.* Berkeley Heights, NJ: Enslow Publishers, 2000.

Shirley, David. *Thomas Nast: Cartoonist and Illustrator.* New York: Franklin Watts, 1998.

PERIODICALS

Murrell, William. "Nast, Gladiator of the Political Pencil." *American Scholar* (Autumn 1936): 472–85.

WEB SITES

HarpWeek Presents the World of Thomas Nast. http://www.thomasnast.com/ (accessed on September 4, 2006).

"Political Cartoons of Thomas Nast." *United States Senate.* http://www.senate. gov/artandhistory/art/exhibit/nast_cartoons.htm (accessed on September 4, 2006).

"Thomas Nast Biography." *The Ohio State University Libraries: Cartoon Research Library.* http://cartoons.osu.edu/nast/bio.htm (accessed on September 4, 2006).

Theodore Roosevelt

BORN: October 27, 1858 • New York, New York
DIED: January 6, 1919 • Oyster Bay, New York

U.S. president; conservationist

"A vote is like a rifle: Its usefulness depends upon the character of the user."

Theodore Roosevelt came into his American presidency as the result of a tragedy. He endeared himself to Americans with his love of controversy and enthusiasm for life. Roosevelt was a man with a firm commitment to his beliefs. He believed he knew what was best for everyone else and made no secret of his opinions. The era's most popular president, historians generally rank him as one of the most effective presidents in American history.

Sickly childhood

Theodore Roosevelt, also known as Teddy, was born on October 27, 1858, into a wealthy family in New York City. The second of four children, Roosevelt belonged to the seventh generation of his family to be born in Manhattan. His father, also named Theodore, was a successful glassware merchant. Roosevelt's mother Martha came from a traditional Southern plantation (a large farm, usually with a focus on growing one

Theodore Roosevelt.
© CORBIS.

151

particular crop). The Roosevelts adored their son, who suffered from a serious case of asthma throughout his childhood. Underweight and of poor eyesight, Roosevelt was determined from an early age to overcome his poor health. He lifted weights, exercised, and took boxing lessons. By early adulthood, his asthma symptoms had largely disappeared. He would spend the rest of his life an enthusiastic outdoorsman.

As much as he enjoyed physical activity, Roosevelt was also an avid reader and writer. An eager learner, Roosevelt excelled in his college studies at Harvard University. After college, he married nineteen-year-old Alice Hathaway Lee, a friend of his roommate, on his twenty-second birthday in 1880. Roosevelt's happiness with his beloved wife did not last long. She died at home of Bright's disease (a kidney disorder) in 1884, days after giving birth to their only child, Alice Lee. To add to his grief, Roosevelt's mother died that same day—in the same house—of typhoid fever (an infectious bacterial disease).

Heartbroken, Roosevelt left his infant daughter behind to be cared for by relatives. He headed west for two years of cattle ranching and a stint as a frontier sheriff. For young Alice, this separation from her father would be the first of many. She grew up with very little interaction with, and guidance from, her father, and as a young woman was known for her willful, unconventional (not in keeping with society's norms and expectations) behavior. According to the Web site *American President,* Roosevelt once told a friend, "I can be president of the United States, or I can control Alice. I cannot possibly do both."

Enters politics

Roosevelt's stay in the West left him with a renewed sense of energy and enthusiasm. He returned to New York and ran unsuccessfully for mayor of the city. At that point, he also wrote three books on his experiences in the Wild West. The books were full of descriptive characters and adventure. Roosevelt's writing had an easy style that many American readers came to enjoy.

Roosevelt was elected to the state assembly in 1881. In 1886, he married longtime-friend Edith Kermit Carow. Together with young Alice, the couple moved into a house Roosevelt had built for his first wife in Oyster Bay, New York. The house was called Sagamore Hill. By 1897, four boys and another girl would round out the Roosevelt family.

In 1888, Roosevelt campaigned for the Republican presidential nominee, **Benjamin Harrison** (1833–1901; served 1889–93; see entry).

Harrison was victorious, and after he took office in 1889, he appointed Roosevelt to the U.S. Civil Service Commission. He would keep the position until 1895, when he accepted a job as the president of the New York City Police Board. During his tenure with the Civil Service and his two years on the Police Board, Roosevelt proved himself a rarity in the world of Gilded Age politics. (The Gilded Age was the period in history following the Civil War and Reconstruction [roughly the final twenty-three years of the nineteenth century], characterized by a ruthless pursuit of profit, an exterior of showiness and grandeur, and immeasurable political corruption.) He was honest, unwilling to ignore the law in order to give powerful positions to wealthy businessmen and politicians who asked for favors. He cleaned up the city's police force by getting rid of corrupt officers and officials.

In 1897, fellow Republican and president **William McKinley** (1843–1901; served 1897–1901; see entry) made Roosevelt the assistant secretary of the U.S. Navy.

Theodore and Edith Roosevelt and their family in 1903: (from left) Quentin, the president, Ted, Archie, Alice, Kermit, the first lady, and Ethel. © LIBRARY OF CONGRESS/HULTON ARCHIVE/GETTY IMAGES.

The Spanish-American War

Spanish rule in Cuba was based on repression (the act of dominating and controlling people with force), and the Cubans revolted in 1895. Spain's response was to round up three hundred thousand Cubans and put them in camps where they could not help the rebels. Spain's behavior angered many Americans, who believed Cuba should be independent of Spain's rule.

Throughout 1897, McKinley tried to convince Spain to give Cuba its independence. In November of that year, Spain gave Cuba limited independence and closed the camps. (Limited independence meant that regarding political matters within Cuba, it could govern itself; international matters would still be governed by Spain.) The peace was short lived, when in January 1898, pro-Spanish demonstrators rioted on the streets of Havana, Cuba. McKinley sent the U.S. battleship *Maine* to the Havana harbor to protect American citizens who had arrived to help Cuba, as well as to let Spain know that America still valued its relationship with Cuba.

Spanish minister to the United States Enrique Dupuy de Lôme (1851–1904) wrote a private letter to a friend back in Spain that was intercepted by the Cubans. The Cubans, in turn, leaked the letter to the U.S. media. The letter described McKinley as weak and indicated that the Spanish were not negotiating in good faith with the United States. Published in the *New York Journal,* the letter infuriated Americans, who saw it as an attack on the honor of both their president and their nation.

The situation worsened when the *Maine* exploded and sank on February 15, 1898. The explosion killed 266 crew members. A Navy investigation concluded that the explosion had been caused by an outside source, presumably a Spanish mine. (More recent scholarship has speculated, however, that the explosion more likely occurred because of internal problems with the ship itself.) McKinley did not want to go to war, but he saw no alternative at this point. He ordered U.S. ships to block Cuba's ports; America and its president wanted an end to the Cuban crisis. On April 23, 1898, Spain declared war on the United States. Two days later, America declared war on Spain. The war lasted just over three months. Fewer than four hundred American soldiers died in battle; many more died from disease.

Rough Riders to the rescue When the Spanish-American War broke out in Cuba, thirty-nine-year-old Roosevelt served as commander of the First U.S. Volunteer Cavalry, a unit better known as the Rough Riders. Roosevelt had left his job with the Navy to join the cavalry, which included more than twelve hundred men of all backgrounds from New Mexico, Arizona, Oklahoma, and other western states.

Roosevelt and Colonel Leonard Wood (1860–1927) trained their volunteers so well that the unit was allowed to engage in battle, even though volunteer units were generally not allowed to see action. They formed in Texas and shipped out to Cuba on June 14, 1898. Although they were called Rough Riders, they fought mainly on foot because there was no room for their horses on the ship to Cuba.

The Rough Riders landed in Cuba on June 22 and saw their first battle two days later. Their next assignment was to join trained military forces in the attack on the Spanish city of Santiago on July 1. Roosevelt's unit, along with regular regiments and the Buffalo Soldiers (African American infantrymen), captured Kettle Hill and moved on to San Juan Heights. With the Buffalo Soldiers reaching the crest of the hill first, the Rough

Riders joined in the battle, and the hill was captured. Santiago surrendered soon after, and the war was over in just three months. According to historian Virgil Harrington Jones, no American unit in the Spanish-American War suffered as many deaths as the Rough Riders, which lost 37 percent of its men before leaving Cuba.

The hero returns

Roosevelt returned to New York a war hero and used his popularity and status to get elected as his state's governor in November 1898. He immediately set to work reforming the corrupt political system. In 1900, the Republicans chose Roosevelt as the running mate for President McKinley, who was seeking his second term. (McKinley's first-term vice president, Garret A. Hobart [1844–1899], had died in November 1899.) As a campaigner, Roosevelt covered more than 21,000 miles (33,789 kilometers), and made hundreds of speeches in 567 cities and 24 states. McKinley, in contrast, gave speeches from the front porch of his home in Canton, Ohio. Many historians believe Roosevelt's popularity helped McKinley win the election. When McKinley died from an assassin's bullet on September 14, 1901, the forty-two-year-old Roosevelt became the youngest president of the United States.

A president for the people

Never before had America seen a family in the White House (the name Roosevelt gave the Executive Mansion) quite like the Roosevelt clan. Alice quickly became known as "Princess Alice" and "The Other Washington Monument," because she was so outspoken and wild. The younger children were free to roam through the White House, and Roosevelt allowed the press and media to write about his family. In doing so, he increased his popularity by letting the American public see that his values—as a family man—were no different from their own. Roosevelt's favorite child was his youngest, Quentin. The two were most alike in personality, and Roosevelt was amused when his boy carved a makeshift baseball diamond into the White House lawn. In America's eyes, the president's home might be bigger than most, but for the first time in history, the children inside acted much like those in any other home in any other neighborhood, on any other street.

Like his children, Roosevelt enjoyed the spotlight, and he never hesitated to speak his mind on any given issue. An animated speaker, the president used great sweeping hand and arm gestures to reinforce his points. For him, the presidency was a "bully pulpit," a public position to be used to announce his personal viewpoint. Coming from someone else, the public may have found such directness offensive. Coming from Roosevelt, they found it amusing.

The beginning of the twentieth century was a time of major change, and not all for the better. As it never had before, big businesses (and the men who ran them) influenced almost every aspect of American society. A huge proportion of the country's wealth was in the hands of a few select men, and that kind of power tended to lead to corruption. From the start, Roosevelt recognized America's need for a committed government. He led his administration with the idea that government should work for not just the wealthy citizens but for all people.

A selective trustbuster

The president recognized the need for the kinds of reforms expressed in the writings of new journalists called muckrakers. It was Roosevelt who gave these journalists their nickname in a 1906 speech; the writers who exposed scandalous and unethical practices among established institutions in America "raked" through "muck," digging through the dirt and filth of corruption to expose the truth. Some of the more famous muckrakers were Ida Tarbell (1857–1954), for her series on the Standard Oil Company; **Upton Sinclair** (1878–1968; see entry), for exposing the dangers and poor working conditions of the meatpacking industry in Chicago; and Lincoln Steffens (1866–1936), for his investigation of the scandals among city and state politicians. Although the president disliked the negative focus of muckraking, he believed in what the writers did because they were committed to uncovering the truth.

Like much of the American voting public, Roosevelt did not approve of the majority of economic power resting in the hands of a wealthy few. His primary mission was the regulation of big business so that healthy competition could take place. He became known as a "trustbuster" because of his determination to break up trusts. (A trust was formed when several companies banded together to limit competition by controlling the production and distribution of a product or service.) Trusts were illegal under the 1890 Sherman Anti-Trust Act, and Roosevelt began to enforce the act more vigorously than it had been in the past decade. Roosevelt's administration began more than forty lawsuits against companies. Curiously, the president was more in favor of regulating trusts than he was of dissolving them; he called the Sherman Anti-Trust Act "foolish." Congress refused to enact his suggestions for the federal licensing and regulation of interstate companies, which would have limited their power. The only choice Roosevelt had, then, was to enforce the Sherman Anti-Trust Act. Still, he made it clear that in his eyes, some trusts were good, while others were bad.

Roosevelt took action in 1902 against both the beef trust and the Northern Securities Company, a railroad monopoly. (In a monopoly, one company dominates a sector of business, leaving the consumer no choices and other businesses no possibility of success.) Northern Securities had been established by some of the country's wealthiest businessmen: John D. Rockefeller (1839–1937), J. P. Morgan (1837–1913), James Hill (1838–1916), and **Edward Harriman** (1848–1909; see entry). Roosevelt ordered the Justice Department to file a suit to dissolve the company. Within a few months, the president filed suit against a Chicago meatpacking company called Swift & Company. America cheered as it watched the unethical companies struggle against the law. Roosevelt had made his point: Big business would have to deal with the federal government if it broke the law.

Roosevelt's "Square Deal" In May 1902, coal miners in Pennsylvania went on strike (refused to work). They had tried for months to meet with management and mine owners to negotiate better pay, shorter hours, and safer working conditions. When negotiations failed, the workers refused to enter the mines.

Anthracite (hard) coal was used to fuel trains and to heat houses and businesses. In 1902, as spring passed into summer and then into fall, Americans became concerned that the continued strike would result in a coal shortage. Businesses would close and citizens would freeze. President Roosevelt also felt concerned, and in October he invited representatives from the miners and the coal operators to the White House. In doing so, he became the first president in history to mediate (act as a go-between in) a labor strike. The meeting was called the Coal Strike Conference of 1902. During the conference, Roosevelt expressed his concerns. The miners agreed to go back to work if they could get a small, immediate pay increase and a promise that negotiations would continue. The coal operators refused, despite the president's involvement.

When Roosevelt realized the strike would continue, he took direct action. He threatened to send military troops to take over operation of the mines. If this were to happen, miners and owners alike would lose money. Both sides entered into negotiations with a committee appointed by Roosevelt, and miners returned to work on October 23. They had received a 10-percent increase in wages as well as a guarantee of shorter work days.

Roosevelt's involvement in the mining dispute set a precedent (an established example) of what could happen in future labor-management conflicts. The working class realized it had the support of an intelligent, influential president. Big business was all too aware that its authority was no longer limitless. Roosevelt called his program the "square deal," meaning both sides got fair treatment and consideration.

The president showed his support of business regulation again in 1903 when he passed a bill to establish the U.S. Department of Commerce and Labor, and again when he passed the Elkins Act. This law prohibited railroads from giving rebates (refunds) to those shippers who used their services most. Those refunds were discriminatory because they favored only the big companies; smaller companies did not do enough shipping to qualify for these refunds.

Big Stick diplomacy

Days before President McKinley was shot in 1901, Roosevelt spoke at the Minnesota State Fair. During his speech, he explained his stance on foreign policy by reciting an African proverb, "Speak softly and carry a big stick." By quoting this saying, Roosevelt expressed his belief that to be effective, one did not have to be the mightiest, but just needed the power to fight back if necessary. His ideas about foreign policy became known as Big Stick diplomacy. The president embraced this policy throughout his two terms in office.

Roosevelt proved the effectiveness of his philosophy in 1902. During that year, the Venezuelan government found itself heavily in debt to other countries. Germany, Italy, and Great Britain wanted to invade Venezuela to claim some of its territory as repayment. Roosevelt stepped in to help the countries reach an acceptable agreement, thereby avoiding war.

"Conservationist President"

Roosevelt carried his love of the outdoors into adulthood. He was an avid big-game hunter. When he realized America's bison herds were being hunted to near extinction, it concerned him. As the years passed, that concern was extended to wilderness lands and their wildlife.

Working closely with conservationists such as **John Muir** (1838–1914; see entry) and Gifford Pinchot (1865–1946), Roosevelt used his power of office to pass protective legislation to guarantee the preservation of America's natural resources. In 1902, Congress passed the Newlands Act, also known as the Reclamation Act. Reclamation is the process of altering or restoring a region or land to a healthy ecosystem. The new law used money from the sale of public lands in sixteen western states to build irrigation systems to maintain the country's arid (dry) regions. Settlers who benefited from these systems would repay the costs so that a revolving fund was available. Roosevelt eventually approved twenty-one reclamation projects.

Roosevelt has a national park named after him in North Dakota. He is also represented on Mt. Rushmore in South Dakota. Arizona is home to the Theodore Roosevelt Dam, which forms Theodore Roosevelt Lake. Both of these projects were completed under the Newlands Act in 1911.

Campaign and election of 1904

Roosevelt knew he had not earned his first years in the White House; no one elected him. But when it came time for another presidential election, he had proved himself a highly capable leader in the political and business worlds. His own Republican Party trusted him without reservation. The southern African American population supported him; this was an impressive feat, given that Roosevelt did not truly believe African Americans were equal to whites. He thought that African Americans were not able to govern themselves and that white Christians had the responsibility to look after the race.

Roosevelt broke the race barrier in 1901 when he invited African American reformer **Booker T. Washington** (1856–1915; see entry) to lunch at the White House. Washington was an advisor and consultant to many powerful white politicians of the day. He embraced the idea of the time that African Americans should be satisfied with whatever rights were given them by white society and work hard to prove themselves. He believed that only through hard work and determination would African Americans gain equal rights.

The Republican Party nominated Roosevelt for president unanimously. Roosevelt was fairly certain he would win the presidency. The Republican Party (also known since 1880 as the Grand Old Party, or GOP) was the majority party in national politics. The Democratic

The Making of the Teddy Bear

A portrait of Theodore Roosevelt is shown behind a teddy bear, which was named after the president. NINA LEEN/ TIME LIFE PICTURES/GETTY IMAGES.

While visiting the South to settle a border dispute between Mississippi and Louisiana in 1902, Roosevelt went bear hunting in Mississippi. In order to guarantee the president would go home with a trophy, some men had a pack of hounds chase a bear cub. After wounding the creature, they then roped the cub to a tree. Roosevelt found the situation appalling and refused to kill the bear (although he ordered a companion to shoot it and put it out of its misery). The press caught wind of the story and printed it in newspapers across the country.

Newspaper cartoonist Clifford K. Berryman (1869–1949) of the *Washington Post* ensured a place in history for the story with a November 16, 1902, front-page cartoon entitled "Drawing the Line in Mississippi."

Berryman's original drawing made the bear look fierce. He redrew the animal, however, to look more cuddly, less dangerous. The story became so popular that within a year, a stuffed "Teddy Bear" appeared on the market. Several stories circulated about how the bear was invented, but this is the most widely accepted version:

Morris Michtom was a New York City candy store owner. After seeing Berryman's cartoon, he came up with the idea to memorialize the popular incident. His wife created a stuffed bear, for which Michtom asked permission from the president to name Teddy. Released in 1903, the Teddy Bear became such a hit that the Michtoms quit the candy-store business and opened the Ideal Novelty and Toy Company in 1906. Their bear remained the president's mascot for the rest of his life. One of the original teddy bears is housed at the National Museum of American History.

The Ideal Company went on to produce some of the most popular toys in American history. Ideal toys include dozens of inventive dolls (the company was the first to make dolls whose eyes closed when laid down); the Evel Knievel toys popular in the 1970s; and the award-winning Rubik's Cube of 1980s fame.

Party continued to be split from within, which weakened whatever political power it had.

Although William Jennings Bryan (1860–1925) had been the Democratic candidate in the presidential elections in 1896 and 1900 (and would be again in 1908), Democrats did not nominate him for the 1904 race. Instead, they selected Alton B. Parker (1852–1926), chief judge of the New York Court of Appeals. Roosevelt and his running mate, U.S. senator Charles W. Fairbanks (1852–1918) of Indiana, did not travel extensively during the campaign. Roosevelt instead directed the campaign from the front porch of his home in Oyster Bay, New York. In addition, he turned to some of the nation's wealthiest businessmen for funding. Edward Harriman, Henry Frick (1849–1919), and J. P. Morgan (1837–1913) donated 70 percent of the more than $2 million raised by the Republican Party. The size of these donations raised the ethical issue of campaign contributions by large corporations, a practice that logically gave one political party an advantage over the other (in this case, the Republican Party over the Democratic Party). Within three years, Congress would prohibit contributions by national banks and corporations, but not by their officers as individuals.

Roosevelt beat Parker, 336 electoral votes to 140. Electoral votes are the votes a presidential candidate receives for having won a majority of a state's popular vote (citizens' votes). The candidate who receives the most popular votes in a particular state wins all of that state's electoral votes. Each state receives two electoral votes for its two U.S. senators and an amount for the number of U.S. representatives it has (which is determined by a state's population). A candidate must win a majority of electoral votes (over 50 percent) in order to win the presidency. Roosevelt also won the popular vote by a majority never before seen in the country's history: 57.4 percent. Roosevelt was the first man to be elected president on his own after serving out his deceased predecessor's term. In addition, he was viewed by many as the most popular president in history at that point.

Four more years

Roosevelt became more aggressive in his domestic policy during his second term as president, mostly because the changing times required it. Two major reforms were established, both in June 1906. On June 29, Roosevelt directed the passage of the Hepburn Act (named after U.S. representative William P. Hepburn [1833–1916] of Iowa, chairman of the Committee on Interstate and Foreign Commerce). The act strengthened the Interstate Commerce Commission (ICC) by adding two more members and allowing the committee to determine fair rates after complaints surfaced of a railroad shipper charging unfair rates. The ICC had

Political cartoon from the Utica Saturday Globe *shows President Theodore Roosevelt holding his nose at the investigation into the meatpacking scandal. The caption reads, "A nauseating job, but it must be done."* © BETTMANN/CORBIS.

been established as a result of the Interstate Commerce Act, which had passed in 1887. This act demanded that all railroad shipping rates be fair and reasonable. The Commission's job was to enforce the new laws.

The other major reform applied to the food industry. One day after signing the Hepburn Act into law, Roosevelt passed the Pure Food and Drug Act. This act was designed to protect consumers from fraudulent (untrue) food labeling and unsafe food. Although individual states had enacted food laws, they were difficult to enforce. Harvey Wiley (1844–1930), head of the Bureau of Chemistry in the U.S. Department of Agriculture, lobbied for stricter laws regarding food handling. Wiley enlisted the support of the more ethical food producers and drug manufacturers. Even so, his concerns were largely drowned out by the powerful Beef Trust (the five biggest meatpacking companies) as well as by large pharmaceutical companies and small producers of patent medicines.

During the Spanish-American War, America experienced a beef scandal. Meat was being sent overseas to U.S. troops. Soon reports were printed claiming the beef was tainted (made less wholesome) with embalming fluid to preserve it. (Embalming fluid is what corpses are injected with to delay the decaying process.) Shortly after the war ended, muckraker Charles Edward Russell (1860–1941) wrote a serial documentary exposing the greed and corruption of the Beef Trust. In 1906, journalist Upton Sinclair wrote the groundbreaking novel *The Jungle,* which detailed horrifying accounts of how meat was handled and processed in Chicago's meatpacking industry. With the public in an uproar over this health issue, Roosevelt signed the Pure Food and Drug Act as well as its accompanying Meat Inspection Act. The Meat Inspection Act required the U.S. Department of Agriculture to inspect all slaughtered animals to insure safety in the handling and processing of the meat. Lawbreakers could be jailed, fined, or both. These two food-related pieces of legislation were considered major efforts in progressive reform. Although the president did not introduce them, he is often given credit for doing so.

Panic of 1907 Roosevelt's views on trusts did not change. He spent his second term committed to ridding society of what he felt were "evil" trusts. He filed suits against DuPont, Standard Oil, American Tobacco, and New Haven Railroad. These lawsuits did nothing to improve the president's relations with the business community. The situation was only made worse with the Panic of 1907.

In the summer of 1907, several businesses and financial firms went bankrupt (declared themselves unable to pay their debts; often, this means the business closes). In October of that year, the Knickerbocker Trust in New York and the Westinghouse Electric Company closed their doors to business, setting off what became known as the Panic of 1907. Stock market prices decreased, and people and businesses began pulling their money out of banks for fear they would lose it. Banks began closing rapidly.

Just as President **Grover Cleveland** (1837–1908; served 1885–89 and 1893–97; see entry) had done when he was in office, Roosevelt called upon J. P. Morgan to restore order to the American economy. Morgan was a financier, an investment banker who works on a grand scale with large amounts of money. Morgan called upon the best bankers and financial experts, and together the men gathered in Morgan's home. From there, they channeled money to the weaker businesses and institutions in an effort to keep them from going bankrupt. Economic conditions improved within weeks, and the crisis passed.

The Panic of 1907 led reformers from both political parties to call for change in the banking business and its procedures. Various banking reforms and legislation were passed throughout the ensuing years. In 1913, the Federal Reserve System was established and became the banking headquarters of the United States.

Through it all, a conservationist Roosevelt continued passing conservation and environmental legislation throughout his second term. In 1905, with the help and advice of his good friend Pinchot, Roosevelt moved the Division of Forestry from the Department of the Interior to the Department of Agriculture and renamed it the U.S. Forest Service. That department would eventually come to be known as the National Forest Service. Under Pinchot's leadership for the first five years, America's national forests grew from 56 million acres (226,624 square kilometers) to 172 million acres (696,059 square kilometers).

In 1906, Roosevelt signed into law the American Antiquities Act, which gave him the authority to proclaim historic landmarks and structures as well as other areas of historic interest, such as national monuments. Although the law specifically stated that the president should include in the monument the smallest amount of land needed, Roosevelt interpreted the guidelines loosely. His first dedication was Devil's Tower in Wyoming. In 1906, he proclaimed a very generous amount of land, 800,000 acres (3,237 square kilometers) of the Grand Canyon, to be a national monument.

Throughout his years as president, Roosevelt used his power and authority to establish 150 national forests, 5 national parks, 18 national monuments, 51 bird reserves, and 4 game preserves. Altogether, he set aside for preservation 230 million acres (930,777 square kilometers) of land.

Meanwhile, overseas . . .

Winning the Spanish-American War made America a world power. The victory gave the United States the territories of Guam and Puerto Rico and allowed America to purchase the Philippine Islands. Taking over foreign countries and controlling their political and economic systems is known as imperialism, and Roosevelt firmly believed in it. Many Americans disagreed with him. Called anti-imperialists, they felt that imperialism was too costly and would eventually attract too many non-whites into the country. They also believed that the United States did not have the right to impose its values on another country and that it should not govern countries so far outside its own boundaries.

Roosevelt approached foreign policy using the doctrine of "New Imperialism." Nations he personally believed were uncivilized would gain independence only once they conformed to the American model of government and democracy. The president believed in the superiority of his own country's morals and history and thought that his belief justified America's involvement in countries with which it normally had little interaction. Under this direction, the United States became a sort of watchdog throughout the western half of the world. Under Roosevelt's leadership, America's empire grew to include the Philippines, Cuba, Haiti, the Dominican Republic, and Puerto Rico. In 1906, Cuba revolted against the United States's authority. According to the Platt Amendment, which had been passed in 1903, Cuba was forbidden to make independent treaties with other nations. The amendment also gave the United States the right to intervene in Cuban affairs in order to maintain order and the island's independence. Finally, the amendment required Cuba to lease a naval base (Guantanamo Bay) to the United States for an unstated length of time. Cuban nationalists (people who put the good of the country above all else, including individual rights) were deeply grieved by the power given to the United States; they wanted complete freedom and were willing to fight and die for it. Roosevelt sent in Marine Corps troops, beginning an occupation that would last until 1909.

The Panama Canal Perhaps the most famous of Roosevelt's foreign policy initiatives involved the creation of the Panama Canal (a man-made waterway). For years, American naval leaders wanted to build a passage between the Atlantic and the Pacific oceans through Central America. The United States now owned territory on both sides, so a canal took on even greater importance, as it would drastically reduce the amount of shipping and travel time.

Building of the canal across the Isthmus of Panama (then a territory of Colombia) had officially begun in 1878 by Ferdinand de Lesseps (1805–1894), the French engineer who had built the Suez Canal in Egypt. Construction came to a halt when laborers contracted tropical diseases and engineering problems arose. Even so, a French company retained rights to the project, so no one else could continue the construction. Roosevelt tried to buy those rights for $40 million. He also offered to pay $10 million for a 50-mile (80.47-kilometer) stretch across the isthmus, but Colombia refused. Roosevelt correctly predicted a revolution in Panama against Colombian rule. He then sent a naval ship and military troops to support Panama's rebellion. When Roosevelt presented the rebels with the $10-million offer, they happily accepted, and America had total control of a 10-mile (16.1-kilometer) canal zone.

Thousands of workers began digging the canal. For ten years, thirty thousand workers, most from the West Indies, were paid 10 cents an hour for ten-hour shifts. Many died of yellow fever, a disease carried by mosquitoes. Despite the disapproval of many Americans who felt Roosevelt had acted in an unconstitutional manner in obtaining the canal zone, work continued. On August 15, 1914, the Panama Canal opened for business. In addition to building the canal, workers also constructed three railroads and created a man-made lake.

The project cost $400 million and was considered one of the world's greatest engineering projects. By 1925, more than five thousand merchant ships had traveled the Panama Canal. The waterway shortened the trip from San Francisco, California, to New York City by nearly 8,000 miles (12,872 kilometers). Equally as important, the canal became a major military asset that made the United States the dominant power in Central America.

The Panama Canal remained an American asset until December 31, 1999, at which time it (and its surrounding land) was handed over to Panamanian authorities. During his presidency, Jimmy Carter (1924–; served 1977–81) had signed a transfer agreement. During the twenty years between the signing of the agreement and the actual transfer, a transitional committee ran the Canal. An American leader led the committee during the first decade, followed by a Panamanian leader for the second. Along with the canal, Carter offered Panama his apologies and acknowledged that although Roosevelt's vision was to be praised, the feelings of American colonialism in Panama created controversy. The agreement holds that the United States can interfere if the Canal loses its neutrality or threatens American interests in any way.

Russo-Japanese War War erupted between Russia and Japan in 1904. Both countries had plans for Korea and Manchuria, a large region in northeast Asia. At the time, China had control of a port in Manchuria that Russia wanted to take over. It convinced China to lease the port, which gave Russia occupation within southern Manchuria. Japan was angered over this move because Russia had forced Japan to give up its own right to be in Manchuria when Japan beat China in the Sino-Japanese War (1894–95). Then in 1896, Russia ended an alliance with China against Japan and won the rights to extend the Trans-Siberian Railroad across parts of China-controlled Manchuria. This gave Russia control of an important territory in Manchuria. Roosevelt had been expecting the conflict, and his sympathies lay with Japan. America had long wanted to put an end to Russia's plan to take over Manchuria. Now that Japan was fighting the battle, America would not have to.

The war ended in 1905 with Japan defeating Russia's navy and overrunning Manchuria's neighbor, Korea. This defeat prohibited Russia from expanding its power in the Far East. At the same time, Japan became the first Asian power to defeat a European power. This victory suddenly made Japan a much stronger nation than it had been in the past, which concerned Roosevelt. To add further worry, Japan had already established an alliance (a partnership with another country or countries) with the powerful Great Britain in 1902. This alliance threatened the United States's ability to be the dominant superpower.

Roosevelt also kept in mind the Open-Door policy the United States had with China. This policy stated that all trading nations of the world would have access to China's market. In order to keep the policy in action, the president invited leaders from Japan and Russia to New Hampshire to work out an agreement that would become known as the Treaty of Portsmouth (named after the city in which negotiations were held). Japan, though victorious in its war against Russia, was in trouble financially, and both countries agreed to negotiate. Roosevelt would later be awarded the Nobel Peace Prize for his peacekeeping efforts. Although Roosevelt's mediation brought peace, the conference did not go quite as he had hoped. The president had to give Japan a similar position and influence in China that America demanded for itself in the Western Hemisphere. This was power he had not intended to share.

In keeping with his belief that the world could be made up of great superpowers that maintained stability even as they competed, Roosevelt negotiated a secret deal with Japan in 1905 called the Taft-Katsura Agreement. This deal assured the United States that Japan had no interest in the Philippines, which had remained an important interest for America; in return, America pledged not to interfere in Japan's relations in Korea. Soon after, Korea became a Japanese protectorate (a region under the protection and partial control of a country).

The personal becomes the public

Roosevelt was a prolific (productive) writer. In his lifetime, he authored twenty-seven books and countless articles. His writing and many speeches covered a wide range of topics, and included everything from football to birth control, morals to women's equality. Roosevelt knew his beliefs and did not miss an opportunity to share them with anyone who would listen.

On the subject of women's rights, he was uncharacteristically silent, though he did support woman's suffrage (right to vote) and educational equality. In keeping with the traditional, conservative views of his times, however, the president believed that the education of females should include an awareness of what was going on in the world but no encouragement to participate in it, whereas the education of males should encourage them to make use of their fighting instincts. Roosevelt had no patience for cowardice.

Roosevelt was popular and he knew it. But in keeping with his 1904 campaign promise not to seek reelection in 1908, Roosevelt hand-picked Secretary of War William Howard Taft (1857–1930) to run as the Republican candidate in the presidential race. He easily won nomination. Taft's opponent was William Jennings Bryan, and Taft won with 51.6 percent of the popular vote.

Goes on safari

Needing some relaxation, fifty-year-old Roosevelt and his son Kermit spent a year in Africa on safari, where he hunted and killed thousands of animals. Among these were five elephants, nine lions, thirteen rhinos, and seven hippos.

News reports of political trouble back in the United States reached Roosevelt while on safari, but when he and Kermit reached Egypt, Roosevelt's wife Edith joined them for a grand tour of Europe. The family returned to New York City, where they were met with the largest reception in the city up to that time. By then, Roosevelt was angry at Taft over some of the anticonservation measures Taft signed into law. He was also upset that Taft was not running the presidency as he himself had. Roosevelt considered his old friend's behavior an act of betrayal.

Back in the running

By 1912, Roosevelt was disgruntled enough with Taft's job as president that he decided to run for the top office again. The year 1912 was the first year in which there were presidential primaries (elections to pare down the candidates so that there is just one per political party). At that early stage of primary elections, only twelve states held Republican primaries. That left thirty-six states without a primary election. Of the

Former president Theodore Roosevelt (front) rides a camel in the desert of Khartoum, Sudan, during his safari to Africa in 1909.
© BETTMANN/CORBIS.

twelve Republican primaries, Roosevelt beat Taft in landslide victories. In those other thirty-six states, delegates were chosen by state convention. To get to the state convention, a delegate had to be nominated by the local convention. At that level, professional politicians easily dominated the proceedings.

In the 1912 campaign, 254 delegate seats were up for grabs. The Republican National Committee was in a position to decide the outcome. In 1912, Taft supporters dominated that committee; they were not about to let Roosevelt disgrace their candidate. They awarded Roosevelt 19 seats, while Taft was given 254. Taft was renominated. The stubborn Roosevelt then decided his only option was to run for president as a third-party candidate on the Progressive, or Bull Moose, Party (see box) ticket.

With the Republican Party now split in two, it was highly unlikely either Roosevelt or Taft would win the election. New Jersey governor

Who Was the Progressive Party?

No professional politicians ran the Progressive Party. The membership of the party was well educated and respectable, including in its numbers many professional and civic-minded women. As a result of this mix, it was the only major political party of the election to support women's rights. Aside from women's rights, the central idea of the party was to redistribute the nation's wealth so that more Americans could enjoy a better quality of life. Despite this concern for the nation's workforce, the Progressives were not a labor party. They wanted to help but not engage the participation of the workers themselves. Progressives were cultured, middle-class Americans, and that is how they intended the party to stay.

Woodrow Wilson (1856–1924) claimed victory, the first Democrat to serve in the White House in sixteen years. Wilson won 435 electoral votes, compared with Roosevelt's 88 and Taft's 8. Wilson received 41.9 percent of the popular vote, leaving 27.4 percent to Roosevelt and 23.1 percent to Taft. The remaining votes were divided between Socialist Eugene V. Debs (1855–1926) and Prohibition Party leader Eugene W. Chafin (1852–1920).

Life goes on

After his defeat, Roosevelt once more headed for the jungle with his son Kermit, this time in Brazil. While away, he continued to write. He churned out history books as well as essays for publication in magazines. Most of those essays were scientific in nature, but he also published some in which he tried to persuade America that its participation in World War I (1914–18) was inevitable.

Roosevelt lost his beloved son Quentin in the war. With his son's passing went the former president's enthusiasm. A sadness he had never known before came over Roosevelt. German propagandists (those who publish one-sided information to rally support for a specific cause) published photos of Quentin's disfigured body alongside his plane for all the world to see.

Roosevelt died in his home on Oyster Bay on January 6, 1919. His physically and mentally stressful life had taken its toll on his sixty-one-year-old body, and he died from a blood clot in his heart. Five hundred invited guests attended his funeral, while thousands of respectful mourners waited outside the church. His service was simple, without music or eulogy, and his oak coffin was covered by a wreath from the Rough Riders. He was buried in a cemetery on Oyster Bay.

For More Information

BOOKS

Chambers, John Whiteclay II. *The Tyranny of Change: America in the Progressive Era, 1890–1920.* 2nd ed. New Brunswick, NJ: Rutgers University Press, 2000.

Ingram, Scott. *The Panama Canal (Building World Landmarks)*. San Diego: Blackbirch Press, 2003.

Kraft, Betsy Harvey. *Theodore Roosevelt: Champion of the American Spirit*. New York: Clarion Books, 2003.

Lansford, Tom, and Robert P. Watson, eds. *Theodore Roosevelt (Presidents & Their Decisions)*. San Diego: Greenhaven Press, 2003.

McPherson, Stephanie Sammartino. *Theodore Roosevelt (Presidential Leaders)*. Minneapolis: Lerner Publications, 2005.

Painter, Nell Irvin. *Standing at Armageddon: The United States, 1877–1919*. New York: W. W. Norton, 1987.

Wiebe, Robert H. *The Search for Order, 1877–1920*. New York: Hill and Wang, 1967. Reprint, Westport, CT: Greenwood Press, 1980.

WEB SITES

"The Funeral of Theodore Roosevelt." *Theodore Roosevelt Association.* http://www.theodoreroosevelt.org/life/Religion.htm#FUNERAL (accessed on September 4, 2006).

"In His Own Words." *Theodore Roosevelt Association.* http://www.theodoreroosevelt.org/life/quotes.htm (accessed on September 4, 2006).

"Life of Theodore Roosevelt." *Theodore Roosevelt Association.* http://www.theodoreroosevelt.org/life/lifeoftr.htm (accessed on September 4, 2006).

National Park Service. "Theodore Roosevelt." *Theodore Roosevelt National Park.* http://www.nps.gov/thro/tr_cons.htm (accessed on September 4, 2006).

"Teddy Bear." *National Museum of American History.* http://americanhistory.si.edu/news/factsheet.cfm?key=30&newskey=6 (accessed on September 4, 2006).

"Theodore Roosevelt and Big Stick Diplomacy." *Mt. Holyoke College.* http://www.mtholyoke.edu/~jlgarner/classweb/worldpolitics/bigstick.html (accessed on September 4, 2006).

"Theodore Roosevelt: Icon of the American Century." *National Portrait Gallery.* http://www.npg.si.edu/exh/roosevelt/ (accessed on September 4, 2006).

"Theodore Roosevelt (1901–1909)." *American President.* http://www.americanpresident.org/history/theodoreroosevelt/ (accessed on September 4, 2006).

"Theodore Roosevelt: The Nobel Peace Prize 1906: Biography." *Nobelprize.org.* http://nobelprize.virtual.museum/nobel_prizes/peace/laureates/1906/roosevelt-bio.html (accessed on September 4, 2006).

Upton Sinclair

BORN: September 20, 1878 • Baltimore, Maryland

DIED: November 25, 1968 • Bound Brook, New Jersey

Writer; socialist

Upton Sinclair.
© BETTMANN/CORBIS.

"I aimed at the public's heart, and by accident I hit it in the stomach."

U pton Sinclair was a struggling writer until the publication of his fifth novel, *The Jungle,* in 1906. Then, seemingly overnight, the twenty-seven-year-old author found fame. That novel secured him a place among the ranks of famous muckrakers, journalists who took it upon themselves to uncover scandal and corruption among America's big businesses and politics.

Early life of struggle

Upton Sinclair was born in Baltimore, Maryland, on September 20, 1878. His father was a liquor salesman, a job that contributed to his alcoholism. Sinclair's mother, Priscilla Harden, despised alcohol and refused to drink tea or coffee because they contain caffeine. These conflicting attitudes were the source of much tension in the future writer's childhood home. The Sinclair family moved to New York when Upton was ten. A hat salesman by day, his father spent his nights at local bars. Sinclair later revealed in his writing that those early years were filled with uncertainty. As reported on *ClassicReader.com,* "As far back as I can remember, my life was a series of Cinderella transformations; one night I would be sleeping on a vermin-ridden sofa in a lodging house, and the next night under silken coverlets in a fashionable home. It all depended on whether my father had the money for that week's board." When conditions in the Sinclair home got particularly bad, Sinclair would be sent to live with his wealthy grandparents. This back-and-forth lifestyle gave him early insight into the many differences between those who have wealth and those who do not.

Reading and writing became a means of escape for a young Sinclair. By the age of fifteen, he was writing dime novels (popular, inexpensive books with simple plots, and always written with much drama; usually adventures, mysteries, or romances). To help pay his tuition at New York City College, he supplemented his meager income by writing for pulp magazines. These periodicals were cheaply produced and sold for twenty-five cents in the late 1880s, when they first hit newsstands. Most pulp magazines were all fiction, though some included true stories as well.

Sinclair enrolled in New York's Columbia University in 1897; he helped finance his educational endeavor by writing adventure stories for boys weeklies. The weeklies were small newspapers written specifically for a young, male audience. They could be bought for two or three pennies. Every issue contained serial fiction (stories told, one adventure at a time, throughout each edition of the paper). These stories involved young boys in familiar settings, such as public school. Each story included likeable characters engaging in activities familiar to readers, like playing football, getting into trouble with teachers or parents, and telling jokes. At this point, Sinclair had two secretaries to whom he would dictate his stories. At the same time he was writing almost non-stop, he was completing his studies. He even managed to teach himself how to speak French in just six weeks. This intense work habit would stay with him throughout his life. By the time of his death at the age of ninety, he had written and published nearly one hundred books.

A socialist is born

In 1900, Sinclair married Meta Fuller, the daughter of a friend of his mother's. The marriage was unfulfilling and ended in 1913, but not before producing a son, David. Sinclair wrote several novels during that decade of marriage, but they did not sell well, and the family lived a life of intense poverty. Even though his novels were unsuccessful, Sinclair refused to find other work. His books were largely autobiographical, with fictional characters whose lives resembled many aspects of the author's life.

Around this time, Sinclair became interested in socialism (an economic, political, and social theory in which the public owns all property and resources and controls the means of production as well as the distribution of goods). In socialism, there is no room for private ownership. The focus instead is on collective ownership and equality for all. Socialism is the direct opposite of capitalism, which is the economic system used in America. Capitalism is founded on the idea that individual ownership promotes healthy competition among businesses, which in turn gives consumers more choices.

The industrialization (the move from an agricultural economy to one based on industry and business) of America underscored both the negative and the positive aspects of capitalism. On the one hand, individuals had the opportunity to gain vast amounts of wealth through business. On the other hand, most individuals did not have the business sense or the means through which to become wealthy. Instead, the rich got richer by hiring the poor, who became so desperate for work that they accepted low-paying jobs in unsafe work conditions. They worked ten-hour shifts or more, for a few dollars a day, and barely got by. The capitalist society of the Gilded Age and the early Progressive Era required the lower classes to send their children to factories instead of schools, resulting in a system that worked only for those who were in control. (The Gilded Age was the period in history following the Civil War and Reconstruction [roughly the final twenty-three years of the nineteenth century], characterized by a ruthless pursuit of profit, an exterior of showiness and grandeur, and immeasurable political corruption. The Progressive Era was the period that followed the Gilded Age [approximately the first twenty years of the twentieth century]; it was marked by reform and the development of a national cultural identity.)

Socialism provided an alternative to capitalism, and it became a popular theory among laborers and others who struggled just to survive. It was a threat to those who thrived in capitalist America, however. Opponents of the theory painted it as nothing more than total control of government over citizens who would sacrifice all rights and opportunities. The upper and middle classes of American society as a whole came to fear socialism. But Sinclair was one of those who struggled, and he took up the socialist cause with a vengeance. He officially joined the Socialist Party in 1902. Socialism became the driving force for his writing, and his passion showed through in the novel that was to skyrocket him to fame.

Sinclair was a devoted reader of and writer for the socialist newspaper *Appeal to Reason*. In 1904, his editors sent him to Chicago to investigate the lives and working conditions of the city's stockyard workers (employees in the enclosed yards where food animals are temporarily kept before being slaughtered). The writer spent seven weeks living among the poor and mostly immigrant workers (people who move from one country to another, permanently). As poor as Sinclair was, he did not have to do much to blend in with the overworked, underpaid employees. He worked alongside them, lived among them, and interviewed hundreds of them. At night, he would write about what he saw and heard. He had always understood the troubles of the working-class poor, but now he also had details on how the meatpacking industry worked. He returned to New York with a full report.

The Jungle

Appeal to Reason published Sinclair's report as a serial, one chapter in each issue of the newspaper beginning in 1905. Reaction to Sinclair's work was so strong and immediate that the author began searching for a book publisher. No publisher would touch the book, however. According to journalist Chris Bachelder's article "The Jungle at 100," a manuscript reader from Macmillan (a publishing company) rejected Sinclair's novel with the words, "Gloom and horror unrelieved. As to the possibilities of a large sale, I should think them not very good." Sinclair would find similar reactions in the rejections from five more publishing houses before his manuscript was accepted by Doubleday, Page & Company.

Editors at Doubleday believed the novel as it was published in serial format was too graphic (uncomfortably realistic), and they insisted that Sinclair cut out some of his descriptions. The edition of *The Jungle* published in February 1906 was not the version that the author had originally written, but public reaction reassured Sinclair that it was still a disturbing, thought-provoking work. The book sold fifty-five hundred copies in one day, and within months was translated into seventeen languages. *The Jungle* was an international best-seller. Among its admirers were President **Theodore Roosevelt** (1858–1919; served 1901–9; see entry), Nobel Prize writer George Bernard Shaw (1856–1950), and feminist Charlotte

Perkins Gilman (1860–1935; see box). Gilman, according to Bachelder, wrote Sinclair a letter telling him "that book of yours is unforgettable."

Socialism, no; reform, yes

Sinclair and Roosevelt struck up an extensive correspondence as a result of the novel and its impact on society, but it was clear that Roosevelt—and the public at large—missed the essential message Sinclair tried to communicate in *The Jungle*. At the end of the novel, the workers discover and embrace socialism, Sinclair's answer to society's problems. Readers, including Roosevelt, finished the book not with a desire for a socialist society but with a sense of horror regarding the filth and health hazards of the meat industry. But Sinclair continued to write the president, passing along suggestions and talking about socialism. As Bachelder wrote in his article, Roosevelt had to go over Sinclair's head, straight to Frank Doubleday. "Tell Sinclair to go home and let me run the country for a while."

The book jacket of an early edition of Upton Sinclair's The Jungle. © BETTMANN/ CORBIS.

Roosevelt defended individualism with the same stubbornness that Sinclair defended socialism, but the president did share the author's disdain for capitalist greed. Earlier in the phase of their correspondence, Roosevelt explained in detail why he would never agree with socialism, but he promised Sinclair that he would use his power as president to reform the meatpacking industry.

Roosevelt kept his promise. When Congress was reluctant to pass the Pure Food and Drug bill for fear of angering some of the politicians' wealthiest supporters (whose businesses were in the meatpacking industry), he encouraged Congress to pass the bill into law. On June 30, 1906, the first federal laws regulating the food and drug industries were put into effect. Testing would be required to ensure the safety of all food and drugs meant for human consumption. The Food and Drug Administration would be established to carry out the enforcement of the new laws. Furthermore, some drugs would require a doctor's prescription before purchase, and drugs that were habit-forming would carry a warning on the label.

Charlotte Perkins Gilman: Defender of Justice

Feminist Charlotte Perkins Gilman. © CORBIS.

Charlotte Perkins Gilman was one of the most influential writers of the late nineteenth and early twentieth centuries. In her hundreds of novels, essays, and short stories, she argued against the societal norm of the day that kept women in the home, taking care of husbands and families. Gilman believed this oppressed women (kept them from realizing their potential).

Gilman was born in Hartford, Connecticut, the daughter of a librarian and author father. Harriet Beecher Stowe (1811–1896), author of the famous abolition (antislavery) novel *Uncle Tom's Cabin,* was her father's aunt. Gilman's father abandoned the family in 1866, and they lived in great poverty, moving from relative to relative.

Gilman studied at the Rhode Island School of Design from 1878 to 1880; she then began earning a living by designing greeting cards. She married another artist, Charles Walter Stetson (1858–1911), in 1884. The birth of daughter Katharine soon followed, and the new mother fell into a deep depression. In 1886, she began seeking treatment for her condition from Dr. Silas Weir Mitchell (1829–1914), who recommended that she live as domestic a life as

Another piece of legislation related solely to the meatpacking industry was passed that same day. The Meat Inspection Act required that certified officials inspect all animals before slaughter to ensure their health. Any found with disease would not be fit for eating. Once the animals were slaughtered, they again were inspected because some disease was not evident until the animals were cut open. Finally, the new law required slaughterhouses and stockyards to maintain specific health standards, which would be enforced on a regular basis by officials from the Department of Agriculture.

Despite the book's popularity and his assurance of a place in history, Sinclair was disappointed with the reaction to his novel. He wanted the world to recognize socialism as the answer to every workingman's prayers.

possible. He advised her to never pick up a pen or a brush or a pencil again. As strange as the doctor's advice may sound, it reflected the common idea of the day that women were not physically or emotionally capable of handling a life beyond cooking, cleaning, and taking care of children. Many highly respected minds of the day promoted the idea that it was dangerous to their health and well-being for women to pursue activities outside the household.

Gilman wrote about her experiences with Mitchell and what happened when she followed his advice in her most famous short story, "The Yellow Wallpaper." The main character of the story is a young mother who suffers from nervous depression, brought on by the birth of her daughter. The woman's husband is a doctor, who forces her to rest in the bedroom of their rented house, doing nothing. The patterns of the room's ugly yellow wallpaper begins to haunt the woman as she slowly goes insane.

Gilman divorced Stetson in 1894 and moved to California, where she began writing books that would one day be labeled feminist, though the author herself refused such a label. In 1898, she attacked the traditional divisions of social and gender roles in her most famous nonfiction work, *Women and Economics*. "There is no female mind," she wrote in her book. "The brain is not an organ of sex." She also argued that in order to achieve equality between men and women, women needed a way to make their own money.

Gilman married her cousin George in 1902; the union would be a happy one until his death in 1934. In 1909, Gilman founded a feminist magazine titled *The Forerunner*. The magazine's life lasted for seven years. Gilman and her husband moved to Connecticut in 1922. Ten years later, she was diagnosed with breast cancer. After the death of her husband, Gilman returned to California to spend time with her daughter. Rather than die a slow death by cancer, she chose to end her life by taking an overdose of chloroform (a substance used as an anesthetic during surgery). Gilman died on August 17, 1935, in California. Her work was largely ignored for more than twenty years, but enjoyed a significant revival with the birth of the feminist movement in the 1960s.

He wanted the burdens of the common laborer to be acknowledged and then relieved. When it became clear that his dreams would go unrealized, he later wrote in the book he believed to be his most important, *The Brass Check: A Study of American Journalism,* "I aimed at the public's heart, and by accident I hit it in the stomach." Yet no book had more social impact during the Gilded Age and Progressive Era than did *The Jungle.*

Never gives up

Sinclair used the proceeds from *The Jungle* to establish a socialist commune (a community where most property is shared and little is privately owned) called Helicon Home Colony in Englewood, New Jersey. Within a year, the commune burned to the ground, and Sinclair was once again penniless.

Meat plant workers and inspectors check hanging meat at a packing plant, following the passage of the Meat Inspection Act of 1906. © BETTMANN/CORBIS.

Driven by the success of his 1906 novel, Sinclair continued to write novels that exposed controversial issues and irregularities in various industries in America. *The Metropolis,* published in 1908, was a behind-the-scenes look at New York's elite society. He followed that with the 1917 publication of *King Coal,* which revolved around a coal-mining strike that took place in 1914. This novel was an argument for the establishment of labor unions. *Oil!,* published in 1927, is considered to be one of Sinclair's greatest novels. Its plot revolves around two friends, one a poor laborer, the other the son of a wealthy oil magnate. This fictitious account paints a detailed portrait of the lives of the two men as they go through life. *Boston* was published one year later. The real-life inspiration for the book was the infamous Sacco-Vanzetti case, in which two Italian immigrants, Nicola Sacco (1891–1927) and Bartolomeo Vanzetti (1888–1927), were accused and eventually executed for the death of two men. Although both men had alibis (excuses), they were the only two people ever accused of the crime.

While active in the Socialist Party, Sinclair ran unsuccessfully for Congress on the Socialist ticket in 1906. He left the party in 1917 to support Democratic president Woodrow Wilson (1856–1924; served 1913–21), but returned to socialism when the president supported intervention in the Soviet Union.

Sinclair remarried in 1913. He and Mary Craig Kimbrough stayed together until her death in 1961. The couple moved to California in the 1930s. In 1934, he ran for governor on the Democratic ticket (figuring he had a better chance than if he ran as a Socialist). He surprised everyone by winning nearly nine hundred thousand votes, but no one was surprised when he did not win the election.

The 1940s found Sinclair writing a series of books featuring central character Lanny Budd. The series consisted of eleven historical novels. Together, they covered much of Western political history in the first half of the twentieth century. His 1942 novel in the series, titled *Dragon's Teeth,* won the Pulitzer Prize for fiction in 1943. The book covered Germany's descent into Nazism.

Sinclair and his wife moved to Arizona in 1953, where he continued to write, but not at his former hectic pace. He published his autobiography in 1962, in which he declared that his lifelong commitment to the ideals of socialism had not changed. After his second wife's death, the author remarried; his third wife, Elizabeth Willis, died in 1967. Sinclair spent his last year in a nursing home, where he died on November 25, 1968.

For More Information

BOOKS

Arthur, Anthony. *Radical Innocent: Upton Sinclair.* New York: Random House, 2006.

Mattson, Kevin. *Upton Sinclair and the Other American Century.* New York: Wiley, 2006.

Sinclair, Upton. *The Brass Check: A Study of American Journalism.* Pasadena, CA: Self-published, 1919. Multiple reprints.

Sinclair, Upton. *The Jungle.* New York: Doubleday, 1906. Multiple reprints.

Sinclair, Upton. *Oil!* New York: Albert and Charles Boni, 1927. Multiple reprints.

PERIODICALS

Bachelder, Chris. "The Jungle at 100: Why the Reputation of Upton Sinclair's Good Book Has Gone Bad." *Mother Jones* (January-February 2006): pp. 71–74. Also available at http://www.motherjones.com/arts/books/2006/01/the_ jungle_at_100.html.

WEB SITES

Blackwell, John. "1906: Rumble Over 'The Jungle.'" *The Capital Century: 1900– 1999.* http://www.capitalcentury.com/1906.html (accessed on September 4, 2006).

"Charlotte Perkins Gilman." *Pegasos.* http://www.kirjasto.sci.fi/gilman.htm (accessed on September 4, 2006).

Nakao, Annie. "Upton Sinclair Made His Mark as a Muckraker; His Vision for California Now Takes the Spotlight." *San Francisco Chronicle.* http://sfgate. com/cgi-bin/article.cgi?f=/c/a/2005/01/12/DDGB9AOANQ1.DTL (accessed on September 4, 2006).

"Upton Sinclair." *Classic Reader.* http://www.classicreader.com/author.php/aut. 100/ (accessed on September 4, 2006).

Sitting Bull

BORN: c. 1831 • Grand River Valley, South Dakota

DIED: December 15, 1890 • Standing Rock, South Dakota

Native American tribal chief

"What treaty that the whites have kept has the red man broken? Not one. What treaty that the whites ever made with us red men have they kept? Not one."

Sitting Bull was a Sioux chief and holy man who defended his people and their way of life until the end of his own life. An honorable warrior and leader, Sitting Bull always put the well-being of his tribe before anything else. As their chief, he refused to sign his name to a treaty that would allow the U.S. government to take Sioux land. His death in 1890 remains a mystery, and historians have never been able to disprove the theory that he was assassinated for political reasons. He is most famous for his participation in the Battle of Little Bighorn, commonly referred to as "Custer's Last Stand."

A typical childhood

Sitting Bull.
THE LIBRARY OF
CONGRESS.

Sitting Bull was born around 1831, in South Dakota's Grand River Valley. He was born into a Lakota tribe, which is a member of the Sioux (pronounced SUE) Nation. His given name was Tatanka Iyotanka,

183

which describes a buffalo sitting on its haunches, immovable. Sitting Bull lived up to the name, always giving much thought to every situation before making a move.

Sitting Bull, a serious youth, lived an uneventful childhood until the age of fourteen. At that time, he engaged in a successful raid on the Crow, a tribe known for its courage. His complete lack of fear made him known throughout neighboring tribes as a dedicated warrior. In 1847, at just fifteen, Sitting Bull proved the truth of his reputation when he galloped his horse past the skirmish line in a battle with the Flatheads. With arrows flying from all directions at him, the young warrior laughed and teased his enemies and managed to suffer only minor injuries. This convinced the Sioux that he must have been born with strong medicine powers.

In 1856, Sitting Bull became a leader in both the Strong Heart and the Kit Fox warrior societies. Native Americans and others considered these Lakota societies to be the finest light cavalry in the world, and it was an honor to be a member. A few years later, Sitting Bull became a respected member of the Silent Eaters, an organized group concerned with tribal welfare.

Goes head to head with U.S. soldiers

Sitting Bull first fought U.S. soldiers in June 1863, when the U.S. army engaged in a campaign to seek revenge on Native American tribes that had rebelled against the government and killed hundreds of white settlers, including women and children. This event was known as the Santee Rebellion (named after the primary warring tribe), and it took place in 1862 in Minnesota. Sitting Bull's people took no part in the killings, but the army was not particular in which Native Americans it targeted for revenge.

Throughout the next five years, Sitting Bull fought against the U.S. cavalry time and time again. In 1868, as proof of the respect he commanded, the fearless warrior was named head chief of the Lakota Nation.

Sitting Bull was made chief just two years into the Plains Indian Wars (1866–90). During the span of the wars, the federal government was trying to force Native Americans from their tribal lands so that white settlers could move into the region. Although most Plains tribes were peaceful and lived together harmoniously, they were not about to let white men take their land without a fight.

Sitting Bull was a dedicated enemy of the U.S. government and military. He knew that defeat would mean an end to his people's way of life and culture. Even in the first years of the wars, he saw the slaughter of the buffalo, the animal his people depended on for food, clothing, and shelter. He watched as white men brought their diseases and bad habits, such as drinking alcohol, into the native villages and camps.

The worst years

Hostilities peaked between 1869 and 1878. More than two hundred battles were fought during those years. By the late 1870s, the goal of the federal government became the Americanization of those whom many American officials and citizens called "savages." The tribes were expected to live on specific parcels of land. They were also forced to participate in American schooling and to learn to live the way white American society lived. In their speech, dress, and behavior, Native Americans were expected to turn their backs on their cultures and beliefs.

In 1874, General George Armstrong Custer (1839–1876) led an expedition into the Black Hills of Dakota Territory, searching for gold. When they found what they were after, prospectors (those hopeful of finding gold) rushed into the Black Hills. This territory had formerly been off-limits to white settlers because it was considered sacred ground by many tribes. (The Fort Laramie Treaty of 1868 provided the official protection.) The Lakota living in those hills were forced to defend themselves against the criminal prospectors. The government then tried to buy the land from the tribes, but the Lakota refused to sell. Since buying the land did not work, the treaty was simply ignored, and the government informed the Lakota that if they had not willingly moved to reservations by January 31, 1876, they would be considered hostile. Sitting Bull, true to his name, did not move.

In March 1876, federal troops began moving into the area. Sitting Bull knew they were coming, and he summoned the Lakota, Cheyenne, and Arapaho to his camp in Montana Territory. They held a sun dance ritual, and during the ceremony, Sitting Bull had a vision. In it, he saw soldiers falling from the sky into the Lakota camp.

Sitting Bull shared his vision with other chiefs and leaders, and on June 17, Chief Crazy Horse (1842?–1877) set out with five hundred of his men. They surprised U.S. troops on their way to Montana and forced their retreat.

The Battle of Little Bighorn To celebrate their major victory, Sitting Bull moved the Lakota camp to the valley of Little Big Horn River, where they met with three thousand more Native Americans who left their reservations to follow the great chief. On June 25, Custer and the Seventh Cavalry attacked the camp. Greatly outnumbered, Custer and his men were killed. Sitting Bull's vision had come true.

Custer's death outraged the American public. Although the general had defied orders and moved into battle sooner than he was told to do, and despite the fact that he was completely unaware that Crazy Horse had forced the retreat of U.S. troops, Custer became an overnight hero. His life and death were exaggerated in songs, poems, and tall tales. His career before his "last stand" had been ordinary, but now he was portrayed as a courageous hero whose life had been snuffed out by bloodthirsty savages. America wanted revenge.

Exile and surrender

Custer's defeat brought thousands more soldiers into the region, and the Lakota were specific targets. In May 1877, Sitting Bull took his tribe into Canada, where the United States could not capture him. When the government sent an official across the border to offer the chief a pardon (formal forgiveness for his "crime") in exchange for settlement on a reservation, an angry Sitting Bull refused.

As recorded in *Great Speeches by Native Americans,* Sitting Bull's response to the government was, "For sixty-four years you have kept me and my people and treated us bad. What have we done that you should want us to stop? We have done nothing. . . . Don't you say two more words. Go back home where you came from. . . . This part of the country does not belong to your people. You belong on the other side; this side belongs to us."

Sitting Bull and his people lasted four long years in Canada. When the buffalo were all but extinct and he could no longer keep the tribe fed and healthy, he crossed the border once more. On July 19, 1881, he surrendered at Fort Buford, Montana. According to the PBS Web site *New Perspectives on the West,* the great chief said, "I wish it to be remembered that I was the last man of my tribe to surrender my rifle." For Sitting Bull, surrender was the beginning of the end. But surrendering during the Plains Indian Wars was often used as a strategy to buy more time and eventually escape, and other famous Native American warriors used it to their advantage.

Officials sent Sitting Bull to Standing Rock Reservation. When they realized how popular he still was and saw how welcomed he was there, they feared he might instigate an uprising, so he was sent down the Missouri River to Fort Randall. He was held as a prisoner of war for two years.

Returns to Standing Rock

In May 1883, Sitting Bull was reunited with his Lakota tribe at Standing Rock. The chief worked alongside his people in the fields, but it was common knowledge that he still had authority over the Native Americans there. When government officials visited to tell the tribes of their desire to open part of the reservation to white settlers, Sitting Bull spoke out against the plan.

He left the reservation for four months in 1885 to join Buffalo Bill's Wild West show. This variety show featured several famous figures of the West, including Buffalo Bill Cody (1846–1917). It traveled the country entertaining settlers whose only knowledge of the wild frontier came from books and stories. For his part in riding around the arena once during each performance, Sitting Bull earned $50 a week. White society became too much for the aging chief, and he returned to his cabin at Standing Rock.

Although the rules of the reservation required Sitting Bull to embrace Christianity and other white cultural norms, the chief refused. He lived with his two wives and children and never gave up his traditional lifestyle. Not long after he returned, Sitting Bull had another vision. In it, he was told that he would be killed by one of his own people.

Vision comes true

Sitting Bull was visited by a Lakota named Kicking Bear (Mato Wanahtaka; 1846–1904) in the fall of 1890. Kicking Bear shared with the chief news of a ceremony that was supposed to get rid of white people and give back to the Native Americans their traditional way of life. The ceremony was known as the Ghost Dance, and Lakota at other reservations had already adopted it.

Officials at those reservations called in the military to keep the tribes under control. Those in charge at Standing Rock feared Sitting Bull would join the Ghost Dancers. If he did that, the movement would have a power beyond control. Before dawn on December 15, 1890, forty-three Lakota police officers broke down Sitting Bull's front door

Geronimo: Famous Apache Warrior

Apache chief Geronimo. © CORBIS.

Geronimo was born in 1829 in either Arizona or New Mexico. Regardless, the region belonged to Mexico at the time. He was born into an Apache tribe and given the name Goyakla, which means "one who yawns." For unknown reasons, Mexican soldiers gave him the name he is known by: Geronimo.

Although not himself a hereditary leader, Geronimo was often mistaken for one by outsiders because he acted as spokesman for his brother-in-law, an Apache chief named Juh (c. 1825–1883). Juh had a speech impediment, which made him unable to speak clearly.

Geronimo had a wife and three children by the 1850s, and he was also responsible for the care of his widowed mother. In the summer of 1858, his tribe traveled to Mexico to trade with the Mexicans in a town the Apaches called Kaskiyeh. They set up camp, and women and children remained behind while the men went to town to trade. When the men returned to camp on the third day, they found most of their women and children murdered. Mexican soldiers from a neighboring town had attacked the camp, and

and dragged the chief to his front porch. Word of the arrest had already spread, and Sitting Bull's followers were waiting for him outside to lend their support.

A gunfight broke out, and in the chaos, Sitting Bull was shot and killed by a Lakota policeman. Catherine Weldon, a missionary and teacher who lived among the Lakota, described the chief in these words, as reported by Sally Roesch Wagner in her article "Sitting Bull: In Memory": "As a friend . . . sincere and true, as a patriot devoted and incorruptible. As a husband and father, affectionate and considerate. As a host, courteous and hospitable to the last degree." Weldon believed Sitting Bull was murdered so that he could not ever tell of secrets he knew that would disgrace the U.S. government.

Geronimo's wife, children, and mother were among the massacred. The loss of his family sent the warrior in search of vengeance, and he led his tribe in raids on Mexican towns and villages. He attacked people in New Mexico and Arizona along the way.

Geronimo was a role model for other Apaches, who saw in him the values they held most dear. He was aggressive and courageous in battle, and his vow of vengeance was considered an honorable way to live. Many Apaches believed Geronimo had powers, which began to come to him in visions shortly after that fateful day in 1858. Legend claims he could walk without leaving footprints. His powers earned him the highly respected title of medicine man.

As the U.S. government began forcing Native Americans from their lands and onto reservations (assigned lots of land), Geronimo and his Apaches fought fiercely. Although many people credited him with being the last Native American to surrender to the United States, in fact he surrendered more than once. The first time came in 1884, and his tribe members were taken to the San Carlos Indian Reservation. He and 144 Apaches escaped the following year, but surrendered ten months later when they were found in Mexico. As they were being brought back across the border, Geronimo and a small group of his men escaped. Although the United States had fifty-five hundred soldiers searching for the escapees, it took them five months and more than 1,600 miles (2,574.4 kilometers) to find them.

Geronimo's final surrender took place near Douglas, Arizona, in September 1886. The U.S. government sent the warrior, along with 450 Apache men, women, and children, by train to Florida, where they lived for a year at Fort Pickens and Fort Marion. In 1888, they were moved to Mount Vernon, Alabama, where they stayed until 1894, when they were sent to Fort Sill, Oklahoma. Throughout all these years, the Apaches were technically considered prisoners of war.

Geronimo died at Fort Sill in 1909. He was eighty-five years old. Despite having requested to be allowed to die in his native land of Arizona, he was never set free.

Wagner also claims that the government and military both were guilty of changing census records to reduce the number of Native Americans required to sign agreements to sell their land (as required by the Treaty of 1868). In addition, she declares that officials used illegal means to gather signatures to reach the required numbers.

Weldon and Wagner voiced opinions that reflected those of others. According to Wagner's article, the *New York World* newspaper reported on December 21, 1890, that "The lying, thieving Indian agents wanted silence touching past thefts and immunity to continue their thieving." The editor of that paper supported his reporter's claims and said a military official's report of Sitting Bull's death gave evidence of the claims. "As it stands now it was organized butchery, and one of the most

American showman Buffalo Bill Cody (right) and Sioux leader Sitting Bull stand together during "Buffalo Bill's Wild West Show" in the early 1890s. © HULTON ARCHIVE/GETTY IMAGES.

shameful incidents in our 'century of dishonor' toward the Indians," wrote the editor.

An investigation into the murder was never made, and the assassination charges have never been found to be untrue. Wagner's article includes a quote from General Leonard Colby, head of the Nebraska National Guard. Colby claimed there was an "understanding between the officers of the Indian and military departments that it would be impossible to bring Sitting Bull to Standing Rock alive, and even if successfully captured, it would be difficult to tell what to do with him." Colby further reports that there was an arrangement between the commanding officers and the Indian police that the death of Sitting Bull would be preferable to his capture, and that "the slightest attempt to rescue him should be the signal for his destruction."

Sitting Bull was buried without ceremony. It was not until 1953 that his remains were moved to Mobridge, South Dakota, where his grave was marked with granite.

For More Information

BOOKS

Blaisdell, Bob, ed. *Great Speeches by Native Americans.* Mineola, NY: Dover Publications, 2000.

Geronimo. *Geronimo: His Own Story.* Edited by S. M. Barrett. New York: Dutton, 1970. Reprint, New York: Meridian, 1996.

Marker, Sherry. *Plains Indian Wars (America at War).* New York: Facts on File, 2003.

Roop, Connie, and Peter Roop. *Sitting Bull.* Scholastic Paperbacks, 2002.

Utley, Robert. *The Lance and the Shield: The Life and Times of Sitting Bull.* New York: Henry Holt, 1993.

WEB SITES

"Chief Sitting Bull." *History Channel.* http://www.historychannel.com/exhibits/sioux/sittingbull.html (accessed on September 4, 2006).

"Geronimo." *Arizona State Museum.* http://www.statemuseum.arizona.edu/artifact/geronimo.shtml (accessed on September 4, 2006).

"Geronimo." *Indians.org.* http://www.indians.org/welker/geronimo.htm (accessed on September 4, 2006).

"History of Sitting Bull." *Canada's Digital Collections.* http://collections.ic.gc.ca/beaupre/promme92.htm (accessed on September 4, 2006).

McLaughlin, James. "An Account of Sitting Bull's Death." *PBS: Archives of the West.* http://www.pbs.org/weta/thewest/resources/archives/eight/sbarrest.htm (accessed on September 4, 2006).

PBS. "Sitting Bull." *New Perspectives on the West.* http://www.pbs.org/weta/thewest/people/s_z/sittingbull.htm (accessed on September 4, 2006).

Wagner, Sally Roesch. "Sitting Bull: In Memory." *First Nations: Issues of Consequence.* http://www.dickshovel.com/sittingbull.html (accessed on September 4, 2006).

Hannah Solomon

BORN: January 14, 1858 • Chicago, Illinois
DIED: December 7, 1942 • Chicago, Illinois

Social pioneer

"In a democracy, all are responsible."

H annah Solomon is best remembered as the founder of the National Council for Jewish Women (NCJW), a volunteer organization that sought to improve the lives of women and children throughout the United States. Solomon spent her entire life in Chicago, Illinois, where her tireless efforts in social welfare brought her into contact with leading social activists of her day, including **Jane Addams** (1860–1935; see entry) and Susan B. Anthony (1820–1906). She formed lasting friendships with both women. The social activist was a writer as well and published a volume of essays and speeches in 1911. Her autobiography, *The Fabric of My Life,* was published in 1946, four years after her death.

Activism in her blood

Hannah Greenebaum Solomon was the fourth of ten children born to German immigrants Sarah and Michael Greenebaum. She was born on January 14, 1858, into a close-knit Jewish community in Chicago. Within that community, Solomon's parents were active in civic and social organizations. In 1883, Sarah founded the city's first Jewish Ladies

Hannah Solomon.

193

Sewing Society, a club whose members made clothing for the needy. In 1907, a sister branch of that club was established and named after Sarah. Michael was a volunteer firefighter and helped establish the Zion Literary Society, a book discussion group for youth, in 1877.

Solomon's extended family—aunts, uncles, cousins, grandparents—had also immigrated to Chicago and were equally active in civic and social activities. Having grown up in a household that frequently included these family members as well as friends and activists, Solomon was instilled with a sense of duty as well as a great love of family. As stated in her autobiography, "Even in our formative years, we children of Sarah and Michael Greenebaum were unconsciously affected by their spirit of joyous citizenship in a beloved country whose reverse side, our parents never forgot, imposed civic obligation." Her achievements in later years would surprise no one who knew her.

Another important aspect of Solomon's family life was religion. The Greenebaums kept a kosher home (a household adhering to strict guidelines for food preparation and rituals) and honored traditional Jewish rituals and ceremonies. Yet Michael Greenebaum helped establish Chicago's first Reform synagogue (Jewish temple). Reform Judaism broke away from the Orthodox (strict, traditional) practice of the Jewish religion and incorporated a more modern interpretation of both Jewish religious texts and practices. In the twenty-first century, Reform Judaism is the largest Jewish denomination in America.

Begins a life of activism

Solomon's father was a prosperous hardware merchant in the city. His success allowed him to send his children to the best schools in the area. Solomon attended a religious school, where she was taught both Hebrew and German. From there, she attended and graduated from public high school. In 1876, Solomon and her older sister were invited to join the elite (upper-class) and newly formed Chicago Woman's Club (CWC). They became the organization's first Jewish members. The CWC had been established by women who wanted to become involved in civic work on an organized basis without having to gain approval from men's civic organizations.

In her work on the subject of civic women in Chicago, author Maureen Flanagan explained how male and female reformers of the Gilded Age and the Progressive Era went about their work differently. (The Gilded Age was the period in history following the Civil War and Reconstruction [roughly the final twenty-three years of the nineteenth century], characterized by a ruthless pursuit of profit, an exterior of showiness and grandeur, and immeasurable political corruption. The Progressive Era was the period that followed the Gilded Age [approximately the first twenty years of the twentieth century]; it was marked by reform and the development of a national cultural identity.) Men's charity efforts were more concerned with who was the most deserving among the poor. Each men's organization had a basic set of guidelines to follow when determining how money and relief efforts would be spent. Women reformers were traditionally less concerned with who was considered worthy of assistance; they saw need and were less likely to compare the degree of neediness. Without their own civic clubs and associations, women could not help out in the ways they believed were most beneficial to the greatest number of people.

The CWC operated with a strong sense that education was the key to success and prosperity. Many of its philanthropic (charitable) efforts focused on this idea. Among its first causes was the improvement of public schools and work conditions for female teachers. In order to be a member, a woman had to complete a course of study that was as rigorous and demanding as many college courses. Solomon, the club's youngest member, wrote several academic papers as part of her course. One of them, titled "Our Debt to Judaism," was the first religious paper ever presented to the CWC.

Whereas the earlier efforts of the CWC focused on social improvement and education, the focus by the end of the club's first decade had switched to reforms at the state level. The CWC was the driving force behind a movement to improve state facilities for orphans and female prisoners. The women of the CWC also successfully pushed for the passage of laws to restrict child labor and to enforce mandatory education for children (the idea that children had to go to school instead of work). In 1899, Illinois was the first state to create a juvenile court system. Members of the CWC were among the most active and vocal advocates of such a system.

Family and activism: her greatest loves

Solomon married businessman Henry Solomon in May 1879 when she was twenty-one years old. She devoted those early years of her marriage to raising her young family, which would eventually include three children: Herbert, Helen, and Frank. She gave up all outside activities willingly, as her love of family and her desire to be a supportive wife and mother consumed all her energy.

In 1890, Chicago was chosen as the site for the World's Columbian Exposition, a cultural event that would celebrate the discovery of America by Christopher Columbus (1451–1506) and the country's progress since that time. America wanted the fair to prove to the world that as a nation, it had become an advanced, enlightened society. By 1891, the fair's Board of Lady Managers decided to organize events for women of all religions. Hannah Greenebaum Solomon was the obvious choice to lead the Jewish population. Even though her civic activism had taken a backseat to raising her family, she maintained her social connections with people who had the money and power to make important decisions.

The next two years were spent planning and organizing. Solomon wanted to establish a women's congress (a gathering of people, usually for a political purpose) to represent Jewish women across the nation. In an initial effort to get the group established, Solomon handwrote more than ninety letters seeking participants and assistance. By the time the National Council of Jewish Women (NCJW) was founded in 1893, more than two thousand letters had been exchanged between Solomon and others.

The National Council of Jewish Women is formed

Jewish men were preparing their own congress, the Jewish Denominational Congress, and they approached Solomon to join them. Despite asking, the men expected the women to do nothing more than support the men's efforts by showing up. Solomon explained that the women desired their own representation and would join the men if they could guarantee active participation. Her request was denied.

The Columbian Exposition opened in 1893. The Jewish Women's Congress was a four-day event, held that year from September 4 through 7. Speakers from across the country came to lecture on subjects such as religion, philanthropy, and Jewish history. The event was so popular that each day, all the seats were filled and women stood in the hallways for hours, just to hear the speakers. By the end of the fourth day, the enthusiastic crowd voted to form the National Council of Jewish Women. The organization's goals were to fulfill its commitment to Judaism through social reform, education, and activities against anti-Semitism (hatred of the Jews). Solomon was unanimously elected president of the NCJW.

The enthusiasm of NCJW members did not diminish after the close of the Congress. By the time of the council's first triennial (every three years) convention in 1896, the organization boasted more than three thousand members across the country. Reforms were already in place; the council was proving itself to be an effective, dedicated group of women. Already in the first three years of the NCJW's existence, the organization worked closely and tirelessly in the settlement house movement, which provided much-needed social services to the urban poor. Together, they designed programs to train girls and women so that they would have the skills needed to get steady jobs. They also developed free health clinics and programs that went door-to-door to help those who needed it most. The NCJW advocated for children in court during an era when children had few rights. In a very short period of time, these women had made their mark on society, and they had only just begun.

As often happens when an organization is still in its early stages of growth and development, the NCJW began to question its identity. Would it be primarily a religious organization, or a philanthropic organization? Solomon's belief was that philanthropy was a way to uphold a Jew's commitment to her religion; charity was an expression of faith. She encouraged members to make their Judaism the defining element of the council.

By the end of the nineteenth century, Jewish men relied on their women to take over the responsibility of religious observance. It was up to the women to keep homes kosher, to see that the children obtained religious instruction and faith, and to prepare for religious holidays and rituals. The council took their obligations seriously and focused their efforts on fighting the assimilation (absorption of one culture into another) of Jews into American society. They did this through study circles, which was basically the religious education of Jewish women. This was a radical (extreme) idea at the time, as only men had religious authority in the synagogues.

The council's argument was hard to combat, though. How could women be expected to uphold the religious responsibility of her family if she did not know what that responsibility was? Solomon had the idea of inviting rabbis (Jewish religious leaders) to speak at and lead the study circles. This idea was in keeping with the traditional belief that the true power of Jewish women lay not in their authority but in their ability to influence others.

Controversy amidst the council

Part of Reform Judaism involved the moving of the Sabbath (Holy Day) from Saturday to Sunday. Solomon supported this shift because she believed American Jews could more fully observe the Sabbath if it were held on the same day as the Christian Sabbath. It was, in a sense, assimilation, and this point did not escape the more conservative Orthodox Jews in the council. To them, the movement of the Sabbath was the first step toward converting to Christianity.

Much of that first triennial convention was spent debating this all-important issue. Those who were against it were intensely outspoken about their beliefs. So firm were they on their stance that they tried to block Solomon's reelection to the presidency of the council. When attacked as a blasphemer (one who speaks disrespectfully of sacred things) and one who does not consecrate (observe) the Sabbath, Solomon's famous response, as reported on the Jewish Women's Archive Web site, was, "I do consecrate the Sabbath. I consecrate every day of the week!" Solomon won the reelection, but her presidency continued to be plagued with problems rising from the Sabbath issue. In an effort to avoid the conflict, the organization agreed to refrain from discussing religious principles and dedicated its efforts solely to philanthropy. Solomon resigned from her position in 1905 and was given an honorary presidency for life. Meanwhile, her eldest son, Herbert, had died suddenly in 1899. His death would have a major impact on both her physical and her mental health.

Beyond the council

Although her work with the NCJW took much of her time, it was not Solomon's only civic activity. In 1897, she founded the Bureau of Personal Service, an organization that gave much-needed assistance to the Russian Jewish immigrants who flooded Chicago in the 1890s. With financial assistance from the NCJW, the Bureau worked with other relief organizations to give new immigrants legal advice and guidance during those first overwhelming months in a new land. Solomon was the Bureau's head for thirteen years.

In addition to her work within the Jewish community, Solomon teamed with Susan B. Anthony (1820–1906) and led activists in the fight for women's suffrage (right to vote). Regardless of Solomon's firm belief in suffrage, she was never able to convince the NCJW of the value of having a political voice. Its members believed women did not need the power of the vote to make a positive change in society.

Solomon herself identified her role as president of the Illinois Industrial School for Girls as the one that affected her most. The school was for girls who were wards of the state (those who had been orphaned or abused). The facility had fallen into serious disrepair because of a lack of money, but by the end of her first year as its president in 1907, the school's debt had been paid. Solomon improved school policies and procedures, which in turn improved the care the girls received.

Solomon worked with city officials to improve Chicago's sanitation system, and she is credited with establishing a penny lunch program for the city's poor children within the public school system.

A lasting legacy

In 1910, Solomon helped establish the Chicago Women's City Club, an organization whose members worked to improve and increase social offerings in Chicago. One of its first major efforts was the Public Beach Campaign. Members researched various locations throughout Chicago and worked with various commissions to clean up the sites so they could be turned into public swimming beaches. The following year, the reformer published *A Sheaf of Leaves,* a collection of essays and speeches.

The second decade of the twentieth century was not entirely kind to Solomon. Her husband and most devoted supporter died in 1913. Yet she turned her grief into constructive effort. During World War I (1914–18), she worked with people of more than forty various nationalities living within the city to coordinate war efforts to support troops overseas.

Solomon's reform activities—and those of many other women (see box)—made life in Chicago during the Gilded Age and the Progressive Era easier for its residents. She was a prime example of the ideal Jewish woman: strong, tireless, and compassionate, able to use her influence to better her community and the city in which its members lived. The NCJW in the twenty-first century has branched out to become a global organization, with members around the world who work together to improve the quality of life in both America and Israel. The organization joins with human rights groups, reproductive rights groups, and child

Rebel Women of Chicago

During the Gilded Age and the Progressive Era, Chicago was an active city, filled with women who chose to dedicate their lives to the betterment of all. Chicago has a rich history of women activists, each of whom impacted her society in a unique way. Here is a very brief list of some of the Windy City's lesser-known female movers and shakers.

Alice Hamilton (1869–1970): Resident of Jane Addams's Hull-House settlement; developed the field of industrial medicine and was the first woman appointed to the Harvard Medical School faculty.

Katherine Dunham (1909–2006): Dancer and choreographer who established the Chicago Negro School of Ballet.

Marion Lucy Mahoney Griffin (1871–1961): First woman to earn her architect's license in the state of Illinois and second woman to graduate from the prestigious Massachusetts Institute of Technology. Designed the Woman's Building for the 1893 Columbian Exposition.

Bessie Abramowitz Hillman (1889–1970): One of several leaders of the 1910 garment workers' strike in Chicago; founding member of the Amalgamated Clothing Workers of America labor union.

Ella Flagg Young (1845–1918): First woman superintendent of the Chicago public school system (1901–15).

Ida Platt (1863–c. 1940): First African American female lawyer admitted to the Illinois bar in 1894; she would be the only African American female attorney in the state until 1920. She was also the second African American woman allowed to practice law in the United States.

welfare groups to enact legislation that protects men, women, and children from all walks of life.

For More Information

BOOKS

Diner, Hasia R., and Beryl Lieff Benderly. *Her Works Praise Her: A History of Jewish Women in America from Colonial Times to the Present.* New York: Basic Books, 2002.

Felder, Deborah G., and Diana Rosen. *Fifty Jewish Women Who Changed the World.* New York: Citadel Press, 2003.

Flanagan, Maureen A. *Seeing With Their Hearts: Chicago Women and the Vision of the Good City, 1871–1933.* Princeton, NJ: Princeton University Press, 2002.

Slater, Elinor, and Robert Slater. *Great Jewish Women.* Middle Village, NY: Jonathan David Publishers, 1994.

Solomon, Hannah G. *The Fabric of My Life: The Autobiography of Hannah G. Solomon.* New York: Bloch Publishing Co., 1946.

WEB SITES

"Chicago Women's History." *Chicago Public Library.* http://www.chipublib.org/003cpl/chgowomen.html (accessed on September 5, 2006).

"Clubs, Women's." *Encyclopedia of Chicago.* http://www.encyclopedia.chicagohistory.org/pages/306.html (accessed on September 5, 2006).

"Hannah Greenebaum Solomon." *National Women's Hall of Fame.* http://www.greatwomen.org/women.php?action=viewone&id=148 (accessed on September 5, 2006).

Library of Congress. "American Jewish Women." *American Memory: American Women.* http://memory.loc.gov/ammem/awhhtml/awas12/jewish.html (accessed on September 5, 2006).

PBS. "The Golden Land, 1654–1930s; Jewish Cultural Life in Chicago." *Heritage: Civilization and the Jews.* http://www.pbs.org/wnet/heritage/episode7/documents/documents_8.html (accessed on September 5, 2006).

"Women of Valor: Hannah Greenebaum Solomon." *Jewish Women's Archive.* http://www.jwa.org/exhibits/wov/solomon/ (accessed on September 5, 2006).

Elizabeth Cady Stanton

BORN: November 12, 1815 • Johnstown, New York
DIED: October 26, 1902 • New York, New York

Women's rights activist

"The voice of woman has been silenced in the state, the church, and the home, but man cannot fulfill his destiny alone, he cannot redeem his race unaided."

Elizabeth Cady Stanton was one of the most prominent women's rights activists of the nineteenth century. Suffrage (the right to vote) was the cause most dear to Stanton's heart. She dedicated her life to ensuring that women's voices were heard. In 1851, she met another tireless activist, Susan B. Anthony (1820–1906), and together the women spearheaded the suffrage movement. Although neither would live to see women get the vote, their dedication and courage were the basis for the passage of the Nineteenth Amendment, in 1920.

Father wanted a boy

Elizabeth Cady Stanton.
THE LIBRARY OF
CONGRESS.

Elizabeth Cady Stanton was born to Margaret and Daniel Cady, well-known residents of Johnstown, New York, on November 12, 1815. Daniel was a lawyer and a judge. Stanton's parents never hid their preference for their two sons over their four daughters. According to the

National Women's Hall of Fame Web site, when Stanton's brother died, her father cried to her, "Oh my daughter, I wish you were a boy!"

Not wanting to disappoint her father, Stanton did everything in her power to make herself her brother's equal in her father's eye. She obtained a quality education and excelled in Latin, Greek, and mathematics. She learned to debate and ride horses. She took a genuine interest in learning law from her father. Stanton would be considered well educated in any era of American society, but she was especially well educated for a woman in the early nineteenth century. Most women of the time did not receive formal schooling of any kind.

Marries and becomes active in politics

Stanton's early activism in two other social movements, abolition (the antislavery movement) and temperance (a movement encouraging moderation in drinking alcohol or not drinking at all) brought her into contact with other like-minded people. She married abolitionist Henry B. Stanton (1805–1887) in 1840. Already an individual thinker at the age of twenty-five, Elizabeth had the word "obey" removed from the couple's wedding vows. The Stantons would have five sons and two daughters between 1842 and 1859.

The Stantons honeymooned at the World's Anti-Slavery Convention, which was held in London in 1840. When it became clear to Stanton that male delegates were considered more important than female delegates (only men were allowed to speak; women were not given seating, but had to stand), she decided then and there that women should hold a convention for their own rights. The idea stayed with her, even though her busy schedule prohibited her from acting on it right away. A chance meeting at the convention with Lucretia Mott (1793–1880), another key figure in the suffrage movement, laid the groundwork for an event that would not happen for another eight years.

The Stantons spent the early years of their marriage in Boston, but in 1847, they moved to Seneca Falls, New York. This move marked a turning point in Stanton's life. In Boston, she had been surrounded by domestic servants who took care of the daily chores and tasks such as laundry, cooking, and caring for the children. Stanton had no idea what life without servants was like. In Seneca Falls, however, she had no live-in help. With three young children and a large house to care for, she experienced what life was like for the average woman. According to the *Elizabeth Cady Stanton House* Web site, Stanton wrote,

"I now fully understood the practical difficulties most women had to contend with."

Living in Seneca Falls with a more normal lifestyle left Stanton isolated from other enlightened, reform-minded people. Her activism was confined largely to writing, and she published articles in newspapers and magazines. In July 1848, Stanton met with Mott and three of her friends in a nearby town called Waterloo. The women decided the time was right to hold the first women's rights convention. According to *The Seneca Falls Convention* Web site of the Smithsonian Institution, they would discuss "the social, civil, and religious condition and rights of woman."

The Seneca Falls Convention

Stanton, the obvious writer in the group, developed the Declaration of Sentiments, which outlined the purpose of the convention. In the Declaration, she put forth the idea that men and women were equal. She also listed eighteen ways in which men did not treat women as their equals. Stanton also developed eleven resolutions, one of which stated that women had the duty to secure the right to vote. When some of the more conservative women of the group protested against this particular resolution, Stanton stood her ground. She recognized that having power in making laws would grant them more power to secure other rights.

The Seneca Falls Convention took place on July 19 and 20, 1848, at the local Wesleyan Methodist Church. Little promoting of the event took place; a small ad ran in the local newspaper. The women did not expect a great turnout. July was the busy season for farmers, and Seneca Falls was a rural area.

The convention was attended by three hundred people, including forty men. Since no woman felt she was capable of leading the meeting, Mott's husband, James Mott (1788–1868), presided over the ceremonies. Ten of the eleven resolutions passed, but not the resolution on suffrage. Suffrage was still just too foreign a concept for most Americans in the mid-nineteenth century, but especially to a mostly Quaker audience. (Quakers, also known as the Religious Society of Friends, practice a religion that denounces violence of any kind, and their members rarely vote on legal matters.) One hundred men and women signed the Seneca Falls Declaration, though some later removed their names due to pressure and criticism.

Suffragists Susan B. Anthony (left) and Elizabeth Cady Stanton. © BETTMANN/ CORBIS.

The press did not cover the convention favorably but instead ridiculed its ideas and delegates openly. Stanton was frustrated by the misrepresentation of her cause, but its coverage in the press at all was a step in the right direction. As reported by the Smithsonian Institution, Stanton said, "Imagine the publicity given to our ideas by thus appearing in a widely circulated sheet like the *Herald*. It will start women thinking, and men too; and when men and women think about a new question, the first step in progress is taken."

Meets Susan B. Anthony

Because both women were dedicated activists, it was only a matter of time before Stanton met Susan B. Anthony. In 1851, that meeting took place, and the two formed an immediate partnership that would last throughout their lifetimes. Stanton was limited to how much she could travel and how many hours she could dedicate to her activism because she was raising a large family. Anthony, on the other hand, was not married, had no children, and could devote as much time as she wanted to her endeavors. As a result, Stanton was the one who came up with ideas and the words with which to convey them, and Anthony took those ideas and words to the world. In her memoir *Eighty Years and More,* Stanton wrote, "It has been said that I forged the thunderbolts and she fired them." Anthony was more visible in the public's eye, and therefore she became more famous. But in fact, the two women needed each other's strengths to make as much progress as they did.

By the time the Civil War (1861–65) ended, Stanton's children were older and she felt more comfortable traveling and being away from them if necessary. She focused her efforts on suffrage at this time because freed slaves had been given the right to vote, but women still could not. When their efforts saw no progress being made, Stanton, Anthony, Matilda Joslyn Gage (see box), and other women activists founded the National Woman Suffrage Association (NWSA) in May 1869. Stanton was the first president; Anthony was its first vice president.

A movement divided

Stanton and Anthony formed the NWSA for a price; they broke from their abolitionist supporters, who they claimed were more interested in getting rights for African Americans than they were for women. The NWSA denounced the Fifteenth Amendment, which granted suffrage for African American men, and it allowed only female members. In response, some activists from New England began a separate rights group (also in 1869), the American Woman Suffrage Association (AWSA). The AWSA was considered a more conservative group, and it focused only on getting the vote. The NWSA, on the other hand, included in its mission other issues that affected women, such as employer discrimination and divorce law.

By the 1880s, Stanton had grown weary of traveling. She changed her focus to writing, and along with Anthony and Gage produced *The History of Woman Suffrage,* a three-volume set that details and documents the activism of the women's suffrage movement.

When it became evident that the suffrage movement was failing because it was divided from the inside, Stanton and Anthony made the controversial decision to merge with the AWSA. In 1890, under Stanton's leadership, the groups combined forces to become the National American Woman Suffrage Association (NAWSA). Stanton remained president until 1892, at which time Anthony took over the helm. At her announcement of her retirement, Stanton gave her famous speech, *Solitude of Self.* In it, she talked about the many reasons why women should be considered the equals of men. The speech is considered Stanton's masterpiece, and even in the twenty-first century, it is considered the most complete and articulate explanation of the ideology upon which the feminist movement was built.

Toward the end of her life, Stanton returned to exploring her interests in the relationship between organized religion and women's subordination (inferior position) to men. She wrote countless articles on the topic. In 1895 and 1898, she published two volumes of controversial biblical commentaries under the title *Woman's Bible.* In these volumes, she declared her beliefs that the Bible was partial to men and that women who held fast to traditional Christianity obstructed their own abilities to become independent. For her views, Stanton was criticized mightily in the press and from the pulpit. Many fellow women's rights activists turned their back on Stanton at that point for fear that her radicalism would harm their movement. Anthony was not one of them.

Matilda Joslyn Gage: Forgotten Women's Rights Activist

Matilda Joslyn Gage. THE LIBRARY OF CONGRESS.

Although never as famous as Stanton or Anthony, Matilda Joslyn Gage (1826–1898) was an abolitionist who entered the women's rights movement in 1852. She worked closely with Anthony and Stanton in the National Woman Suffrage Association (NWSA), and the leadership roles of these three women often overlapped.

Gage helped organize the Virginia and New York state suffrage associations and was an officer in her home-state New York branch for twenty years. The NWSA's official newspaper, *National Citizen and Ballot Box,* was published from her New York home from 1878 to 1881.

In 1880, the New York Woman Suffrage Association gained the right for the women of the state of New York to run for office in school elections and to vote in them as well. Gage organized meetings in her Fayetteville home to help women of the town get comfortable with

Stanton died of heart failure on October 26, 1902, in the New York City apartment she shared with two of her grown children. As reported on the PBS Web site *Not for Ourselves Alone,* her dear friend Anthony told a reporter, "I am too crushed to speak."

The Nineteenth Amendment to the U.S. Constitution granted women the right to vote. The amendment became law on August 26, 1920. On November 2, 1920, more than eight million American women exercised their newly acquired right to vote. It had taken them 144 years to achieve full citizenship. Stanton was inducted into the National Women's Hall of Fame in 1973.

For More Information

BOOKS

Bohannon, Lisa Frederiksen. *Women's Rights and Nothing Less: The Story of Elizabeth Cady Stanton.* Greensboro, NC: Morgan Reynolds Publishing, 2000.

the voting process, and they elected an all-woman slate of officers to the school district. Gage was the first to cast her ballot.

Together, Stanton, Anthony, and Gage edited the first three volumes of the six-volume *History of Woman Suffrage (1881–1887)*. Most of the work was done in Gage's home. Anthony became such a regular figure around the Gage household that the guest room was called the Susan B. Anthony Room.

As years passed, the NWSA became more conservative, and it considered Gage's views on religion radical (extreme). Gage believed that Christianity contributed to women's oppression by men, and she publicly said so. The NWSA did not want to offend its conservative Christian members, who wanted the vote so that they could create a more Christian nation. Gage believed in the separation of church and state. In 1890, when the NWSA merged with the American Woman Suffrage Association, Gage left Stanton and Anthony to form the Woman's National Liberal Union (WNLU). The WNLU was an antichurch organization whose members included anarchists (believers in a society without government), prison reformers, labor leaders, and feminists. It was considered a radical organization. As a result of her participation in it, Gage lost her friendship with Stanton and Anthony.

Gage wrote a great deal about her causes, but left behind no diary or journal. Other than letters and some newspaper clippings, she left no written record of her personal life. The lack of information about her makes it clear why the name Matilda Joslyn Gage is not as well known as that of Elizabeth Cady Stanton or Susan B. Anthony.

Gage's other claim to fame was that she was mother-in-law to L. Frank Baum (1859–1919), author of the popular classic *The Wizard of Oz*. Gage encouraged her son-in-law to think about social reform. Their discussions contributed to Baum's literary creation of Oz, a utopian (perfect) city.

Brammer, Leila R. *Excluded from Suffrage History: Matilda Joslyn Gage, Nineteenth-Century American Feminist.* Westport, CT: Greenwood Press, 2000.

Stanton, Elizabeth Cady. *Eighty Years and More (1815–1897): Reminiscences of Elizabeth Cady Stanton.* New York: European Publishing Co., 1898. Reprint, Amherst, NY: Humanity Books, 2002.

Stanton, Elizabeth Cady. *The Woman's Bible.* New York: European Publishing Co., 1895–98. Reprint, Mineola, NY: Dover Publications, 2002.

Ward, Geoffrey C. *Not for Ourselves Alone: The Story of Elizabeth Cady Stanton and Susan B. Anthony.* New York: A. A. Knopf, 1999.

WEB SITES

"Elizabeth Cady Stanton." *National Park Service: Women's Rights National Historical Park.* http://www.nps.gov/wori/ecs.htm (accessed on September 5, 2006).

"Elizabeth Cady Stanton House." *Places Where Women Made History.* http://www.cr.nps.gov/nr/travel/pwwmh/ny10.htm (accessed on September 5, 2006).

Library of Congress. "Votes for Women: Selections from the National American Woman Suffrage Association Collection: 1848–1921." *American Memory.*

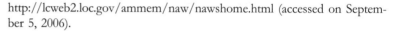

http://lcweb2.loc.gov/ammem/naw/nawshome.html (accessed on September 5, 2006).

PBS. *Not for Ourselves Alone: The Story of Elizabeth Cady Stanton and Susan B. Anthony.* http://www.pbs.org/stantonanthony/index.html (accessed on September 5, 2006).

"The Seneca Falls Convention." *Smithsonian Institution National Portrait Gallery.* http://www.npg.si.edu/col/seneca/senfalls1.htm (accessed on September 5, 2006).

Stanton, Elizabeth Cady. "Address: First Women's-Rights Convention." *Institute for the Study of Civic Values.* http://www.libertynet.org/edcivic/stanton.html (accessed on September 5, 2006).

Wagner, Sally Roesch. "Matilda Joslyn Gage: Forgotten Feminist." *New York History.* http://www.nyhistory.com/gagepage/gagebio.htm (accessed on September 5, 2006).

Wagner, Sally Roesch. "The Mother of Oz." *The Matilda Joslyn Gage Foundation.* http://www.matildajoslyngage.org/motherofoz.htm (accessed on September 5, 2006).

"Women of the Hall: Elizabeth Cady Stanton." *National Women's Hall of Fame.* http://www.greatwomen.org/women.php?action=viewone&id=149 (accessed on September 5, 2006).

Mark Twain

BORN: November 30, 1835 • Florida, Missouri
DIED: April 21, 1910 • Redding, Connecticut

Writer; humorist

Mark Twain.
© BETTMANN/CORBIS.

"Always do right. This will gratify some people and astonish the rest."

Writer Samuel Langhorne Clemens, whose pen name was Mark Twain, lived when America was changing from an agricultural nation to an industry and business giant. His musings on and insight into human nature provided readers with a glimpse into the Gilded Age—the good and the bad of it. (The Gilded Age was the period in history following the Civil War and Reconstruction [roughly the final twenty-three years of the nineteenth century], characterized by a ruthless pursuit of profit, an exterior of showiness and grandeur, and immeasurable political corruption.) Whether writing about people, politics, or current events, Twain's sharp wit and good-natured humor made his subjects interesting.

Even during his lifetime, Twain was a favorite among writers, journalists, and magazine cartoonists, who would quote him and draw his likeness at every opportunity. At a time when America was at once fearful of and hopeful about the future, Twain gave the country something to laugh about: itself. In the process, he became something of a folk hero.

Sam Clemens is born

Samuel Langhorne Clemens was born in Florida, Missouri, on November 30, 1835. He was the sixth of seven children. The Clemens family moved to Hannibal, Missouri, when Sam was just four years old. Young Clemens grew up playing along the banks of the Mississippi River. This region would be the setting for two of his most famous novels, *The Adventures of Tom Sawyer* and *The Adventures of Huckleberry Finn.*

Missouri was a new state at the time, one with a high slave population. Clemens's father owned a slave; his uncle owned a handful. Clemens spent many summers playing with children his age in the slave quarters, listening to tall tales and slave spirituals. He developed an appreciation for storytelling from his time spent with the slaves. Childhood days were also spent exploring nearby forests and swimming holes or floating down the Mississippi in makeshift rafts. It was an ideal childhood for a young, curious boy.

Clemens's father died in 1847. Eleven-year-old Clemens left school with a fifth-grade education and took a job as a printer's apprentice (student helper) at a local newspaper. His job, which required him to arrange the type for each story, allowed the boy to read news from around the world as he worked. After three years at this job, he went to work for his older brother, who owned several newspapers. Under the pseudonym (false name) S. L. C., Clemens wrote a humorous essay and published it in the *Carpet-Bag,* a Boston magazine.

Heads east

The Clemens brothers were not skilled businessmen, and soon their newspapers were in trouble financially. Clemens's brother managed to save part of his business, but the younger Clemens had had enough. He left Missouri and headed to New York City and Philadelphia when he was eighteen years old. There, he worked at various newspapers and began writing articles. Clemens traveled throughout the East and wrote about his observations in the form of tall tales and short stories for numerous newspapers, including those his brother still owned. Four years later, in 1857, he returned home and began a completely new career as a riverboat pilot on the Mississippi River. He spent the first two years as an apprentice and earned his own pilot's license in 1859.

As a riverboat pilot, Clemens came into contact with people from all backgrounds. His ability to entertain and observe simultaneously gave him endless topics for writing. During his time on the river, he sent in stories and articles to newspapers. When the Civil War (1861–65) broke out, all traffic on the Mississippi River stopped. Clemens joined a Confederate volunteer regiment called the Marion Rangers. Military life was not to his liking, however, and he quit within three weeks.

Becomes Mark Twain

Needing a way to earn a living, Clemens traveled west in July 1861 to join his brother Orion Clemens (1825–1897), who had just been appointed secretary of the Nevada Territory. Samuel Clemens had great dreams of striking it rich in Nevada's silver rush. During his stagecoach ride across the country, Clemens came across tribes of Native Americans for the first time. He also met various westerners, whose mannerisms and behavior were far different than those of the southerners he had known all his life (or the easterners he had come to know). His impressions of these people would eventually find their way into a number of his novels.

Clemens never did strike it rich, so he began writing for a Nevada newspaper called the *Territorial Enterprise.* For the first time, he wrote under the pseudonym (false name) Mark Twain, the professional name he would keep for the rest of his life. According to the PBS Web site *American Experience: Ulysses S. Grant,* it means "water that is 2 fathoms [12 feet, or 3.2 meters] deep." The Mississippi River can be dangerous for boats. The river is full of sandbars, rocks, and debris whose locations were always changing in the strong currents. Growing up along the river, and as a pilot on the river, Twain would have often heard rivermen calling out the nautical term "Mark Twain!" to let boat pilots know that the water was safe, but only just safe, for navigation.

Twain, never one to stay in one place for long, wanted a change of scenery. In 1864, he left Nevada for San Francisco, California, where he again wrote stories for local papers.

Catches his first big break

Twain published a short story titled "Jim Smiley and His Jumping Frog" in 1865. The story was an instant hit and was published in newspapers across America. Suddenly, people knew who Mark Twain was. The story was included in a collection published in 1867 under the title *The Celebrated Jumping Frog of Calaveras County; and Other Sketches.*

Twain was hired in 1866 by the *Sacramento Union* newspaper to travel to and report on the Sandwich Islands, which would eventually be known as Hawaii. Twain sent his reports home from the islands. His popularity soared so much that he began his first lecture tour upon his return to the United States. While on tour, he established himself as a fascinating stage performer.

The year 1867 found Twain in New York City. He had been hired by the *Alta California,* a San Francisco newspaper, to continue his travel writing. Twain signed up for a five-and-a-half-month-long steamship cruise. The steamer stopped at ports throughout Europe on its way to the Holy Land (Israel). Twain sent the paper letters full of descriptions and humorous observations. They proved so popular that they were compiled into his first best-selling book, *The Innocents Abroad,* in 1869.

Meets his life's love

The trip to Europe turned out to be beneficial to him in his personal life as well. On the ship, he met a man named Charles Langdon, who showed Twain a photo of his sister, Olivia. Twain fell in love with her upon sight, and the two married in 1870. After a brief stay in Buffalo, New York, the couple moved to Hartford, Connecticut, with their son in 1871. They rented a home in Nook Farm, a colony of writers and artists. The following year, Twain published a book of his frontier adventures and recollections. He called it *Roughing It.* That same year, daughter Susy was born. Langdon, Twain's only son, died at the age of 2 years of diphtheria (an infection of the throat resulting in high fever, breathing difficulty, and sometimes heart and brain damage).

One night at a dinner party at Nook Farm, Twain was complaining to his dinner guests that there was nothing of literary value available on the market. He was challenged to remedy that situation by writing something of merit. Together with friend Charles Dudley Warner (1829–1900), who also happened to be a publisher, he wrote *The Gilded Age* in 1873. The novel attacked political corruption, big business, and America's obsession with wealth. Although the novel did not sell as well as some of his others, Twain was credited with coming up with the term "Gilded Age," the name that would be given to the historic era in which he lived.

In 1874, Twain's nineteen-room mansion in Hartford was built. The author designed the house himself, and it was architecturally unlike any other house in the neighborhood. Twain had incorporated various styles

Mark Twain's house in Hartford, Connecticut. © AP IMAGES.

and elements from buildings he had visited throughout his world travels. The $40,000 home had three floors, each with its own unique decorations and style.

Twain and his family lived in their Hartford home for seventeen years. The writer spent his happiest and most productive years there, as two more daughters were born during that time and he published his most famous novels, *The Adventures of Tom Sawyer* (1876) and *The Adventures of Huckleberry Finn* (1884). Twain was hailed as the era's greatest humorist. Wherever he went, crowds gathered to hear him speak.

Twain wrote several other novels during those years, and all sold well. In 1884, Twain established the Charles L. Webster Company, his own publishing firm. He would now have control over his work and make sizeable profits. In 1885, he agreed to write the memoirs of former U.S. president Ulysses S. Grant (1822–85; served 1869–77). The two-volume set sold around three hundred thousand copies, giving Twain a profit of about $100,000. Grant's widow earned four times that much on royalties (percentage of the cost of each volume sold).

Mark Twain Said ...

"The church is always trying to get people to reform; it might not be a bad idea to reform itself a little, by way of example."

"Lie—an abomination unto the Lord and an ever present help in time of trouble."

"It is good to obey all the rules when you're young, so you'll have the strength to break them when you're old."

"It is better to take what does not belong to you than to let it lie around neglected."

"We adore titles and heredities in our hearts and ridicule them with our mouths. That is our democratic privilege."

"In fact, the more things are forbidden, the more popular they become."

"Always obey your parents, when they are present. Most parents think they know more than you do; and you can generally make more by humoring that superstition than you can by acting on your own better judgement."

Loses beloved daughter and home

Twain's writing made him a great deal of money, but the author was not as wise with investments as he was with words. After years of making poor investments, Twain was near bankruptcy (the formal declaration of being unable to repay financial debt). When his publishing company failed, Twain was forced to find some way to make money. He and his family embarked on a lecture circuit that took them traveling around the world. This type of traveling literary show was known as a Chautauqua (pronounced shuh-TAW-kwuh; see box).

In 1896, Susy Clemens was visiting the family home in Hartford. At just twenty-four, she died of meningitis (an infection of the lining of the brain) there and was found in the bathtub. Unable to return to a home that could no longer bring them happiness, the Twain family never lived in Hartford again. They sold the property in 1903.

The traveling lecture series, along with the publication of a book of essays regarding the experience, restored Twain's finances, but the writer's final years were dark. During his travels, he witnessed various wars. The Spanish-American War and Philippine War, both in 1898, especially angered Twain, who viewed the U.S. government as greedy in its expansionist policy (efforts to increase the number of America's territories). From 1901 until his death, Twain publicly declared himself an anti-imperialist (one who is against territorial expansion). He even served as vice president of the Anti-Imperialist League.

The Chautauqua Movement

Along with all the other changes and reforms going on throughout the Gilded Age and the Progressive Era were educational and religious reforms. In 1874, a Methodist minister named John H. Vincent (1832–1920) partnered with an Akron, Ohio, businessman named Lewis Miller (1829–1899). Miller, who made his fortune by inventing farm machinery, happened to be the father-in-law of inventor Thomas Edison. Vincent and Miller created a series of summer courses aimed at Sunday-school teachers. These in-depth training seminars were held at Lake Chautauqua in New York and had a summer-camp atmosphere. The event quickly became well known throughout America. Soon, subjects other than religion were added. Before the turn of the century, hotels, lecture buildings, and permanent homes were built at the lake.

Not everyone who wanted to attend could afford to travel to the summer school, so smaller assemblies similar to the one at the lake were organized in various parts of the country. Usually these assemblies were held at campgrounds near a lake or a wooded area.

The Chautauqua, as the event became known, took to the road and began traveling the nation in 1904. In addition to lectures and speakers, the event expanded to include live music, theatrical shows, and even magic shows. Many famous celebrities and reformers spoke at the Chautauqua, with Mark Twain being perhaps the most famous. Twain was a gifted storyteller who fascinated his audience for hours. Even two U.S. presidents, Ulysses S. Grant and Theodore Roosevelt, made appearances during the early years of the event.

The railroads made it possible for middle-class folks to attend a Chautauqua, even if it was not coming to their hometown. The traveling show brought New York–style culture to even the most rural corners of America. At one point in time, one in five Americans had attended a Chautauqua.

The Chautauqua, once a traveling phenomenon of culture and entertainment, lost its appeal after World War I (1914–18), when cars, radio programs, and movies gained a place in society. Yet even in the twenty-first century, Chautauqua continues to travel on a reduced scale throughout the country.

Mark Twain's writing in the later years reflected his attitude toward government and his sadness over the loss of Susy. His public appearances took on the same tone, and his antigovernment writings and speeches threatened his financial situation. Some considered him a traitor to his country. Magazines began to refuse to publish his works because of his political beliefs.

Despite the controversy, many Mark Twain fans remained devoted to the humorist. His popularity overseas rivaled that of his appeal at home; anti-imperialist or not, he was still one of America's most popular celebrities.

Mark Twain traveled a great deal on the lecture circuit; here, he takes a little rest. © CORBIS.

The final years

By 1903, the Twains had been living in New York City for three years. Twain's wife, Livy, had never enjoyed particularly robust health, and after the tragic loss of Susy, her emotional health suffered as well. In hopes a change of climate would help her, Livy's doctor suggested the couple travel to Italy. All hopes remained unfulfilled, and she died there in the spring of 1904. Twain was devastated and returned to their home in New York City. He began dictating his memoirs that year. His autobiography remained unfinished at his death, and was published ten years later.

In 1905, President **Theodore Roosevelt** (1858–1919; served 1901–9; see entry) invited Twain to the White House. That same year, Twain celebrated his seventieth birthday with 170 friends and fellow writers. The party, hosted by *Harper's Weekly* editor George Harvey (1864–1928), featured a forty-piece orchestra and fifteen formal speeches and toasts. The event was the talk of New York, and reports of it appeared in newspapers and magazines.

Twain's advancing years did little to slow him down, and he continued to immerse himself in work to keep busy. That year, he traveled the country, lecturing and performing. By this time, Twain had taken to wearing a white linen suit in public. Very few photos taken in his later years show him wearing anything else.

In 1906, Twain reluctantly agreed to let his daughter Jean be committed to an asylum. She was an epileptic (one who suffers from uncontrollable seizures caused by a brain disorder) and could no longer be cared for by loved ones. She died from a seizure in 1909. In 1908, Twain moved to what would be his final house. The estate, located in Redding, Connecticut, was named Stormfield. The following year, Twain's daughter Clara married.

Twain's health was deteriorating, and on April 21, 1910, he died of heart failure. He was seventy-four years old. His death made front-page news in newspapers across the globe. Tributes to Twain's life were published for weeks after his death, as well as examples of his humor, quotations, and other writings. As evidence of his universal appeal, many different regions claimed the great writer, raised in Hannibal, Missouri, as their own. Articles in western papers talked about his western-ness; to those in the East, he was an easterner. Twain was one of those rare writers who belonged to all of America.

Twain wrote simply about simple things, though he also had an edgy side, as demonstrated by his antigovernment slants. But he showed America its weaknesses and strengths, even as they sometimes blurred into one another. He examined not only his own life but also that of everyone else around him, whether cowboy or farmer, king or poor person, criminal or businessman. America came to depend on Twain to show them how, despite all the changes the country was going through, its people came together to form a nation. Perhaps inventor **Thomas Edison** (1847–1931; see entry) said it best. As reported on the PBS site *American Experience: Ulysses S. Grant,* Edison quipped, "An American loves his family. If he has any love left over for some other person he generally selects Mark Twain."

For More Information

BOOKS

Powers, Ron. *Mark Twain: A Life.* New York: Free Press, 2005.

Twain, Mark. *The Autobiography of Mark Twain.* New York: Sheldon & Company, 1924. Multiple reprints.

Twain, Mark. *Mark Twain's Helpful Hints for Good Living: A Handbook for the Damned Human Race.* Edited by Lin Salamo, Victor Fischer, and Michael B. Frank. Berkeley: University of California Press, 2004.

Twain, Mark. *The Wit and Wisdom of Mark Twain.* Edited by Alex Ayres. New York: Harper & Row, 1987. Reprint, New York: Perennial, 2005.

Twain, Mark, and Charles Dudley Warner. *The Gilded Age.* Hartford, CT: American Publishing, 1874. Reprint, New York: Modern Library, 2006.

Willis, Resa. *Mark and Livy: The Love Story of Mark Twain and the Woman Who Almost Tamed Him.* New York: Maxwell Macmillan International, 1992. Reprint, Routledge, 2004.

WEB SITES

The Mark Twain House and Museum. http://www.marktwainhouse.org/theman/bio.shtml (accessed on September 5, 2006).

PBS. *Mark Twain.* http://www.pbs.org/marktwain/learnmore/activities.html (accessed on September 5, 2006).

PBS. "People & Events: Samuel Langhorne Clemens, 1835–1910." *American Experience: Ulysses S. Grant.* http://www.pbs.org/wgbh/amex/grant/peopleevents/p_twain.html (accessed on September 5, 2006).

"Quotations." *Twainquotes.com.* http://www.twainquotes.com/quotesatoz.html (accessed on September 5, 2006).

Railton, Stephen. "Mark Twain in His Times." *University of Virginia Library.* http://etext.virginia.edu/railton/index2.html (accessed on September 5, 2006).

Cornelius Vanderbilt

BORN: May 27, 1794 • Staten Island, New York

DIED: January 4, 1877 • New York, New York

Entrepreneur; railroad magnate

"I have been insane on the subject of moneymaking all my life."

Although Cornelius Vanderbilt died just as the Gilded Age began, he is included in that era's history because of his phenomenal wealth. (The Gilded Age was the period in history following the Civil War and Reconstruction [roughly the final twenty-three years of the nineteenth century], characterized by a ruthless pursuit of profit, an exterior of showiness and grandeur, and immeasurable political corruption.) Considered the first robber baron (a businessman who becomes wealthy by unethical means), Vanderbilt made a large part of his fortune in the railroad industry. Vanderbilt's lifestyle is the perfect example of Gilded Age grandeur and prosperity, the levels of which had never before been realized.

Born of modest means

Cornelius Vanderbilt.
© BETTMANN/CORBIS.

Cornelius Vanderbilt, born May 27, 1794, was the fourth of nine children born to Cornelius and Phebe Vanderbilt. His father was a farmer and ferryman, and Vanderbilt worked in the ferry business from an early age. By the age of eleven, he had quit school; his formal education would go no further. When Vanderbilt failed to convince his father to expand the family business, he secured a loan from his mother to start his own ferry company. By age sixteen, he was ferrying passengers and cargo between Staten Island and Manhattan, a direct rival of his father's business.

The War of 1812 proved profitable for the young entrepreneur (self-employed business owner). The federal government contracted with Vanderbilt to transport goods and supplies to forts around New York City. He did so using sailing schooners, and it was during this time that he earned the nickname "Commodore," a name that would stay with him throughout his lifetime.

Enters the steamship industry

As the number of steamboats on New York's waters increased, Vanderbilt realized his chances for success would also increase if he switched his focus to these more advanced sailing vessels. In 1818, at the age of twenty-four, he sold his ferries and schooners and went to work for a man named Thomas Gibbons (1757–1826), who owned a small steamboat. Vanderbilt learned to operate the technologically advanced vessel. Soon, he persuaded his boss to build a steamship of Vanderbilt's design. Gibbons also recognized Vanderbilt's business aptitude and let him run the business.

Breaks up monopoly Vanderbilt used that ship, named *Bellona,* to ferry passengers between Manhattan and New Jersey. That route was already in use by steamboat inventor Robert Fulton (1765–1815) and his partner, Robert R. Livingston (1746–1813). Since 1807, the two men had been granted a monopoly (in which one company has complete control of the production and distribution of a service or product, leaving no room for competition) on that route for thirty years. Vanderbilt was in direct defiance of that monopoly, and he made the situation worse by undercutting Fulton's passage fee. Fulton charged $4; Vanderbilt charged each passenger just $1 to ride his boat. The reduced fare was less than it cost him to take the passenger, so Vanderbilt made zero profit. To make up for making no money on the fare, Vanderbilt charged more for food and drink served in the ship's bar.

Fulton and Livingston sued Vanderbilt, and the case went before the U.S. Supreme Court. Vanderbilt won the case in 1824. The monopoly was declared illegal on the grounds that it violated the commerce clause of the U.S. Constitution, which states that only the federal government can regulate interstate commerce.

With the monopoly dissolved, passengers enjoyed lower rates all around, and other steamboat operators began to run on the route between New Jersey and Manhattan. Vanderbilt was already accustomed to charging low rates, so their business did not suffer with the increase in competition. Vanderbilt invested in updating his boat with new technology, which allowed for faster travel, and soon he was making a huge profit.

Opens own steamboat business By 1829, thirty-five-year-old Vanderbilt had saved $30,000, and he used that money to start his own steamboat business. His first service operated a route between Philadelphia, Pennsylvania, and New York City. Many steamboats already operated on this route. To increase his business, Vanderbilt cut rates, which threatened the other steamship companies. Their owners mistakenly assumed he still worked for Gibbons (who had sold his business, retired, and died during the previous several years). Together, the owners collected a handsome sum to bribe Vanderbilt into leaving their waters. He did so, happily, after just one year on the route.

From there, Vanderbilt took his business to the Hudson River market, where he competed directly with the Hudson River Steamboat Association. Again, he cut fares, this time from $3 to $1 and finally, to nothing. With two boats, he made up for losses by increasing the cost of food and drink on board. The Association paid him $100,000 in advance, and an annual fee of $5,000 for ten years to leave the Hudson River. Again, Vanderbilt complied. From there, he went to the Long Island Sound market and the coastal trade. It was only a matter of time before he dominated both markets. By the 1840s, Vanderbilt had increased his fleet to include one hundred ships run by more men than any other American business. He was worth several million dollars.

Throughout his reign as steamboat king, Vanderbilt established the business sense that would make him the richest man in America. He worked hard and was so competitive that he was willing to cut prices to increase business. And wherever he set up shop, prices in the industry dropped, a bonus for customers.

Like the War of 1812 before it, the California Gold Rush of 1849—which inspired hundreds of thousands of hopeful prospectors to leave their homes from around the country—afforded Vanderbilt an opportunity to make a staggering sum of money. He did just that, by offering a shortcut via Nicaragua to California. In doing so, he cut the journey by 600 miles (965 kilometers) and two days (from thirty-five to thirty-three) and was able to charge $400 instead of the $600-per-person fare charged by those boat operators going through Panama. Vanderbilt eventually cut the rate to $150 per person and still made a profit.

Heads to the Atlantic In 1855, Vanderbilt took his business to the Atlantic Ocean region. As was his habit, he cut fares. At this time, he invested $600,000 to build the *Vanderbilt,* the largest ship ever to sail the Atlantic up to that time. It was 335 feet long and weighed 4,500 tons. Vanderbilt spared no expense and equipped his sailing vessel with the most advanced power plant, which made it the fastest boat on the water.

The Civil War (1861–65) gave Vanderbilt yet another opportunity to make money off of conflict, and he sold or leased most of his ships to the Union (North). By 1863, Vanderbilt was worth $40 million.

Turns to the rails

During the Civil War, Vanderbilt realized that the future of transportation lay not on the high seas but on land. Already in 1857, he had become director of the New York & Harlem Railroad (NY&H). His interest in the steamboat industry had kept him from actively participating in the running of the railroad. In 1862, he began investing in a rival of his railroad, the Hudson River Railroad (HRRR). By 1863, he owned a healthy portion of stock in the HRRR, but his primary interest was still with the NY&H. His interest switched focus that summer, however, when a group of stock traders began selling the HRRR short. (This is a method by which a profit can be made from stock that is declining in value.) Vanderbilt devised a scheme in which he convinced these unethical traders that the supporters of the railroad were low on cash. Supporters sold their stocks to these traders for cash and the option to buy back their stock at a slightly higher price within thirty days. But instead of holding onto the stock, the traders immediately sold it. Little did they know that the very men who sold them that stock bought it back, along with all the other shares on the market. By July, the stocks in the HRRR were cornered and the traders lost large sums of money.

Vanderbilt and his followers took control of the HRRR's board of directors in 1864, and the scheming millionaire became its president the following year. He added one more line to his fold in 1867, when he became president of the New York Central (NYC), one of the largest railroads in operation.

Vanderbilt merged the NYC and the HRRR and doubled the worth of the combined lines to around $90 million by 1869. Without remorse, he watered stock (issued stock in the railroads at a price greater than its actual value) and set the amount according to what he anticipated the railroads would make. He gave himself a $20-million bonus in stock and another $6 million in cash.

Fights the Erie

In 1868, Vanderbilt decided he needed to buy the New York & Erie Railroad (Erie) to put an end to competition for New York City freight. Around that same time, he came to the conclusion that to remain competitive with the other major lines (Pennsylvania and the B&O), he needed to extend his route into Chicago.

The Erie Railroad was owned by Daniel Drew (1797–1879), James Fisk (1834–1872), and **Jay Gould** (1836–1892; see entry), men who, like Vanderbilt, employed unethical tactics to make millions. Vanderbilt tried to undercut the Erie by lowering shipping rates, but his ploy backfired this time. When he lowered the cattle fare to $1 a head, Fisk took advantage of the low rate and bought cattle in Buffalo, New York, which he then shipped home using Vanderbilt's NYC line. Fisk made a hefty profit on the beef when he sold it. Vanderbilt lost money because he had to ship so many head of cattle at a discounted rate that he had little room to ship anything else.

The Erie War, as it came to be known, lasted from 1867 to 1868. Between 1864 and 1872, Gould saturated the market with watered stock. Vanderbilt took advantage of the falsely (but unbeknownst to him) inflated value and bought more and more shares of stock in his competitor's railroad. The more he bought, the more stock Gould issued. Vanderbilt was incredibly wealthy, but even his fortune was not enough to buy out the competition. He took a loss of $1.5 million and admitted defeat. Gould, Fisk, and Drew were left with a railroad company that was nearly bankrupt (unable to pay its debts).

To his good fortune, Vanderbilt had more luck securing railroads that traveled all the way to Chicago. He bought the Lake Shore & Michigan Southern as well as the Northern Indiana railroads. By 1873,

Political cartoon shows railroad tycoons Cornelius Vanderbilt (left), straddling the Hudson River Railroad and New York Central Railroad, and James Fisk, riding the Erie Railroad, fighting it out in the Erie War. © BETTMANN/CORBIS.

Vanderbilt had control of a consolidated system running from New York City to Chicago.

Vanderbilt did not rely solely on acquisition to build his railroad fortune. In the final years of his life, he improved his railroads and expanded them. Despite being publicly scolded for it by fellow railroad tycoons and others who believed it was impractical and foolish, Vanderbilt quadrupled the track for the NYC line from Albany to Buffalo. Two tracks were for passenger trains, the other two for freight. This expansion greatly improved the productivity of the NYC and made Vanderbilt's profits skyrocket.

Dies richest man in America

Unlike some of the other robber barons of the Gilded Age such as Andrew Carnegie (1835–1913) and John D. Rockefeller (1839–1937), Vanderbilt was not generous with his money. He did not engage in

A Prominent Family

A 1996 photo of the Breakers, the Newport, Rhode Island, mansion of Cornelius Vanderbilt II. © KEVIN FLEMING/CORBIS.

In 1813, Cornelius Vanderbilt married his cousin, Sophia Johnson. The couple had thirteen children, one of whom died in infancy. It was the beginning of a family that would produce some famous Americans of the Gilded Age and beyond:

William Henry Vanderbilt (1821–1885): Son of Cornelius. Took over the railroad empire his father established; donated money to establish the New York Metropolitan Opera and the Young Men's Christian Association (YMCA).

Cornelius Vanderbilt II (1843–1899): Favorite grandson of Cornelius. Built one of the most famous Vanderbilt mansions, the seventy-room Newport, Rhode Island, summer home called the Breakers.

Gloria Vanderbilt (1924–): Daughter of Cornelius's youngest son. Began a career as an artist whose work was featured on Hallmark greeting cards; well known for her designer blue jeans.

Anderson Cooper (1967–): Son of Gloria Vanderbilt. As of 2006, was a television journalist employed by CNN Network.

philanthropy (donations of wealth) with any sort of regularity. However, when he was seventy-nine, the millionaire donated $1 million to build Vanderbilt University in Nashville, Tennessee. It was his one major philanthropic act. As of 2006, the university was a private research facility that employed more than two thousand full-time faculty. It was the largest private employer in the state.

Vanderbilt died at the age of eighty-three in New York. His estate was worth approximately $100 million, the bulk of which he left to his eldest son, William Henry. Although the son would live only eight more years after his father's death, his ruthless business tactics allowed him to double his worth, and he, like his father, died the richest man in the country.

Lives of splendor and extravagance

Vanderbilt lived his life in a modestly built New York home, where he and his wife Sophia raised twelve children. His children preferred to live lifestyles only the amazingly wealthy could afford. Throughout the twentieth century, the various members of the family would build ten remarkable mansions, many on New York's Fifth Avenue. One son, Frederick William Vanderbilt (1856–1938), had a fifty-room mansion built there in 1898. This mansion stands as a national historic site in the twenty-first century.

For More Information

BOOKS

Cashman, Sean Dennis. *America in the Gilded Age.* 3rd ed. New York: New York University Press, 1993.

Patterson, Jerry E. *The Vanderbilts.* New York: Harry N. Abrams, 1989.

Stasz, Clarice. *The Vanderbilt Women: Dynasty of Wealth, Glamour and Tragedy.* New York: St. Martin's Press, 1991.

Vanderbilt, Arthur T. II. *Fortune's Children: The Fall of the House of Vanderbilt.* New York: Morrow, 1989.

WEB SITES

"Cornelius Vanderbilt." *U-S-History.com.* http://www.u-s-history.com/pages/h845.html (accessed on September 5, 2006).

"The History of Vanderbilt University." *Vanderbilt University.* http://www.vanderbilt.edu/history.html (accessed on September 5, 2006).

"The House of Vanderbilt." *National Park Service: Vanderbilt Mansion National Historic Site.* http://www.nps.gov/vama/house_of.html (accessed on September 5, 2006).

Poole, Keith T. "Cornelius Vanderbilt." *Voteview.com.* http://voteview.com/vanderb2.htm (accessed on September 5, 2006).

Booker T. Washington

BORN: April 5, 1856 • Franklin County, Virginia
DIED: November 14, 1915 • Tuskegee, Alabama

Educator; writer

"I have learned that success is to be measured not so much by the position that one has reached in life as by the obstacles he has had to overcome while trying to succeed."

Booker T. Washington was one of the most influential African American educators in American history. Born a slave, he sought a formal education and eventually became the first president of the Tuskegee Normal and Industrial Institute, a college for African Americans, established in 1881. Washington's famous autobiography, *Up from Slavery* (1901), continues to be widely read in the twenty-first century.

Born into slavery

Booker Taliaferro Washington was born into slavery on April 5, 1856, in Virginia. At the age of nine, he and his family were emancipated (freed) and moved to West Virginia. There, he learned to read and write when he was not working in the salt furnaces (locations set up to extract salt from springs and reservoirs of trapped sea water) and coal mines of the region.

Booker T. Washington.
© CORBIS.

At sixteen, Washington entered Hampton Institute, a secondary school operated by Samuel C. Armstrong (1839–1883), former brigadier general in the American Civil War (1861–65). The purpose of the school was to train students, most of them Native American, mulatto (mixed race of African American and white), and African American, to be teachers. Armstrong strongly believed every student should learn a trade as well, so in addition, students were taught the skills of a specific trade. Washington's training was in janitorial work. He was one of the students who worked on the school grounds to pay for his education.

After graduation, Washington taught school in Tinkersville, West Virginia, for three years. He briefly attended a seminary (a school for training ministers), but left when Armstrong asked him to return to Hampton as a teacher in 1879. Washington kept that position until 1881, when Armstrong recommended him as the principal of a new school in Alabama.

Founds Tuskegee Institute

Lewis Adams was a former slave and the driving force behind the founding of the Tuskegee Normal and Industrial Institute. Here, *normal* refers to a standard for teaching that would create a model for other such schools. Tuskegee would train educators and students interested in learning occupational skills, such as carpentry, farming, and machine operation. Adams insisted on having an African American principal, and he hired Washington after a brief interview. Washington remained president of the school until his death in 1915.

The first day of class was on July 4, 1881. Although the state had donated $2,000 for teachers' salaries, it had provided no funding for land, buildings, or equipment. The first classes, which were attended by thirty students, were held in an old church building. Adams donated a horse, a lumber wagon, plow, harness, and feed. Washington capitalized on his fund-raising abilities and ties with other professionals and managed to purchase 100 acres (0.4 square kilometers) of farmland that had once been a thriving plantation (large farm, usually with a focus on growing one particular crop) in 1882.

As president, Washington had three goals for his school. He wanted to share with poor rural farmers new and improved methods of farming the land. To do this, he developed an extension program that traveled the countryside. This program trained people who were interested in learning but could not attend formal classes. Eventually, Tuskegee graduates built smaller schools throughout the rural South.

An early view of Tuskegee Institute, shortly after it opened in 1881. © BETTMANN/CORBIS.

Washington also wanted to teach his students craft and occupational skills so they could find work once they graduated. At Tuskegee, students learned about industry and production as well as agriculture. Part of the students' education involved having them build the school's buildings themselves and farm the land on which the buildings sat. In doing so, they developed necessary working skills and nourished themselves with the food that they produced.

Washington's final objective was to develop his students' moral character. He insisted on good manners and a strong work ethic. He encouraged Tuskegee students to take pride in every detail of their lives. Although both men and women attended the school, their studies were kept separate. All students attended daily nondenominational (not associated with a specific religious faith) church services.

The Institute was a great success for two reasons: fund-raising and quality of education. Washington toured the country, telling everyone who would listen about his school. His enthusiasm and commitment to excellence impressed some of the country's wealthiest men. He secured funding from steel-magnate Andrew Carnegie (1835–1919) and industrialist John D. Rockefeller (1839–1937). Students learned from the finest African American professionals in the country. Famed chemist George Washington Carver (1864–1943) taught at Tuskegee Institute. He came up with three hundred uses for peanuts and either invented or improved upon recipes for mayonnaise, ink, bleach, metal polish, and scores of other products. Architect Robert Taylor (1868–1942) and landscape architect David Williston (1868–1962) held positions at the school. Both men were among the first African Americans to graduate in their fields of study. Williston became one of the most highly respected landscape architects in American history.

By 1906, Tuskegee had 1,590 students, 156 faculty members, and owned 2,300 acres (9.31 square kilometers) of land. At the time of Washington's death, the school trained its 1,500 students in forty different fields of study on a campus that included 100 buildings and nearly 200 faculty members.

In the late 1930s, the military chose Tuskegee to train its African American pilots because of its commitment to excellence. Those who graduated from the program were known as the Tuskegee Airmen, and they were among the most highly decorated combat veterans of World War II (1939–45). In 1965, the Institute became a national historic landmark; in 1985, its name changed to Tuskegee University.

Family life

Around the time Washington purchased the land for Tuskegee Institute, he married his first wife, Fannie Smith. Married in the summer of 1882, the couple had a daughter the following year. Fannie died in May 1884.

Washington married his second wife, Olivia Davidson, in 1885. He met her when she came to Tuskegee to teach at his school, and he eventually made her the assistant principal. Olivia gave Washington two sons before dying in 1889.

Washington married Margaret James Murray, a Mississippi native, in 1893. The couple had no children of their own together, but in 1900, the entire Washington family moved into a spacious home called The Oaks, located on the Tuskegee Institute campus. The house doubled as an on-site training facility for students. In addition, most of the home's furniture was made by local craftsmen or students. Washington lived in the house until his death, as did his wife, who died in 1925.

An influential leader

Washington's reputation for commitment, intelligence, and level-headedness made him a frequent consultant to Republican politicians who sought advice concerning potential appointments of African Americans to political positions. He earned praise from whites of all social statuses when he publicly proclaimed that self-reliance was the key factor to improved conditions for African Americans.

The Atlanta Compromise In 1895, Washington spoke at the Cotton States and International Exposition in Atlanta, Georgia. His address, called the Atlanta Compromise, sparked great debate for its message of accommodation. African Americans were generally divided into two groups during this period in history. The accommodators believed African Americans should strive very hard to earn their equality among white society. They believed change would come only through hard work and taking advantage of every opportunity to prove themselves worthy of such equal rights. This is the stance Washington took.

The other group, led by famous abolitionist (antislavery activist) Frederick Douglass (1817–1895), believed agitation, or protest and civil disobedience, was the only way African Americans were going to attain equal rights. This side believed those rights were theirs by law, and they should not have to prove themselves worthy to anyone.

Washington's educational philosophy also caused controversy. He believed in the value of industrial education, or the development of practical skills that would help African Americans lead productive lives. In direct contrast with Washington's philosophy was one embraced by African American scholar W. E. B. Du Bois (1868–1963). Du Bois believed African Americans should obtain a more classical education that would emphasize the intellectualism of what he called the "Talented Tenth." According to Du Bois, the most talented top-tenth African American leaders would save his race. By developing this intellectually gifted minority, he thought that African Americans would find a way to overcome oppression at the hands of whites.

Du Bois also believed in political action and the fight for civil rights. At the time, Washington was the more powerful of the two men. Powerful white politicians and other leaders sought his opinion and advice on

anything pertaining to African Americans. If Washington endorsed an idea, it was embraced as well by those consulting him. If he rejected it, so did they. Du Bois was not offended by Washington's power, but he did object to what he perceived as Washington's hypocrisy (double standard): The educator denounced political activism, but he dictated political outcomes by consulting with and advising politicians.

Du Bois gave Washington the nickname "The Great Accommodator," and what began as a friendship based on mutual respect declined over the years. Du Bois's philosophy of activism became the roots of the civil rights movement that began in the 1950s and peaked in the 1960s.

Booker T. Washington listens to President Theodore Roosevelt speak in 1901 after becoming the first African American to be invited to the White House. PUBLIC DOMAIN.

Publishes *Up from Slavery* In 1900, Washington founded the National Negro Business League, an organization dedicated to promoting the development of the African American as businessman (as opposed to activist). Many of the organization's chapters were in the South, and the League was supported by wealthy white businessmen. Washington was a visionary in that he encouraged women to obtain business skills as well.

In 1901, Washington published his autobiography, *Up from Slavery*. The best-seller immediately became the most influential book written by an African American, and it earned him an invitation to the White House by President **Theodore Roosevelt** (1858–1919; served 1901–9; see entry). It was the first time an African American had been invited to the White House. White Southerners made their disapproval known in newspaper articles.

A lifetime of overwork and too little rest finally took its toll on Washington's health. He died on November 14, 1915, of hypertension (high blood pressure), and was buried on the campus of Tuskegee University. That year also marked the beginning of a shift in attitude of African Americans in general, as they moved to embrace the activist philosophy of W. E. B. Du Bois.

In 1940, Washington became the first African American to be memorialized on a postage stamp. The primitive house he was born in was designated the Booker T. Washington National Monument on April 5, 1956, and a state park in Chattanooga, Tennessee, was named in his honor.

For More Information

BOOKS

Brundage, W. Fitzhugh, ed. *Booker T. Washington and Black Progress: Up From Slavery 100 Years Later.* Gainesville: University Press of Florida, 2003.

Carroll, Rebecca, ed. *Uncle Tom or New Negro? African Americans Reflect on Booker T. Washington and "Up from Slavery" 100 Years Later.* New York: Broadway Books/Harlem Moon, 2006.

Harlan, Louis R. *Booker T. Washington in Perspective: Essays of Louis R. Harlan.* Edited by Raymond Smock. Jackson: University Press of Mississippi, 1988.

Mansfield, Stephen. *Then Darkness Fled: The Liberating Wisdom of Booker T. Washington.* Nashville: Cumberland House, 1999.

Washington, Booker T. *Up from Slavery: An Autobiography.* Garden City, NY: Doubleday & Co., 1901. Multiple reprints.

PERIODICALS

Harlan, Louis R. "Booker T. Washington's West Virginia Boyhood." *West Virginia History* (January 1971): 63–85. Also available at http://www.wvculture.org/history/journal_wvh/wvh32-1.html.

WEB SITES

"Booker T. Washington National Monument." *National Park Service.* http://www.nps.gov/bowa/ (accessed on September 5, 2006).

"Booker T. Washington." *National Park Service: Legends of Tuskegee.* http://www.cr.nps.gov/museum/exhibits/tuskegee/btwoverview.htm (accessed on September 5, 2006).

"The Booker T. Washington Papers." *History Cooperative.* http://www.historycooperative.org/btw/ (accessed on September 5, 2006).

Halsall, Paul. "Booker T. Washington (1856–1915): Speech at the Atlanta Exposition, 1895." *Internet Modern History Sourcebook.* http://www.fordham.edu/halsall/mod/1895washington-atlanta.html (accessed on September 5, 2006).

"History of Tuskegee University." *Tuskegee University.* http://www.tuskegee.edu/Global/story.asp?S=1070392 (accessed on September 5, 2006).

Hynes, Gerald C. "A Biographical Sketch of W. E. B. DuBois." *W. E. B. DuBois Learning Center.* http://www.duboislc.org/html/DuBoisBio.html (accessed on September 5, 2006).

Library of Congress. "Booker T. Washington." *The Progress of a People.* http://lcweb2.loc.gov/ammem/aap/bookert.html (accessed on September 5, 2006).

PBS. "Booker T. & W. E. B." *Frontline: The Two Nations of Black America.* http://www.pbs.org/wgbh/pages/frontline/shows/race/etc/road.html (accessed on September 5, 2006).

Ida B. Wells-Barnett

BORN: July 16, 1862 • Holly Springs, Mississippi
DIED: March 25, 1931 • Chicago, Illinois

Journalist; political activist

Ida Wells-Barnett.
GETTY IMAGES.

"Somebody must show that the Afro-American race is more sinned against than sinning, and it seems to have fallen upon me to do so."

Ida B. Wells-Barnett began life as a slave. As a young woman, she was forcefully removed from a train after refusing to give up her seat to a white man. This prompted her to begin a career in journalism that would eventually make her the most outspoken opponent of lynching (putting a person to death, without a trial and usually by hanging).

Born into slavery

Ida B. Wells was born in Holly Springs, Mississippi, on July 16, 1862, to slave parents. Six months after her birth, President Abraham Lincoln (1809–1865; served 1861–65) signed the Emancipation Proclamation, giving all slaves their freedom. Wells's father was a carpenter who was active in politics and became interested in helping educate the freed slaves, including his own seven children. Wells and her siblings received basic academic and religious training through school and church.

237

When she was just sixteen years old, Wells lost her parents and one brother in a yellow fever epidemic that swept through Holly Springs in 1878. (Yellow fever is a deadly virus transmitted by mosquitoes.) Not quite finished with her high-school education, Wells now had to find a way to care for her five younger brothers and sisters. By pinning up her hair and wearing a long dress, Wells was able to convince the superintendent of a school five miles from home that she was eighteen. She was hired as a teacher, a position that paid $25 a month. During the week, she lived near the school while her siblings stayed with various people in their hometown. On weekends, Wells would return home to care for the children and do all the tasks required for keeping a large family, such as cooking and doing laundry.

In 1882, Wells and her two sisters moved to Memphis, Tennessee, leaving behind their brothers to work as carpenter's apprentices (students). Wells found another teaching job in one of the city's all–African American schools. During the summer, she took classes at Fisk University in Nashville. She had also attended Rust University in Holly Springs for a short time, but never earned a degree from either institution.

Stands up for her rights

In 1884, Wells bought a first-class train ticket to Nashville, Tennessee. Despite having paid for a ticket that would allow her to travel in the first-class car, once onboard, Wells was instructed to move to the back of the train, where African Americans were forced to ride. She refused, and as the conductor was forcibly trying to remove her, Wells bit his hand. It took the help of a baggage handler to get Wells out of the train car and into the back. She rode to the next stop, where she left the train and headed back to Memphis.

Wells filed a lawsuit against the railroad and won a settlement of $500. In 1887, however, the Tennessee Supreme Court reversed the ruling on the grounds that she had intended only to cause difficulty for the railroad company. The final decision was a blow to Wells's belief that justice would win out. She did not let her discouragement stop her from standing up for what she believed was right. Soon the name "Iola" was appearing in African American newspapers. Iola was the name Wells used when she wrote about politics and race issues in the South. In 1887, less than one year after she began writing under an assumed name, the National Afro-American Press named her the most prominent (outstanding) correspondent for the American black press. She was also elected as the assistant secretary of the organization.

Buys a newspaper

In 1891, Wells became co-owner of an African American newspaper, the *Memphis Free Speech and Headlight*. She quickly became the newspaper's editor. Her duties included writing articles, hiring correspondents, and increasing the paper's subscription base. She continued to teach during the school year.

Wells's teaching career came to an abrupt halt when she wrote and published an article criticizing Memphis's school system. The federal law at the time made it a crime for African Americans not to have the same rights as whites, but it upheld the belief that the two races should remain segregated (separated). This concept was known as "separate-but-equal." In reality, African Americans were still not treated equally. Although they had their own restaurants and public places, such facilities were never as good as those reserved for white patrons. This separate-but-equal philosophy infiltrated the South's school systems, and it suffered from the same inequalities. Although African American children were being taught in classrooms, their teachers were paid less, their textbooks were not as good as those used in white classrooms, and their schools received only a small percentage of the funding white schools received.

The school board knew Wells had written the article, even though she did not include a byline (indication of author). Wells was relieved of her duties as teacher, and her time was now freed and completely dedicated to improving the conditions of her race.

The year 1892 was a crucial one for Wells. Three people, one a good friend of Wells, were lynched while defending their grocery store from white attackers who wanted to put the store out of business. In the scuffle, one of the owners shot one of the attackers. A gang of white men seeking vengeance came after the three men and hanged them all. An outraged Wells criticized the event in a series of articles in which she specifically discussed the evils of lynching. She argued that the cruel punishment was not used to keep criminals in line but to enforce white supremacy (the idea that whites were superior to African Americans). She encouraged African Americans to boycott (not shop at) all white businesses, and even to leave town if need be. While visiting New York City shortly after her editorials went to press, a white mob ransacked and destroyed her newspaper office and told her they would kill her if she ever returned.

A lynching victim hangs from a tree. THE LIBRARY OF CONGRESS.

A new job, a continuing mission

Wells knew it was too dangerous to return to Memphis, so she stayed in New York and took a job as a writer at a magazine called *Age*. One of her first stories detailed several dozen recent lynchings, including names of the murderers, dates, and locations. The article was published at a good time. Historians estimate that 233 lynchings took place between 1880 and 1884; 381 from 1885 to 1889. These figures are probably much lower than the actual number of lynchings that took place. Many people never reported lynchings for fear of retaliation from whites.

Although the issue in which Wells's article was published sold ten thousand copies, its readers were primarily African American, and they already knew the horror of lynching. Wells knew she had to reach a white audience if she was to get help in putting an end to the barbaric act that took the lives of so many African Americans.

In an effort to bring her message to people who could help, Wells went on a tour of Europe and the British Isles. While there, she founded the National Afro-American Council and served as chairman of its Anti-Lynching Bureau. With the help of reformers in England, her cause was reported in American newspapers. Unfortunately, those same papers also attacked Wells as a nasty woman who spread lies. Conservative whites disliked her, but so did wealthy African Americans, who saw her as a threat to their security. They enjoyed the life of upper-class society, and to be associated with Wells, even if only by skin color, was not something they wanted.

Wells returned home in 1893 and moved to Chicago, Illinois, where she began working for an African American newspaper called the *Conservator*. That same year, she joined forces with another reformer, abolitionist (antislavery activist) Frederick Douglass (1818–1895), and wrote a pamphlet titled "The Reason Why the Colored American Is Not Represented in the World's Columbian Exposition." Ten thousand copies of the pamphlet were distributed at the Chicago World's Fair, an event that changed the cultural and social landscape of America forever.

Marries and retires, but not really

In 1895, Wells married lawyer Ferdinand Barnett, who happened to also be her editor. Her plan was to go into retirement, but that plan fell through. She did cut back on the amount of international travel she did to speak publicly at conventions, but that same year, Wells-Barnett published a detailed account of all the lynchings she could find information on in a book titled *A Red Record: Tabulated Statistics and Alleged Causes of Lynchings in the United States, 1892–1893–1894*. Wells-Barnett and her husband eventually had four children, and she dedicated her time to raising her family while not losing sight of the importance of her cause.

Wells-Barnett encouraged other African Americans to become active in their local regions. She herself helped establish the first kindergarten in the African American district of Chicago. She also joined **Jane Addams** (1860–1935; see entry), founder of the famous Hull-House Settlement (an early social-services community), in successfully protesting Chicago's plan to segregate its public schools. Wells-Barnett continued to denounce discrimination publicly. In the early 1900s, she exposed the segregationist policies of the popular Young Men's Christian Association (YMCA), causing a handful of wealthy donors to withdraw their financial support of the group. They channeled their money instead into the Negro Fellowship Reading Room and Social Center.

Helps establish the NAACP

Wells-Barnett worked tirelessly for three years with other African American reformers and activists to help found the National Association for the Advancement of Colored People (NAACP). The organization was formally established in 1909 with the goal of ensuring the political, educational, social, and economic equality of all African Americans. Wells-Barnett resigned her membership not long after the formation of the NAACP, however, because she believed the group was not militant (radical) enough. African American activists were basically separated into two groups during those days. One group favored accommodation, which meant they made the best of whatever situation they found themselves in and did not rally for more of anything—rights, money, social equality. The other group believed the only way to attain equality was through insisting on truly equal rights; Wells-Barnett sided with this group.

Her last years

Wells-Barnett spent the last two decades of her life involved in community organization and social work in Chicago. She made herself available to do what she believed needed to be done. For instance, in 1913, she worked as an adult probation officer, a duty she remained committed to for three years. Also in 1913, she formed the first African American women's suffrage (right to vote) organization, the Alpha Suffrage Club of

Chicago. She wrote her autobiography, *Crusade for Justice,* in 1928. In 1930, she unsuccessfully ran for the Illinois state legislature, becoming the first African American woman ever to run for public office.

Wells-Barnett would not live to see the end of lynching as a common southern occurrence. It would be 1968 before regular lynchings would gradually stop. According to Robert Zangrando's article "About Lynching," 1882 was the first year any sort of reliable lynching statistics were kept. Between 1882 and 1968, nearly 5,000 people—3,446 of them African American men, women, and children—were lynched. Mississippi had the most lynchings (539 African American victims, 42 white). Well into the twentieth century, lynchings were social events. White families would bring their children to watch the torture and hanging of victims. Spectators watched, fascinated, as victims were dismembered (had body parts cut off), soaked in oil and set on fire alive, then hanged. Railroads sold tickets to lynchings. Newspapers often carried notices of planned executions so townspeople could be sure to put the event on their calendars.

Wells-Barnett died in Chicago of uremia (toxins in the bloodstream due to kidney disease) on March 25, 1931. She was sixty-nine years old. A low-income housing project was built in Chicago in 1941 and named after her. In 1988, she was inducted into the National Women's Hall of Fame. A commemorative stamp bearing her likeness was issued by the U.S. Postal Service in 1990.

For More Information

BOOKS

Als, Hilton, et al. *Without Sanctuary: Lynching Photography in America.* Santa Fe: Twin Palms Publishers, 2000.

McMurry, Linda O. *To Keep the Waters Troubled: The Life of Ida B. Wells.* New York: Oxford University Press, 1998.

Schechter, Patricia A. *Ida B. Wells-Barnett and American Reform, 1880–1930.* Chapel Hill: University of North Carolina Press, 2001.

Welch, Catherine. *Ida B. Wells-Barnett: Powerhouse with a Pen.* Minneapolis: Carolrhoda Books, 2000.

Wells, Ida B. *Crusade for Justice: The Autobiography of Ida B. Wells.* Edited by Alfreda M. Duster. Chicago: University of Chicago Press, 1970.

WEB SITES

Baker, Lee D. "Ida B. Wells-Barnett and Her Passion for Justice." *Duke University.* http://www.duke.edu/~ldbaker/classes/AAIH/caai/ibwells/ibwbkgrd.html (accessed on September 6, 2006).

Gado, Mark. "Lynchings in America." *Crime Library.* http://www.crimelibrary.com/classics2/carnival/ (accessed on September 6, 2006).

"Ida B. Wells-Barnett." *AfricaWithin.com.* http://www.africawithin.com/bios/ida_wells.htm (accessed on September 6, 2006).

Library of Congress. "The Progress of a People: Ida B. Wells-Barnett." *African American Perspectives.* http://memory.loc.gov/ammem/aap/idawells.html (accessed on September 6, 2006).

Long Island University. "Lynchings in America." *B. Davis Schwartz Memorial Library of the C. W. Post Campus.* http://www.liu.edu/CWIS/CWP/library/african/2000/lynching.htm (accessed on September 6, 2006).

Naill, Katherine. "Ida B. Wells-Barnett 'Southern Horrors: Lynch Law In All Its Phases.'" *University of Arkansas.* http://www.uark.edu/depts/comminfo/women/wells.htm (accessed on September 6, 2006).

PBS. "Ida B. Wells." *The Rise and Fall of Jim Crow.* http://www.pbs.org/wnet/jimcrow/stories_people_wells.html (accessed on September 6, 2006).

Without Sanctuary. http://withoutsanctuary.org/ (accessed on September 6, 2006).

Zangrando, Robert L. "About Lynching." *University of Illinois at Urbana-Champaign: Modern American Poetry.* http://www.english.uiuc.edu/maps/poets/g_l/lynching/lynching.htm (accessed on September 6, 2006).

Frances Willard

BORN: September 28, 1839 • Churchill, New York
DIED: February 17, 1898 • New York, New York

Reformer

"There will be other reforms and reformers when we are gone. Societies will be organized, and parties will divide on the right of men to make and carry deadly weapons, dynamite and other destructive agencies still more powerful, that human ingenuity will yet invent."

Frances Willard was the leader of the temperance movement (the organized effort to minimize the consumption of alcohol) in the late nineteenth and early twentieth centuries. In 1874, she helped establish the Woman's Christian Temperance Union (WCTU), one of the largest women's organizations of the century. Unlike many of her peers in the temperance movement, Willard was in favor of women's suffrage (right to vote). Willard's driving force behind her beliefs and her commitment to reform was her Christian faith.

A Midwestern upbringing

Frances Willard.
THE LIBRARY OF
CONGRESS.

Frances Elizabeth Willard was born on September 28, 1839, in New York City. Until 1841, she lived there with her parents and an older brother. At that time, the family relocated to Ohio, where Willard's younger sister was born. In 1846, they moved to a farm in Wisconsin, where Willard spent the rest of her childhood.

Willard and her family moved to Illinois in 1858, where she attended North Western Female College, a Methodist school. After graduation in 1859, Willard began a teaching career that eventually took her to Pennsylvania and New York. Although she enjoyed two intense romantic relationships in her young life, she would never marry.

Willard became president of a new institution in 1871, the Evanston College for Ladies. The college merged with Northwestern University in 1873, at which time Willard became the first dean of women of the Women's College. Her position did not last long, however; in 1874, she resigned after months of disagreement with the president of the college over how the Women's College should be managed. Willard immersed herself immediately in a new reform movement: the woman's temperance movement. She was elected president of the Chicago chapter of the movement.

Founds the WCTU

Willard lost no time. In 1874, she helped found the Woman's Christian Temperance Union (WCTU) and became its first secretary. In her position, she traveled extensively to small towns and cities throughout the United States, helping other concerned citizens form local chapters of the WCTU. The WCTU members were mostly women—many with children—who had felt the ill effects, from husbands and fathers, of alcohol consumption and its resulting abuse. Their mission was to encourage moderation in the consumption of alcohol, or even abstinence (complete stoppage).

The heyday of the saloon

The temperance goal would not be easy to reach, as the brewing industry was one of the fastest-growing industries in America at the end of the nineteenth century. This was due, in large part, because German immigrants brought with them lager (pale beer, free of sediment) and the knowledge of how to brew it. After 1890, beer was the most popular alcoholic beverage on the market.

The brewing industry was helped by the introduction of the transcontinental railroad in 1869, which allowed brewers to ship their product throughout the country. As beer grew in popularity, so did saloons (bars), as innovative American brewers found a way to make a healthy profit off this new beverage. In the bigger cities, it was common to find a saloon for every 150 to 200 residents. Because competition was so fierce, saloonkeepers had to find other ways to attract customers, so they began introducing activities many considered immoral, such as gambling and prostitution (the selling of sex).

By the final decade of the nineteenth century, saloons and the attractions they offered America's hardworking, underpaid laborers had created a problem for the families of these men. Money that should have gone to support the home and family was being spent on alcohol and its related vices (bad habits). Men came home drunk and abused their wives and children. Families who could not pay their rent were evicted from their homes, left penniless and with no place to go.

Frances Willard (standing), her mother (seated, left), and assistant Anna Gordon.
© CORBIS.

The time was ripe for change, and reformers throughout the nation worked together to encourage temperance, using every form of communication at their disposal.

A life of crusading

Willard met Anna Gordon (who would eventually be elected the fourth president of the WCTU) in 1877 and hired her as her personal secretary. The two remained great friends throughout Willard's life. Gordon's expertise in managing organizations allowed Willard to broaden her reform efforts to include women's rights, education reform, labor reform, and women's suffrage. Willard's tireless efforts were rewarded when she was elected president of the WCTU in 1879.

As president, Willard adopted a "Do Everything" policy that encouraged women to step outside the home and learn to speak in public, champion social issues involving their rights and the protection of children, and even own their own businesses. Most members of the WCTU were simple housewives, many with no education or experience in the outside world. These women could not see the value in obtaining the

Spreading the message

An 1874 Currier and Ives illustration entitled "Woman's Holy War" shows women of the Temperance League destroying barrels of alcohol. © BETTMANN/CORBIS.

The temperance movement became a cause not only for organizations like the WCTU and the Anti-Saloon League (formed in 1893) but for churches, too. Preachers used the pulpit on Sunday mornings to condemn the evils of alcohol. Churches and temperance organizations distributed pamphlets of propaganda (information spread for the purpose of promoting a specific cause) with titles such as "The Holy Bible and Drink." They promoted alcohol as a threat to American values such as morality and productivity, calling it a poison and an evil in society. Some propaganda targeted children and their parents. These pamphlets used stories with

plots involving wrongdoing and intense pain. The cause of all the suffering was alcohol; the solution, temperance.

Pamphlets were not the only forms of temperance propaganda. Posters warning of the evils of alcohol appeared in public places throughout the country. Music also became a popular way to spread the message of temperance. Between the 1840s and the beginning of Prohibition (the outlaw of the sale and consumption of alcohol) in 1919, more than one hundred temperance songbook collections were published in America. These songs relied heavily on sentimentality (an excess of emotions), as demonstrated by one temperance song title, "Father's a Drunkard and Mother Is Dead." Poetry was another popular form of propaganda. Titles such as "The Curse of Rum" and "The Face Upon the Floor" summed up the temperance message.

Illustrations and woodcarvings supported the temperance message as well. Postcards, book illustrations, magazine and newspaper drawings—all featured graphic scenes showing alcohol as a moral sin or a health hazard. Young girls interested in marrying were warned to wait for a nondrinking man. Beverage companies promoted their nonalcoholic drinks as beneficial to health. In 1883, Hires Root Beer advertised its drink on trading cards. As reported on the Web site *Ardent Spirits,* a fan of the carbonated beverage claimed the soda pop "seems to cleanse and purify the system as nothing else will do. My son feels much better than he did before using it."

right to vote. Willard explained her support of woman suffrage at a gathering of the International Council of Women. Author Harriet Townsend heard Willard speak at the conference and shared Willard's words with readers in her 1916 book *Reminiscences of Famous Women.*

> I was in General Washington's kitchen at Mount Vernon last week and had a delightful visit with Aunt Dinah, the presiding genius of the place. Always seeking for information on the suffrage question, I asked her Aunt Dinah, do you want to vote? The old woman stood up at the questions with arms akimbo [hands on hips, elbows outward], [and] exclaimed Well, honey, you know that Uncle Sam's kitchen needs a cl'aring out once in a while, and when you are going to cl'ar out a kitchen you have got to have a woman to do it!

Willard and Gordon visited every American city with a population of more than ten thousand people in 1883. That same year, she organized the World WCTU. Through the World WCTU, Willard ensured the mobilization of concerned women everywhere in matters ranging from the social to the political.

At the age of fifty-three, Willard learned how to ride a bicycle. She was so taken with her newfound hobby that she wrote a book in 1895 about her experience. *A Wheel within a Wheel* offers readers a glimpse into the life of a tireless reformer who dared to try new experiences even as she tried to change the world.

Willard's health declined rapidly in late 1897. She had spent the previous few years still active in the WCTU (which had a membership of more than 150,000) but taking more rest periods in England with friends. In February 1898, she was preparing such a trip when she suddenly became ill with influenza. She died in her hotel room in New York City on February 17. She was just fifty-eight years old.

At the time of her death, Willard was one of the most famous women in America. Twenty thousand mourners paid their respects at the WCTU headquarters in Chicago, where her body lay before burial. A marble statue of her likeness was donated in 1905 and remains as part of the National Statuary Collection at the Capitol building in Washington, D.C.

Willard did not live to see the passage of the Eighteenth Amendment on January 16, 1916. That amendment marked the beginning of a period in history known as Prohibition, in which the sale and consumption of alcohol was outlawed. Prohibition lasted until 1933, when the amendment was repealed. Another victory for the WCTU, which eventually actively supported woman's suffrage, was the passage of the Nineteenth Amendment in 1920, which gave all American women the right to vote.

Perhaps the most influential legacy of Willard's crusade against alcohol is Alcoholics Anonymous (AA), which began as a three-person religious group meeting in 1935. By 1950, one hundred thousand recovered alcoholics had been through AA's twelve-step program. The program advocates total abstinence from alcohol. The AA organization, instead of attempting to regulate the liquor industry, treats alcoholism as a disease to be managed. A 2006 press release from AA indicated that a survey revealed the average member had been sober for more than eight years. The organization had, at the time, over two million members in 150 countries.

For More Information

BOOKS

Bordin, Ruth. *Frances Willard: A Biography*. Chapel Hill: University of North Carolina Press, 1986.

Gordon, Elizabeth P. *Women Torch-Bearers: The Story of the Woman's Christian Temperance Union*. 2nd ed. Evanston, IL: National Woman's Christian Temperance Union Publishing House, 1924.

Townsend, Harriet A. *Reminiscences of Famous Women*. Buffalo: Evans-Penfold Co., 1916. Also available at http://womenshistory.about.com/library/etext/bl_townsend_willard.htm (accessed on September 6, 2006).

Willard, Frances. *Writing Out My Heart: Selections from the Journal of Frances E. Willard, 1855–96*. Edited by Carolyn De Swarte Gifford. Urbana: University of Illinois Press, 1995.

WEB SITES

Alcoholics Anonymous. http://www.alcoholics-anonymous.org/en_information_aa.cfm?PageID=10 (accessed on September 6, 2006).

Berk, Leah Rae. "Temperance and Prohibition Era Propaganda: A Study in Rhetoric." *Alcohol, Temperance & Prohibition*. http://dl.lib.brown.edu/temperance/rhetoric.html (accessed on September 6, 2006).

"The Brewing Industry and Prohibition." *Temperance & Prohibition*. http://prohibition.osu.edu/Brewing/Default.htm (accessed on September 6, 2006).

Davis, George T. B. "The Greatest American Woman." *Temperance & Prohibition*. http://prohibition.osu.edu/Willard/willard_last_interview.htm (accessed on September 6, 2006).

"Frances Willard." *Woman's Christian Temperance Union*. http://www.wctu.org/frances_willard.html (accessed on September 6, 2006).

"Frances's Life." *Frances E. Willard Historical Association.* http://www.franceswillardhouse.org/franceslife/ (accessed on September 6, 2006).

Harvard University Library: Open Collections Program. "Frances Elizabeth Willard (1839–1898)." *Women Working, 1800–1930.* http://ocp.hul.harvard.edu/ww/people_willard_frances.html (accessed on September 6, 2006).

The Library Company of Philadelphia. "Alternatives to Alcohol." *Ardent Spirits.* http://www.librarycompany.org/ArdentSpirits/Temperance-alternatives.html (accessed on September 6, 2006).

"The Temperance Movement." *U-S-History.com.* http://www.u-s-history.com/pages/h1054.html (accessed on September 6, 2006).

Where to Learn More

The following list focuses on works written for readers of middle school and high school age. Books aimed at adult readers have been included when they are especially important in providing information or analysis that would otherwise be unavailable.

Books

Addams, Jane. *The Second Twenty Years at Hull-House.* New York: Macmillan, 1930.

Addams, Jane. *Twenty Years at Hull-House.* New York: Macmillan, 1910. Reprint, New York: Signet Classics, 1999.

Als, Hilton, et al. *Without Sanctuary: Lynching Photography in America.* Santa Fe: Twin Palms Publishers, 2000.

American Presidents in World History. Vol. 3. Westport, CT: Greenwood Press, 2003.

Arthur, Anthony. *Radical Innocent: Upton Sinclair.* New York: Random House, 2006.

Bak, Richard. *Peach: Ty Cobb in His Time and Ours.* Ann Arbor, MI: Sports Media Group, 2005.

Baldwin, Neil. *Edison: Inventing the Century.* New York: Hyperion, 1995. Reprint, Chicago: University of Chicago, 2001.

Bankston, John. *The Life and Times of Scott Joplin.* Hockessin, DE: Mitchell Lane Publishers, 2005.

Berlin, Edward A. *King of Ragtime: Scott Joplin and His Era.* New York: Oxford University Press, 1994.

Blaisdell, Bob, ed. *Great Speeches by Native Americans.* Mineola, NY: Dover Publications, 2000.

Bohannon, Lisa Frederiksen. *Women's Rights and Nothing Less: The Story of Elizabeth Cady Stanton.* Greensboro, NC: Morgan Reynolds Publishing, 2000.

Bordin, Ruth. *Frances Willard: A Biography.* Chapel Hill: University of North Carolina Press, 1986.

Brammer, Leila R. *Excluded from Suffrage History: Matilda Joslyn Gage, Nineteenth-Century American Feminist.* Westport, CT: Greenwood Press, 2000.

Brundage, W. Fitzhugh, ed. *Booker T. Washington and Black Progress: Up From Slavery 100 Years Later.* Gainesville: University Press of Florida, 2003.

Carroll, Rebecca, ed. *Uncle Tom or New Negro? African Americans Reflect on Booker T. Washington and "Up from Slavery" 100 Years Later.* New York: Broadway Books/Harlem Moon, 2006.

Casil, Amy Sterling. *John Dewey: The Founder of American Liberalism.* New York: Rosen, 2006.

Chalberg, John. *Emma Goldman: American Individualist.* New York: HarperCollins, 1991.

Chambers, John Whiteclay II. *The Tyranny of Change: America in the Progressive Era, 1890–1920.* 2nd ed. New Brunswick, NJ: Rutgers University Press, 2000.

Cherny, Robert W. *American Politics in the Gilded Age: 1868–1900.* Wheeling, IL: Harlan Davidson, 1997.

Cobb, Ty, and Al Stump. *My Life in Baseball: The True Record.* Garden City, NY: Doubleday, 1961. Reprint, Lincoln: University of Nebraska Press, 1993.

Cousins, Margaret. *The Story of Thomas Alva Edison.* New York: Random House, 1965. Reprint, 1993.

Curtis, Susan. *Dancing to a Black Man's Tune: A Life of Scott Joplin.* Columbia: University of Missouri Press, 1994.

Davis, Allen F. *American Heroine: The Life and Legend of Jane Addams.* New York: Oxford University Press, 1973. Reprint, Chicago: Ivan Dee, 2000.

Delano, Marfe Ferguson. *Inventing the Future: A Photobiography of Thomas Alva Edison.* Washington, DC: National Geographic Children's Books, 2002.

Diner, Hasia R., and Beryl Lieff Benderly. *Her Works Praise Her: A History of Jewish Women in America from Colonial Times to the Present.* New York: Basic Books, 2002.

Dyer, Daniel. *Jack London: A Biography.* New York: Scholastic Press, 1997.

Ehrlich, Gretel. *John Muir: Nature's Visionary.* Washington, DC: National Geographic Society, 2000.

Elshtain, Jean Bethke, ed. *The Jane Addams Reader.* New York: Basic Books, 2002.

Falk, Candace, Lyn Reese, and Mary Agnes Dougherty. *The Life and Times of Emma Goldman: A Curriculum for Middle and High School Students.* 2nd ed. Berkeley: University of California, 1992.

Felder, Deborah G., and Diana Rosen. *Fifty Jewish Women Who Changed the World.* New York: Citadel Press, 2003.

Flanagan, Maureen A. *Seeing with Their Hearts: Chicago Women and the Vision of the Good City, 1871–1933.* Princeton, NJ: Princeton University Press, 2002.

Freedman, Russell, and Lewis Hine. *Kids at Work: Lewis Hine and the Crusade Against Child Labor.* New York: Clarion Books, 1994.

Gaines, Ann. *Grover Cleveland: Our Twenty-Second and Twenty-Fourth President.* Chanhassen, MN: Child's World, 2002.

Geronimo. *Geronimo: His Own Story.* Edited by S. M. Barrett. New York: Dutton, 1970. Reprint, New York: Meridian, 1996.

Glassgold, Peter, ed. *Anarchy!: An Anthology of Emma Goldman's Mother Earth.* Washington, DC: Counterpoint Press, 2001.

Goldberg, Vicki. *Lewis W. Hine: Children at Work.* New York: Prestel Publishing, 1999.

Goldman, Emma. *Living My Life.* New York: Alfred Knopf, 1931. Reprint, New York: Penguin Books, 2006.

Goldman, Emma. *Red Emma Speaks: Selected Writings and Speeches.* 3rd ed. Edited by Alix Kates Shulman. Amherst, NY: Humanity Books, 1998.

Gordon, Elizabeth P. *Women Torch-Bearers: The Story of the Woman's Christian Temperance Union.* 2nd ed. Evanston, IL: National Woman's Christian Temperance Union Publishing House, 1924.

Harlan, Louis R. *Booker T. Washington in Perspective: Essays of Louis R. Harlan.* Edited by Raymond Smock. Jackson: University Press of Mississippi, 1988.

Hine, Lewis. *The Empire State Building.* New York: Prestel Publishing, 1998.

Holmes, Dan. *Ty Cobb: A Biography.* Westport, CT: Greenwood Press, 2004.

Joplin, Scott. *Joplin Gold.* London, England: Chester Music, 2004.

Kazin, Michael. *A Godly Hero: The Life of William Jennings Bryan.* New York: Knopf, 2006.

Kent, Zachary. *Grover Cleveland.* Chicago: Children's Press, 1988.

Kershaw, Alex. *Jack London: A Life.* New York: St. Martin's Press, 1998.

Klein, Maury. *The Life & Legend of E. H. Harriman.* Chapel Hill: University of North Carolina Press, 2000.

Klein, Maury. *The Life and Legend of Jay Gould.* Baltimore: Johns Hopkins University Press, 1997.

Kraft, Betsy Harvey. *Theodore Roosevelt: Champion of the American Spirit.* New York: Clarion Books, 2003.

Kramer, Sydelle. *Ty Cobb: Bad Boy of Baseball.* New York: Random House, 1995.

Lansford, Tom, and Robert P. Watson, eds. *Theodore Roosevelt (Presidents & Their Decisions).* San Diego: Greenhaven Press, 2003.

London, Jack. *The Best Short Stories of Jack London.* Garden City, NY: Sun Dial Press, 1945. Reprint, Greenwich, CT: Fawcett, 1992.

London, Jack. *The Call of the Wild.* Philadelphia: D. McKay, 1914. Multiple reprints.

Mansfield, Stephen. *Then Darkness Fled: The Liberating Wisdom of Booker T. Washington.* Nashville: Cumberland House, 1999.

Mattson, Kevin. *Upton Sinclair and the Other American Century.* New York: Wiley, 2006.

Maxcy, Spencer J., ed. *John Dewey and American Education.* Bristol, England: Thoemmes Continuum, 2002.

McMurry, Linda O. *To Keep the Waters Troubled: The Life of Ida B. Wells.* New York: Oxford University Press, 1998.

McPherson, Stephanie Sammartino. *Theodore Roosevelt (Presidential Leaders)*. Minneapolis: Lerner Publications, 2005.

Mercer, Lloyd. *E. H. Harriman: Master Railroader*. Boston: Twayne, 1985. Reprint, Washington, DC: Beard Books, 2003.

Morris, Charles R. *The Tycoons: How Andrew Carnegie, John D. Rockefeller, Jay Gould, and J. P. Morgan Invented the American Supereconomy*. New York: Holt and Co., 2005.

Muir, John. *Edward Henry Harriman*. New York: Doubleday, Page and Company, 1911. Also available at *Sierra Club: John Muir Exhibit*. http://www.sierra-club.org/john_muir_exhibit/frameindex.html?http://www.sierraclub.org/john_Muir_exhibit/writings/edward_henry_harriman.html (accessed on September 2, 2006).

Muir, John. *Meditations of John Muir: Nature's Temple*. Edited by Chris Highland. Berkeley, CA: Wilderness Press, 2001.

Muir, John. *Our National Parks*. Boston: Houghton, Mifflin and Company, 1901. Reprint, Washington, DC: Ross and Perry, 2001.

Muir, John, and Lee Stetson. *The Wild Muir: Twenty-Two of John Muir's Greatest Adventures*. Yosemite National Park, CA: Yosemite Association, 1994.

Okkonen, Mark. *The Ty Cobb Scrapbook: An Illustrated Chronology of Significant Dates in the 24-Year Career of the Fabled Georgia Peach*. New York: Sterling, 2001.

Painter, Nell Irvin. *Standing at Armageddon: The United States, 1877–1919*. New York: W. W. Norton, 1987.

Panzer, Mary. *Lewis Hine*. New York: Phaidon Press, 2002.

Pflueger, Lynn. *Thomas Nast: Political Cartoonist*. Berkeley Heights, NJ: Enslow Publishers, 2000.

Powers, Ron. *Mark Twain: A Life*. New York: Free Press, 2005.

Renehan, Edward J. Jr. *The Dark Genius of Wall Street: The Misunderstood Life of Jay Gould, King of the Robber Barons*. New York: Basic Books, 2005.

Riehecky, Janet. *William McKinley: America's 25th President*. New York: Children's Press, 2004.

Rolde, Neil. *Continental Liar from the State of Maine: James G. Blaine*. Gardiner, ME: Tilbury House, 2006.

Roop, Connie, and Peter Roop. *Sitting Bull*. Scholastic Paperbacks, 2002.

Schechter, Patricia A. *Ida B. Wells-Barnett and American Reform, 1880–1930*. Chapel Hill: University of North Carolina Press, 2001.

Shirley, David. *Thomas Nast: Cartoonist and Illustrator*. New York: Franklin Watts, 1998.

Sievers, Harry J. *Benjamin Harrison: Hoosier President*. Newtown, CT: American Political Biography Press, 1997.

Sinclair, Upton. *The Jungle*. New York: Doubleday, 1906. Multiple reprints.

Slater, Elinor, and Robert Slater. *Great Jewish Women*. Middle Village, NY: Jonathan David Publishers, 1994.

Solomon, Hannah G. *The Fabric of My Life: The Autobiography of Hannah G. Solomon.* New York: Bloch Publishing Co., 1946.

Stanton, Elizabeth Cady. *Eighty Years and More (1815–1897): Reminiscences of Elizabeth Cady Stanton.* New York: European Publishing Co., 1898. Reprint, Amherst, NY: Humanity Books, 2002.

Stanton, Elizabeth Cady. *The Woman's Bible.* New York: European Publishing Co., 1895–98. Reprint, Mineola, NY: Dover Publications, 2002.

Stevens, Rita. *Benjamin Harrison, 23rd President of the United States.* Ada, OK: Garrett Educational Corp., 1989.

TIME for Kids Editors. *Thomas Edison: A Brilliant Inventor.* New York: HarperCollins, 2005.

Twain, Mark. *The Autobiography of Mark Twain.* New York: Sheldon & Company, 1924. Multiple reprints.

Twain, Mark, and Charles Dudley Warner. *The Gilded Age.* Hartford, CT: American Publishing, 1874. Reprint, New York: Modern Library, 2006.

Utley, Robert. *The Lance and the Shield: The Life and Times of Sitting Bull.* New York: Henry Holt, 1993.

Ward, Geoffrey C. *Not for Ourselves Alone: The Story of Elizabeth Cady Stanton and Susan B. Anthony.* New York: A. A. Knopf, 1999.

Washington, Booker T. *Up from Slavery: An Autobiography.* Garden City, NY: Doubleday & Co., 1901. Multiple reprints.

Welch, Catherine. *Ida B. Wells-Barnett: Powerhouse with a Pen.* Minneapolis: Carolrhoda Books, 2000.

Wells, Ida B. *Crusade for Justice: The Autobiography of Ida B. Wells.* Edited by Alfreda M. Duster. Chicago: University of Chicago Press, 1970.

Wiebe, Robert H. *The Search for Order, 1877–1920.* New York: Hill and Wang, 1967. Reprint, Westport, CT: Greenwood Press, 1980.

Willard, Frances. *Writing Out My Heart: Selections from the Journal of Frances E. Willard, 1855–96.* Edited by Carolyn De Swarte Gifford. Urbana: University of Illinois Press, 1995.

Williams, Jean Kinney. *Benjamin Harrison: America's 23rd President.* New York: Children's Press, 2004.

Wilson, Margie, ed. *The Wit and Wisdom of Jack London: A Collection of Quotations from His Writing and Letters.* Santa Rosa, CA: Wordsworth Pub. Co., 1995.

Wolfe, Linnie Marsh. *Son of the Wilderness: The Life of John Muir.* New York: A. A. Knopf, 1945. Reprint, Madison: University of Wisconsin Press, 1978.

Periodicals

Bak, Richard. "Forget the Babe, Baseball's Best Is Named Tyrus Raymond Cobb." *USA Today (Society for the Advancement of Education).* (September 2005). This article can also be found online at http://findarticles.com/p/articles/mi_m1272/is_2724_134/ai_n15727520.

Bly, Nellie. "Nelly [sic] Bly Again: She Interviews Emma Goldman and Other Anarchists." *New York World* (September 17, 1893). Available at http://sunsite. berkeley.edu/Goldman/Samples/bly.html (accessed on September 2, 2006).

Goldman, Emma. "Was My Life Worth Living?" *Harper's Magazine* (May 1, 2000).

Goldman, Emma. "What Is There in Anarchy for Women?" *St. Louis Post Dispatch Sunday Magazine* (October 24, 1897). Available at http://sunsite.berkeley.edu/ Goldman/Samples/whatis.html (accessed on September 2, 2006).

Harlan, Louis R. "Booker T. Washington's West Virginia Boyhood." *West Virginia History* (January 1971): 63–85. Also available at http://www.wvculture.org/ history/journal_wvh/wvh32-1.html.

Meyer, John M. "Gifford Pinchot, John Muir, and the Boundaries of Politics in American Thought." *Polity* (December 21, 1997).

Millstein, Barbara Head. "Lewis Wickes Hine: The Final Years." *Magazine Antiques* (November 1998): p. 714.

Murrell, William. "Nast, Gladiator of the Political Pencil." *American Scholar* (Autumn 1936): 472–85.

Web Sites

Albrecht, Theodore. "Joplin, Scott." *The Handbook of Texas Online.* http:// www.tsha.utexas.edu/handbook/online/articles/JJ/fjo70.html (accessed on September 3, 2006).

Baker, Lee D. "Ida B. Wells-Barnett and Her Passion for Justice." *Duke University.* http://www.duke.edu/~ldbaker/classes/AAIH/caai/ibwells/ibwbkgrd. html (accessed on September 6, 2006).

Beals, Gerald. *Thomas Edison's Home Page.* http://www.thomasedison.com/ (accessed on September 1, 2006).

"Benjamin Harrison." *American President.org.* http://americanpresident.org/history/ benjaminharrison/biography (accessed on September 2, 2006).

"Benjamin Harrison." *The White House.* http://www.whitehouse.gov/history/ presidents/bh23.html (accessed on September 2, 2006).

Berk, Leah Rae. "Temperance and Prohibition Era Propaganda: A Study in Rhetoric." *Alcohol, Temperance & Prohibition.* http://dl.lib.brown.edu/ temperance/rhetoric.html (accessed on September 6, 2006).

Berkeley Digital Library Site. *The Emma Goldman Papers.* http://sunsite.berke-ley.edu/Goldman/ (accessed on September 2, 2006).

Berlin, Edward A. "A Biography of Scott Joplin." *The Scott Joplin International Ragtime Foundation.* http://www.scottjoplin.org/biography.htm (accessed on September 3, 2006).

Blackwell, John. "1906: Rumble Over 'The Jungle.'" *The Capital Century: 1900–1999.* http://www.capitalcentury.com/1906.html (accessed on September 4, 2006).

"Booker T. Washington National Monument." *National Park Service.* http:// www.nps.gov/bowa/ (accessed on September 5, 2006).

"Booker T. Washington." *National Park Service: Legends of Tuskegee.* http://www.cr.nps.gov/museum/exhibits/tuskegee/btwoverview.htm (accessed on September 5, 2006).

"The Booker T. Washington Papers. *History Cooperative.* http://www.historycooperative.org/btw/ (accessed on September 5, 2006).

"Charlotte Perkins Gilman." *Pegasos.* http://www.kirjasto.sci.fi/gilman.htm (accessed on September 4, 2006).

"Chester Alan Arthur." *American President.* http://ap.beta.polardesign.com/history/chesterccrthur/biography/LifeBeforePresidency.common.shtml (accessed on August 17, 2006).

"Chief Sitting Bull." *History Channel.* http://www.historychannel.com/exhibits/sioux/sittingbull.html (accessed on September 4, 2006).

"Child Labor in America 1908–1912: Photographs of Lewis W. Hines." *The History Place.* http://www.historyplace.com/unitedstates/childlabor/index.html (accessed on September 3, 2006).

Davis, George T. B. "The Greatest American Woman." *Temperance & Prohibition.* http://prohibition.osu.edu/Willard/willard_last_interview.htm (accessed on September 6, 2006).

Davis, Kay. "Lewis Hine." *Documenting "The Other Half": The Social Reform Photography of Jacob Riis and Lewis Hine.* http://xroads.virginia.edu/~MA01/davis/photography/hine/hine.html (accessed on September 3, 2006).

Due, Tananarive. "Excerpt: 'Joplin's Ghost.'" *National Public Radio.* http://www.npr.org/templates/story/story.php?storyId=5346117 (accessed on September 3, 2006).

"Edison National Historic Site." *National Park Service.* http://www.nps.gov/edis/home.htm (accessed on September 1, 2006).

"The Edison Papers." *Rutgers University.* http://edison.rutgers.edu/ (accessed on September 1, 2006).

"Edward H. Harriman (1848–1909)." *Forbes.com.* http://www.forbes.com/business/2005/07/06/harriman-railroads–northern-securities-cx_0706harriman.html (accessed on September 2, 2006).

"Elizabeth Cady Stanton." *National Park Service: Women's Rights National Historical Park.* http://www.nps.gov/wori/ecs.htm (accessed on September 5, 2006).

"Elizabeth Cady Stanton House." *Places Where Women Made History.* http://www.cr.nps.gov/nr/travel/pwwmh/ny10.htm (accessed on September 5, 2006).

"Exhibit: Women of Valor: Emma Goldman." *Jewish Women's Archive.* http://www.jwa.org/exhibits/wov/goldman/ (accessed on September 2, 2006).

Flanagan, Frank M. "John Dewey." *University of Limerick.* http://www.ul.ie/tilde_accs/philos/www/vol1/dewey.html (accessed on August 21, 2006).

"Frances Willard." *Woman's Christian Temperance Union.* http://www.wctu.org/frances_willard.html (accessed on September 6, 2006).

"Frances's Life." *Frances E. Willard Historical Association.* http://www.franceswillardhouse.org/franceslife/ (accessed on September 6, 2006).

Gado, Mark. "Lynchings in America." *Crime Library.* http://www.crimelibrary.com/classics2/carnival/ (accessed on September 6, 2006).

"Geronimo." *Arizona State Museum.* http://www.statemuseum.arizona.edu/artifact/geronimo.shtml (accessed on September 4, 2006).

"Geronimo." *Indians.org.* http://www.indians.org/welker/geronimo.htm (accessed on September 4, 2006).

Goldman, Emma. "I Will Kill Frick." *History Matters.* http://historymatters.gmu.edu/d/99/ (accessed on September 2, 2006).

"The Great Southwest Strike—1886." *The Institute for Labor Studies.* http://www.umkc.edu/labor-ed/history6.htm (accessed on September 2, 2006).

"Grover Cleveland." *The White House.* http://www.whitehouse.gov/history/presidents/gc2224.html (accessed on August 17, 2006).

Halsall, Paul. "Booker T. Washington (1856–1915): Speech at the Atlanta Exposition, 1895." *Internet Modern History Sourcebook.* http://www.fordham.edu/halsall/mod/1895washington-atlanta.html (accessed on September 5, 2006).

"Hannah Greenebaum Solomon." *National Women's Hall of Fame.* http://www.greatwomen.org/women.php?action=viewone=148 (accessed on September 5, 2006).

HarpWeek Presents the World of Thomas Nast. http://www.thomasnast.com/ (accessed on September 4, 2006).

Harvard University Library: Open Collections Program. "Frances Elizabeth Willard (1839–1898)." *Women Working, 1800–1930.* http://ocp.hul.harvard.edu/ww/people_willard_frances.html (accessed on September 6, 2006).

Harvard University Library: Open Collections Program. "Jane Addams (1860–1935)." *Women Working, 1800–1930.* http://ocp.hul.harvard.edu/ww/people_addams.html (accessed on August 17, 2006).

"Hazardous Business: The Fight for the Commission." *Texas State Library and Archives Commission.* http://www.tsl.state.tx.us/exhibits/railroad/fight/page4.html (accessed on September 2, 2006).

"History of Sitting Bull." *Canada's Digital Collections.* http://collections.ic.gc.ca/beaupre/promme92.htm (accessed on September 4, 2006).

"History of Tuskegee University." *Tuskegee University.* http://www.tuskegee.edu/Global/story.asp?S=1070392 (accessed on September 5, 2006).

Howie, Craig. "John Muir." *Scotsman.com.* http://heritage.scotsman.com/profiles.cfm?cid=1=1825412005 (accessed on September 4, 2006).

"Ida B. Wells-Barnett." *AfricaWithin.com.* http://www.africawithin.com/bios/ida_wells.htm (accessed on September 6, 2006).

"The Illustrated History of Baseball Cards: The 1800s." *Cycleback.com.* http://www.cycleback.com/1800s/ (accessed on August 21, 2006).

"In His Own Words." *Theodore Roosevelt Association.* http://www.theodoreroosevelt. org/life/quotes.htm (accessed on September 4, 2006).

"Jack London—His Life and Books." *Jack London State Historic Park.* http:// www.parks.sonoma.net/JLStory.html (accessed on September 3, 2006).

The Jack London Online Collection. http://london.sonoma.edu/ (accessed on September 3, 2006).

"Jack London's Ranch Album." *The World of Jack London.* http://www. jacklondons.net/intro.html (accessed on September 3, 2006).

"James Abram Garfield." *American President.* http://www.americanpresident.org/ history/jamesgarfield/ (accessed on August 17, 2006).

"James Fisk." *U-S-History.com.* http://www.u-s-history.com/pages/h865.html (accessed on September 2, 2006).

"Jane Addams—Biography." *Nobelprize.org.* http://nobelprize.org/peace/laureates/ 1931/addams-bio.html (accessed on August 17, 2006).

"Jane Addams." *Spartacus Schoolnet.* http://www.spartacus.schoolnet.co.uk/ USAaddams.htm (accessed on August 17, 2006).

"John Dewey (1859–1952)." *The Internet Encyclopedia of Philosophy.* http://www. iep.utm.edu/d/dewey.htm (accessed on August 21, 2006).

JohnDewey.Org. http://www.johndewey.org/ (accessed on August 21, 2006).

"John Muir Exhibit." *Sierra Club.* http://www.sierraclub.org/john_muir_exhibit/ (accessed on September 4, 2006).

"John Muir National Historic Site." *National Park Service.* http://www.nps.gov/ jomu/ (accessed on September 4, 2006).

John Muir Trust. http://www.jmt.org/ (accessed on September 4, 2006).

Klein, Maury. "The Robber Barons' Bum Rap." *City Journal.* http://www.city-journal.org/html/5_1_a2.html (accessed on September 2, 2006).

Krain, Jacob B. "Lillian Wald." *The Jewish Magazine.* http://www.jewishmag.com/ 51mag/wald/lillianwald.htm (accessed on August 17, 2006).

Leggat, Robert. "Hine, Lewis Wickes." *A History of Photography.* http://www. rleggat.com/photohistory/history/hine.htm (accessed on September 3, 2006).

Levang, Rex. "100 Years of the Maple Leaf Rag." *Minnesota Public Radio.* http:// music.minnesota.publicradio.org/features/9905_ragtime/index.shtml (accessed on September 3, 2006).

"Lewis Wickes Hine: The Construction of the Empire State Building, 1930– 1931." *The New York Public Library.* http://www.nypl.org/research/chss/spe/ art/photo/hinex/empire/empire.html (accessed on September 3, 2006).

"Lewis Wickes Hine." *Getty Museum.* http://www.getty.edu/art/gettyguide/ artMakerDetails?maker=1601&page=1 (accessed on September 3, 2006).

Library of Congress. "Baseball Cards: 1887–1914." *American Memory.* http:// memory.loc.gov/ammem/bbhtml/bbhome.html (accessed on August 21, 2006).

Library of Congress. "Booker T. Washington." *The Progress of a People.* http://lcweb2.loc.gov/ammem/aap/bookert.html (accessed on September 5, 2006).

Library of Congress. "Inventing Entertainment: The Motion Pictures and Sound Recordings of the Edison Companies." *American Memory.* http://memory.loc.gov/ammem/edhtml/edhome.html (accessed on September 1, 2006).

Library of Congress. "National Child Labor Committee Collection Photographs by Lewis Hine." *Prints and Photographs Reading Room.* http://www.loc.gov/rr/print/coll/207-b.html (accessed on September 3, 2006).

Library of Congress. "The Progress of a People: Ida B. Wells-Barnett." *African American Perspectives.* http://memory.loc.gov/ammem/aap/idawells.html (accessed on September 6, 2006).

Library of Congress. "Votes for Women: Selections from the National American Woman Suffrage Association Collection: 1848–1921." *American Memory.* http://lcweb2.loc.gov/ammem/naw/nawshome.html (accessed on September 5, 2006).

"Life of Theodore Roosevelt." *Theodore Roosevelt Association.* http://www.theodoreroosevelt.org/life/lifeoftr.htm (accessed on September 4, 2006).

"Lillian D. Wald." *National Association for Home Care & Hospice.* http://www.nahc.org/NAHC/Val/Columns/SC10-4.html (accessed on August 17, 2006).

Long Island University. "Lynchings in America." *B. Davis Schwartz Memorial Library of the C. W. Post Campus.* http://www.liu.edu/CWIS/CWP/library/african/2000/lynching.htm (accessed on September 6, 2006).

Lyndhurst: A National Trust Historic Site. http://www.lyndhurst.org/home.html (accessed on September 2, 2006).

The Mark Twain House and Museum. http://www.marktwainhouse.org/theman/bio.shtml (accessed on September 5, 2006).

Maroney, James C. "Great Southwest Strike." *The Handbook of Texas Online.* http://www.tsha.utexas.edu/handbook/online/articles/GG/oeg1.html (accessed on September 2, 2006).

McLaughlin, James. "An Account of Sitting Bull's Death." *PBS: Archives of the West.* http://www.pbs.org/weta/thewest/resources/archives/eight/sbarrest.htm (accessed on September 4, 2006).

Menlo Park Museum. http://www.menloparkmuseum.com/ (accessed on September 1, 2006).

Moss, Charles K. "Scott Joplin: King of Ragtime." *Charles K. Moss Piano Studio.* http://www.carolinaclassical.com/joplin/index.html (accessed on September 3, 2006).

"The Music of Scott Joplin." *Geocities.com.* http://www.geocities.com/BourbonStreet/Bayou/9694/music.html (accessed on September 3, 2006).

Naill, Katherine. "Ida B. Wells-Barnett 'Southern Horrors: Lynch Law In All Its Phases.'" *University of Arkansas.* http://www.uark.edu/depts/comminfo/women/wells.htm (accessed on September 6, 2006).

National Park Service. "Theodore Roosevelt." *Theodore Roosevelt National Park.* http://www.nps.gov/thro/tr_cons.htm (accessed on September 4, 2006).

"The 1906 San Francisco Earthquake and Fire." *The Bancroft Library*. http://bancroft.berkeley.edu/collections/earthquakeandfire/index2.html (accessed on September 3, 2006).

Oden, Lori. "Lewis Hine (1874–1940): Photography for Social Reform." *International Photography Hall of Fame & Museum*. http://www.iphf.org/inductees/LHine.htm (accessed on June 2, 2006).

The Official Web Site of Ty Cobb. http://www.cmgworldwide.com/baseball/cobb/bio.html (accessed on July 6, 2006).

PBS. *American Experience: Emma Goldman*. http://www.pbs.org/wgbh/amex/goldman/ (accessed on September 2, 2006).

PBS. "Booker T. & W. E. B." *Frontline: The Two Nations of Black America*. http://www.pbs.org/wgbh/pages/frontline/shows/race/etc/road.html (accessed on September 5, 2006).

PBS. "Edison's Miracle of Light." *American Experience*. http://www.pbs.org/wgbh/amex/edison/ (accessed on September 1, 2006).

PBS. "The Golden Land, 1654–1930s; Jewish Cultural Life in Chicago." *Heritage: Civilization and the Jews*. http://www.pbs.org/wnet/heritage/episode7/documents/documents_8.html (accessed on September 5, 2006).

PBS. *Harriman Expedition Retraced: A Century of Change*. http://www.pbs.org/harriman/1899/1899_part/participantharriman.html (accessed on September 2, 2006).

PBS. "Ida B. Wells." *The Rise and Fall of Jim Crow*. http://www.pbs.org/wnet/jimcrow/stories_people_wells.html (accessed on September 6, 2006).

PBS. *Mark Twain*. http://www.pbs.org/marktwain/learnmore/activities.html (accessed on September 5, 2006).

PBS. *Not for Ourselves Alone: The Story of Elizabeth Cady Stanton and Susan B. Anthony*. http://www.pbs.org/stantonanthony/index.html (accessed on September 5, 2006).

PBS. "People & Events: Black Friday, September 24, 1869." *American Experience: Ulysses S. Grant*. http://www.pbs.org/wgbh/amex/grant/peopleevents/e_friday.html (accessed on September 2, 2006).

PBS. "People & Events: Jane Addams (1860–1935)." *American Experience: Chicago, City of the Century*. http://www.pbs.org/wgbh/amex/chicago/peopleevents/p_addams.html (accessed on August 17, 2006).

PBS. "People & Events: Samuel Langhorne Clemens, 1835–1910." *American Experience: Ulysses S. Grant*. http://www.pbs.org/wgbh/amex/grant/peopleevents/p_twain.html (accessed on September 5, 2006).

PBS. "Sitting Bull." *New Perspectives on the West*. http://www.pbs.org/weta/thewest/people/s_z/sittingbull.htm (accessed on September 4, 2006).

"Political Cartoons of Thomas Nast." *United States Senate*. http://www.senate.gov/artandhistory/art/exhibit/nast_cartoons.htm (accessed on September 4, 2006).

The President Benjamin Harrison Home. http://www.presidentbenjaminharrison.org/ (accessed on September 2, 2006).

"Quotations." *Twainquotes.com.* http://www.twainquotes.com/quotesatoz.html (accessed on September 5, 2006).

Railton, Stephen. "Mark Twain in His Times." *University of Virginia Library.* http://etext.virginia.edu/railton/index2.html (accessed on September 5, 2006).

Rose, Gene. "The Ghosts of Hetch-Hetchy." *Sierra Club: John Muir Exhibit.* http://www.sierraclub.org/john_muir_exhibit/frameindex.html?http://www.sierraclub.org/john_muir_exhibit/life/ (accessed on September 4, 2006).

"The San Francisco Earthquake, 1906." *Eyewitness to History.* http://www.eyewitnesstohistory.com/sfeq.htm (accessed on September 3, 2006).

"Scott Joplin." *Essentials of Music.* http://www.essentialsofmusic.com/composer/joplin.html (accessed on September 3, 2006).

"The Seneca Falls Convention." *Smithsonian Institution National Portrait Gallery.* http://www.npg.si.edu/col/seneca/senfalls1.htm (accessed on September 5, 2006).

Stanton, Elizabeth Cady. "Address: First Women's-Rights Convention." *Institute for the Study of Civic Values.* http://www.libertynet.org/edcivic/stanton.html (accessed on September 5, 2006).

Stasz, Clarice. "Jack [John Griffith] London." *The Jack London Online Collection.* http://london.sonoma.edu/jackbio.html (accessed on September 3, 2006).

"Stephen Grover Cleveland." *American President.* http://americanpresident.org/history/grovercleveland/biography (accessed on August 17, 2006).

"Teddy Bear." *National Museum of American History.* http://americanhistory.si.edu/news/factsheet.cfm?key=30=6 (accessed on September 4, 2006).

"The Temperance Movement." *U-S-History.com.* http://www.u-s-history.com/pages/h1054.html (accessed on September 6, 2006).

"Theodore Roosevelt and Big Stick Diplomacy." *Mt. Holyoke College.* http://www.mtholyoke.edu/~jlgarner/classweb/worldpolitics/bigstick.html (accessed on September 4, 2006).

"Theodore Roosevelt: Icon of the American Century." *National Portrait Gallery.* http://www.npg.si.edu/exh/roosevelt/ (accessed on September 4, 2006).

"Theodore Roosevelt (1901–1909)." *American President.* http://www.americanpresident.org/history/theodoreroosevelt/ (accessed on September 4, 2006).

"Thomas Nast Biography." *The Ohio State University Libraries: Cartoon Research Library.* http://cartoons.osu.edu/nast/bio.htm (accessed on September 4, 2006).

"Ty Cobb." *Baseball Library.com.* http://www.baseballlibrary.com/baseballlibrary/ballplayers/C/Cobb_Ty.stm (accessed on August 21, 2006).

"Ty Cobb." *National Baseball Hall of Fame.* http://www.baseballhalloffame.org/hofers_and_honorees/hofer_bios/cobb_ty.htm (accessed on August 21, 2006).

University of Illinois at Chicago. *Urban Experience in Chicago: Hull-House and Its Neighborhoods, 1889–1963.* http://www.uic.edu/jaddams/hull/urbanexp/ (accessed on August 17, 2006).

Wagner, Sally Roesch. "Matilda Joslyn Gage: Forgotten Feminist." *New York History.* http://www.nyhistory.com/gagepage/gagebio.htm (accessed on September 5, 2006).

Wagner, Sally Roesch. "The Mother of Oz." *The Matilda Joslyn Gage Foundation.* http://www.matildajoslyngage.org/motherofoz.htm (accessed on September 5, 2006).

Wagner, Sally Roesch. "Sitting Bull: In Memory." *First Nations: Issues of Consequence.* http://www.dickshovel.com/sittingbull.html (accessed on September 4, 2006).

Wehling, Jason. "Anarchy in Interpretation: The Life of Emma Goldman." *Spunk Library.* http://www.spunk.org/texts/people/goldman/sp001520/emmabio.html (accessed on September 2, 2006).

Weiss, Don. "John Muir." *Ecology Hall of Fame.* http://www.ecotopia.org/ehof/muir/bio.html (accessed on September 4, 2006).

"Who Was James Blaine?" *Blaine Amendments.* http://www.blaineamendments.org/Intro/JGB.html (accessed on September 2, 2006).

"William Jennings Bryan." *1896: A Website of Political Cartoons.* http://projects.vassar.edu/1896/bryan.html (accessed on September 4, 2006).

"William McKinley." *American President.org.* http://americanpresident.org/history/williammckinley/biography (accessed on September 4, 2006).

"William McKinley." *1896: A Website of Political Cartoons.* http://projects.vassar.edu/1896/mckinley.html (accessed on September 4, 2006).

"William McKinley. *The White House.* http://www.whitehouse.gov/history/presidents/wm25.html (accessed on September 4, 2006).

Without Sanctuary. http://withoutsanctuary.org/ (accessed on September 6, 2006).

Wolf, Mari Artzner. "A Home of His Own." *Wm. McKinley Presidential Library & Museum.* http://www.mckinleymuseum.org/mckinleyfeature.html (accessed on September 4, 2006).

"Women of the Hall: Elizabeth Cady Stanton." *National Women's Hall of Fame.* http://www.greatwomen.org/women.php?action=viewone&id=149 (accessed on September 5, 2006).

"Women of Valor: Hannah Greenebaum Solomon." *Jewish Women's Archive.* http://www.jwa.org/exhibits/wov/solomon/ (accessed on September 5, 2006).

Zangrando, Robert L. "About Lynching." *University of Illinois at Urbana-Champaign: Modern American Poetry.* http://www.english.uiuc.edu/maps/poets/g_l/lynching/lynching.htm (accessed on September 6, 2006).

Index

Illustrations are marked by (ill.)